Learning Disabilities in the Secondary School

Issues and Practices

Learning Disabilities in the Secondary School
Issues and Practices

9 8 4 8 1

Libby Goodman, Ed.D.

Coordinator of Learning Disabilities Programs

Lester Mann, Ph.D.

Director of Special Education

Montgomery County Intermediate Unit
6198 Butler Pike
Blue Bell, Pennsylvania 19422

LIBRARY

GRUNE & STRATTON
A Subsidiary of Harcourt Brace Jovanovich, Publishers
New York   San Francisco   London

Library of Congress Cataloging in Publication Data

Goodman, Libby.
    Learning disabilities in the secondary school.

    Bibliography: p.
    Includes index.
    1. Learning disabilities—United States.
    2. Ability testing.   3. Education, Secondary—
    United States—Curricula.   I. Mann, Lester, joint
    author.   II. Title.
    LC4705.G66   371.9   76-19050
    ISBN 0-8089-0949-5

Distributed in the United Kingdom by
Academic Press, Inc. (London) Ltd.
24/28 Oval Road, London NW 1

Grune & Stratton, Inc.
111 Fifth Avenue
New York, New York 10003

Library of Congress Catalog Card Number 76-19050
International Standard Book Number 0-8089-0949-5

Printed in the United States of America

Preface

The present book represents an attempt by the authors to come to grips with one of the pressing problems confronting the learning disability specialist: How to deal with the learning-disabled youth at secondary school levels. The preoccupation, until very recently, of the learning disability field with the primary and elementary school age child has meant a neglect of the problems of the older learning-disabled pupil, equally needful of help. It is to assist in the evaluation of, and educational programming for, these pupils that this book is intended.

We have attempted to attack the problems of learning disabilities comprehensively in this volume. Part I, chapters I–V, attends to issues of definition, diagnosis, and placement. Part II, chapters VI–X, deals with programming and instructional concerns. Part III provides a selected bibliography of references relevant to the education of the secondary-level learning disabled pupil. For succinctness of presentation and economy of reading, we have avoided information about materials, techniques, and programs which have already been discussed amply within other contexts.

We do not anticipate that our readers will agree with all of our positions and all of our suggestions; some of them, in fact, go against the grain of existing learning disability philosophies. Controversy and divergences of opinion are, however, to be expected in this uncertain and poorly defined field. For these readers, indeed for all of our readers, we hope that concepts and techniques will nevertheless assist them in their own work with secondary-level learning disabled pupils.

Libby Goodman
Lester Mann

Contents

LIST OF TABLES

Learning Disabilities in the Secondary School

Issues and Practices

PART I

Issues of Identification

CHAPTER 1
An Approach to Secondary-Level Learning Disabilities

INTRODUCTION

This book represents the authors' second effort at understanding and providing solutions to the problems and dilemmas of secondary learning disabled pupils (Mann, Goodman, and Wiederholt, 1977). Our efforts are born of responsibilities for providing public school education for these pupils who have just recently come to the fore in the concerns of special education. We feel that current attention on secondary learning disabilities illustrates the increasing maturity of the learning disability field, a field which, after the initial enthusiasms of its early interests and commitments, is truly coming to grips with its problems.

We have attempted to delineate here various premises and issues in the diagnosis, education, and management of secondary level learning disabled pupils. We have tried to avoid offering simple explanations and glib solutions to complex and resistant problems; instead, we have provided philosophies and guidelines to assist educators in creating pragmatic and effective programs for this urgent area of education.

SECONDARY LEARNING DISABILITIES: A NEGLECTED AREA OF INQUIRY

Learning disabilities, as a field of both inquiry and practice, is now firmly established. Yet proponents still disagree, often violently, about what constitutes a learning disability and what the most appropriate means of evaluating and remediating are. We are not likely to entertain the notion often professed by earlier leaders in the field of reading and remedial education—that the concepts of learning disability, e.g., dyslexia, were not "real" but were essentially errors in understanding the nature of reading problems by people not truly skilled in and appreciative of the problems of academic instruction.

There are learning disabled children! But educators disagree about what their problems are and how the problems can be diagnosed and remediated most effectively. Those entrusted with the preparation of learning disability teachers, should certainly know that any forthright and definitive presentations of techniques and curricula represent oversimplifications of the many complex and unsolved issues.

Unfortunately, oversimplifications continue to confront learning disability practitioners. One of these concepts is that the learning disabled child is between the ages of 6 and 12 and never grows up to leave his cozy self-contained or resource classroom, unless, of course, he is fully remediated and thus no longer learning disabled.

There are, of course, secondary-level learning disabled children. But most of us in the field of learning disabilities appear to have overlooked or deliberately ignored them. This simple observation is readily verified by examining the professional literature on secondary learning disabilities, whether it is opinion or observation, classroom practice or research. Much is written about the young learning disabled child, yet little literature is available on the secondary-level child. Why this neglect?

Perhaps the neglect is a consequence of the fact that most learning disability technologies are oriented almost entirely to the early and elementary school years. Most tests in the field—such as those created by Frostig, Myklebust, Kephart, and Kirk—are all directed to the preliminary or beginning stages of academic acquisition; in fact, the current gaping lacunae of conception and service in the secondary learning disability field are clearly evidenced by the reliance of many practitioners—despite their working with preadolescent and adolescent populations—on such instruments which were intended for younger children.

Partly, too, this exaggerated focus of the field of learning disabilities on young children is a consequence of the modern history of the field. The original challenge was posed by elementary school–aged children, who, despite average or above average intellectual ability, could not grasp or master basic learning skills—reading, arithmetic, spelling, and writing. The focus on young children also appears to be a consequence of learning disabilities' development within the context of the broader field of special education, in which instructional orientation and technology have been directed toward the remediation of basic skills at the primary and elementary levels.

Finally, the neglect of secondary-level learning disabled pupils seems to be due to secondary education's ability to manage or mask the older learning disabled pupil's problems—depending on which standpoint, positive or negative, you assume.

Secondary schools are typically more flexible than elementary schools. The variety of schedules and activities that secondary schools allow permits the learning disabled preadolescent and adolescent to function with some social, if not academic, success. Consequently, the learning disabled pupil's academic limitations may be minimized or obscured at the secondary level. Vocational technical schools also often serve as receiving and habilitation vehicles for learning disabled youth—everyone hoping, the youth included, for successful job and life preparation despite deficient academic skills. In contrast, in elementary schools the learning disabled pupil is exposed to the demands that he or she achieve academically according to teacher and peer standards; these demands may be diminished by judicious assignment at the secondary level—the pupil can even be removed from competition until he or she graduates from or drops out of school. We are not attempting to criticize the secondary schools. As currently financed and constituted, most of these schools can only temporize and compromise with their learning disabled charges. The immediate future does not appear more promising in this respect. However, despite shrinking resources, secondary schools are being asked increasingly to meet the demands of their learning disabled students academically. We hope that this book will provide these schools with some rationales for the most effective deployment of their resources.

Whatever the causes, older learning disabled pupils, preadolescent and adolescent, have been overlooked, ignored, or disregarded over the past years. Hardly anyone has noticed this because we were all too busy remediating the perceptual motor and cognitive deficits of young learning disabled children. We justified concentrating on such a narrow band of children on the basis that we would be able to remediate their deficits or compensate with their strengths so that the children would be able to function effectively later on—and happily ever after. This is the impression that many novice teachers, administrators, and hopeful parents gathered from the broadly reassuring books that they read during the early years of the learning disability movement and from the glittering magic shows that greeted them on the floors of ACLD and CEC conventions. Many of us were sure that we were doing the right thing in "catching" early learning disabilities and correcting them so that there would be, in due time, very few older learning disabled children. This was the natural enthusiasm of a young field excited by the prospect of changing children's lives. We cannot fault ourselves for that original enthusiasm—it inspired many valiant and valuable efforts. Also, we have helped enough children to make us feel that our efforts have not been in vain.

But the field of learning disabilities has matured, and we now realize that the problems of many learning disabled adolescents and adults have resisted our technologies and skills when we attempted to remediate their learning disabilities at the elementary level. The problems of others were not sufficiently acute to draw attention in early grades, and these children muddled through elementary school but cannot now cope with the more complex demands of secondary education. These learning disabled children—now youth—challenge us to meet their needs at the level of secondary learning disabilities.

THE SECONDARY LEARNING DISABLED PUPIL: SOME TENTATIVE CONSIDERATIONS

Who is the secondary learning disabled pupil? The question suggests that there is some simple and unitary answer, that we can describe particular types of youth with particular types of characteristics and learning problems, who are prototypical of the learning disabled preadolescent or adolescent. From our experiences with the enormous diversities of skills and dis-skills in elementary-level learning disabled children, we should all know that this is a vain hope.

Yet we are compelled to try to establish some order out of the phenomena that confront us at the secondary level and to determine which youths should be considered as secondary learning disabled, as contrasted to other problem learners at the secondary level: brain damaged, mentally retarded, emotionally disturbed, culturally deprived, and slow-learning pupils, and the mass of others with nonspecific learning failures who constitute a massive minority with the secondary schools. The determinations that can be made will be difficult and sometimes arbitrary. Yet without an attempt at some categorical or diagnostic distinctions, the appellation of learning disabilities must become a loose catch phrase that simply means *learning problems;* and such a tautological designation will assist little in correcting or managing secondary-level learning disabilities.

We will now attempt to develop an approximate definition of secondary-level learning disabled pupils by exclusion. We will define them more precisely in Chapter 2 by positive criteria. The following paragraphs describe what learning disabled children are not.

1. The secondary learning disabled pupil is not sensorially impaired or physically handicapped to a significant degree. We believe that no extended explanation is needed of these exclusions, which simply recognize that other kinds of services are needed for other types of handicapped youth.

2. The secondary learning disabled pupil is not mentally retarded or a slow learner. Certain mentally retarded pupils suffer from specific weaknesses of or impairments in their learning ability. However, we believe that to delimit the secondary learning disability category, one must establish and maintain definitive psychometric criteria distinguishing the mentally retarded and the slow learner from the learning disabled. The techniques and subject matter of instruction may be the same for each group, i.e., for the educable mentally retarded, the slow learner, and the learning disabled. However, we hold expectations for academic success at levels close to the level of the normal pupil for the learning disabled child—even if he never fulfills them. The same cannot be said for the slow learner or the mentally retarded (unless they have been misdiagnosed). These statements are unpopular and out of step with much of current opinion, and we agree that there are exceptions to them. The authors are also familiar with the problems and imperfections of attempting to determine mental retardation by psychometric means. But, at least by definition, the slow learner and the mentally retarded are comparatively less able than their chronological peers. From such a definition, academic expectations must be lower for the former, just as normal achievement expectations, all problems being corrected, hold for the latter. (Whatever else they are, IQ tests provide measures of academically related or relevant abilities. We define secondary learning disability via academic terms. As such, regardless of the genotypical validity of IQ test results, they are valuable for defining learning disabilities.)

3. The secondary learning disabled pupil is not synonymous with or identical to one with academic deficiencies that have resulted from sociocultural limitations, although the problems of one can exist with or even contribute to the other. The accepted diagnosis of learning

problems associated with sociocultural deprivation emphasizes basically adequate *learning processes,* despite which the student has not learned or is currently failing to learn. The socioculturally deprived pupil is thus distinguished from the learning disabled youth who is presumed to have some type of *process difficulty,* which causes his learning problems. In the learning disabled pupil, something is deficient or impaired in the functioning of his central nervous system; while not necessarily affecting overall cognitive achievement (as measured by standardized intelligence tests), this defect interferes with specific aspects of cognitive operation and makes the youth an inefficient or incapacitated performer in school.

To those who are acquainted with the authors' positions on process assessment and training (Mann and Goodman, 1973; Mann, 1971; Mann, 1970; Mann and Phillips, 1967, Goodman and Hammill, 1973), this definition may be somewhat surprising. It will be clarified as we progress; and we hope to make it clear that the hypothecation of "process" dysfunction or "disability" as basic to the diagnosis of learning disabilities does not necessarily mean a carte blanche acceptance of current process definitions.

Our distinction between socioculturally deprived and learning disabled secondary school pupils may raise even more questions as to the arbitrariness of our definitions than did the distinction we made earlier between learning disabled pupils and the mentally retarded and slow learners. Many people argue that the effects of deprivation may cause massive and pervasive learning disabilities in disadvantaged youth. This may be true, but then such youth should exhibit characteristics similar to those of other learning disabled pupils. And if so, they too become members of our learning disabled group—on the basis of their presenting a "learning disabilities" syndrome of deficits. For we are not concerned with what caused a learning disability as long as we can establish its presence. However, while sociocultural problems are of serious concern to every educator, they are not specifically related to the problems of secondary learning disabilities.

4. The secondary learning disabled pupil is not a so-called brain injured or neurologically impaired youth whose neurological problems have resulted in significant behavior problems. Many of these latter youth have learning problems as well, but their behavior problems are often of a magnitude requiring unusual attention, effort, and time—and in areas other than academic development. The learning disabled pupil's neurological problems are manifested primarily in his inability or disability to master fundamental academic skills, whereas

those of the brain injured child are contributory to and part of a broader constellation of behavior problems. And when behavior problems require first consideration in remediation efforts, we believe it will be beneficial for both "categories" of youth to be clearly distinguished for programming purposes.

5. A secondary learning disabled pupil is not an emotionally disturbed youth. The emotionally disturbed individual frequently has major problems and deficiencies in learning areas. But for him, as with the brain injured, other foci of care, management, and instruction must take precedence in the concerned teacher's mind. The greatest effort should be devoted in working through affective problems, correcting dysfunctional and disabling attitudes and habits, and developing appropriate and effective social coping skills. Presumably, if problems in these areas are corrected or effectively controlled, the emotionally disturbed pupil—like the socially and culturally deprived student—can learn through traditional educational means. There are, of course, learning disabled emotionally disturbed youths who should be provided with the specific technologies of the learning disability field, and they are expected to benefit from that technology.

6. The learning disabled secondary pupil is not simply a member of that vast minority of youth who are the failures of the educational system. This latter group includes those who are not handicapped or socially or culturally deprived and who have adequate mental ability: the emotionally apathetic, the disinterested, the lazy and unmotivated, and those who have been inadequately or inappropriately taught. The recent revelations of the *National Assessment of Education Progress* project indicates that a shocking percentage of high school drop-outs and graduates cannot functionally read, calculate, or write and are abysmally unaware of the fundamental bodies of knowledge that we expect of an educated citizen. But such pupils, once again, are not learning disabled by our definition. To consider them as such would be to make the classification of learning disabilities redundant and useless.

7. Finally, a secondary learning disabled youth is not one who has made adequate, if modest, progress in elementary school, yet is simply unable to cope with the increasingly complex demands of the secondary level. The cognitive apparati of such students are not capable of meeting the increasingly greater quantities and complexities of secondary-level academic instruction. Such youths do not have disabilities; they have insufficiencies in skills that make them the victims of society's insistence on universal education and its require-

ment that they remain in school and perform academically at levels beyond their intellectual means. There is an increasing awareness of the problems that such youth present. They must be provided with more meaningful alternatives than we have so far developed for them. Increasing efforts are being made to do so. Such pupils are not candidates for a secondary-level learning disability program.

In summary, secondary-level learning disabled pupils are not sensorially or physically handicapped, mentally retarded or slow learners, or pupils whose general intellectual levels are insufficient to master the more complex demands of secondary education. Neither are they victims of severe behavioral disturbances caused by brain injury, neurological disturbance, or emotional pathology. They do not suffer from pathologically improverishing social cultural histories; nor do they represent the many dismotivated, disinterested, turned-off constituents, and products, of modern society and its educational systems.

Our diagnosis by exclusion has permitted us to delimit a much narrower group of individuals and to develop positive criteria by which to diagnose secondary learning disabled pupils: They are preadolescents and adolescents who are of average general mental ability and free of significant sensory or physical handicaps. They are also reasonably free of severe emotional and behavioral pathology; they manifest acceptable and manageable behavior. Nevertheless, despite appropriate and ordinarily effective means of instruction, adequate support, and reasonable efforts on their own part, such pupils are unable to cope with academic demands as a consequence of their particular and specific cognitive disabilities.

It may be argued that such a diagnosis severely limits the number of individuals who might be considered as seçondary learning disabled pupils. That is our intention. If we broaden the classification of secondary-level disability, it will lose its value as an explanatory concept. Scientific classification and precise management of educational problems both require limitations. Further, the limitations of our resources, financial and human, necessitate this narrowness. Within the classification of secondary learning disability pupils that we propose, there are sufficient numbers of pupils to whom learning disability specialists can appropriately direct their attention.

REFERENCES

Goodman L, Hammill DD: The effectiveness of the Kephart-Getman activities in developing perceptual-motor and cognitive skills. *Focus Except Child* 4:1–9, 1973

Mann L: Perceptual training: misdirections and redirections. Am J Orthopsychiatry 40:30–38, 1970

Mann L: Psychometric phrenology and the new faculty psychology: the case against ability assessment and training. J Special Education 5:3–53, 1971

Mann L, Goodman L: Perceptual training: a critical retrospect. *In* Schopler E, Reichler RJ (eds): *Psychopathology and Child Development: Research and Treatment.* New York, Plenum, 1976, pp 271–289

Mann L, Goodman L, Wiederholt JL: *The Learning Disabled Adolescent: A Book of Readings.*Boston, Houghton-Mifflin (in press)

Mann L, Phillips WA: Fractional practices in special education: a critique. Except Child 33:311–315, 1967

CHAPTER 2
A Closer Look at Secondary Learning Disabilities

A SECONDARY LEARNING DISABILITY DEFINITION: RECAPITULATION AND PROSPECT

In Chapter 1 we defined secondary-level learning disabilities through diagnosis by exclusion, an often criticized if even more often bootlegged form of diagnostic decision making. From the preceding diagnosis by negatives, we can move to a positive diagnostic position concerning the secondary learning disabled pupil, one that we adumbrated in Chapter 1 and will expand here.

The secondary-level learning disabled pupil has at least average mental ability, his learning is not impeded by physical or sensory problems, and his behavior is acceptable and manageable. Despite having made reasonable efforts and having received ordinarily appropriate instruction and environmental support in the past, he cannot cope with academic demands at the secondary level, as a consequence of specific cognitive disabilities. An environmentally deprived pupil may also be termed a learning disabled one if he meets these criteria. Clearly, our definition is not definitive at this point, i.e., as regards establishing criteria for learning disability selection. We will provide more specific criteria for such selection later.

NATIONAL ADVISORY COMMITTEE'S DEFINITION

The definition put forth by the National Advisory Committee for Handicapped Children (NACHC) in 1968 varies considerably from our own:

> Students with special learning disabilities exhibit a disorder in one or more of the basic psychological processes involved in understanding or in using spoken or written languages. These may be manifested in disorders of listening, thinking, talking, reading, writing, spelling, or arithmetic. They include conditions which have been referred to as perceptual handicaps, brain injury, minimal brain dysfunction, dyslexia, developmental aphasia, etc. They do not include learning problems which are due primarily to visual, hearing, or motor handicaps, to mental retardation, emotional disturbance or to environmental disadvantage.

This definition is an omnibus one, based on the concensus and agreement of specialists from a variety of disciplines. According to the analysis of two distinguished scholars in the field (Myers and Hammill, 1969), the definition establishes four criteria for diagnosing learning disabilities: (1) the principal of disparity, (2) the role of demonstrable central nervous system dysfunction, (3) basic disorders of the learning processes, and (4) children excluded by the definition.

There are few programs for the learning disabled which have not adopted or adapted the central tenets of the NACHC's definition as operational bases for their own programs. Nevertheless, we have rarely found learning disability programs in which these tenets have not been violated in practice. In fact, many of the programs currently operated for learning disabled children provide service to the mentally retarded (test scatter presuming normal intellectual potential is usually the basis for justifying the inclusion of such children), as per psychometric definitions, or otherwise include children with behavior problems and/or poor learners who have no clear identifying characteristics of specific learning disability. Many learning disability programs also include the disadvantaged, although some programs may not do so since the learning disabilities movement has been largely a white middle class one.

The NACHC's definition is unsatisfactory from our standpoint. First, it presents problems for those who are attempting to work with secondary-level learning disabled pupils since the definition has emerged from work at the primary and elementary levels. Further, the labeling of disorders ". . . in one or more of the basic psychological processes" is too vague and nonspecific. Psychological processes are ill defined in the committee's statement. "Imperfect ability to listen, think, speak, write, spell or do mathematical calculations" probably characterizes the bulk of the world's population.

Such a vague definition of learning disabilities permits each university, professor, school district, special education administrator, teacher, remedial specialist, and parent to make his own decisions as to what constitutes a recognizable (for classification and treatment) learning disability. Thus, learning disabilities classes become catch-alls for a variety of problem learners who cannot be accommodated instructionally or for political reasons in other programs. It omits guidelines for the practicing educator in his or her development of instructional programs for the learning disabled; and a definition of learning disabilities should have the most implications for the educator, among other professionals.

Furthermore, the NACHC's definition of learning disabilities offers a conglomorate diagnosis encompassing other handicaps—brain injury, minimal brain dysfunction, dyslexia, developmental aphasia, perceptual handicaps. We protest, among other things, the specification of perceptual handicaps as a unitary, free-standing syndrome. (Even though the myths of perceptual handicap and perceptual training have been slain repeatedly in the literature, they survive all the same; apparently, nothing serves the public's needs like a good myth.) We also protest NACHC's inclusion of developmental aphasia (another term that has created enough confusion to merit complete retirement), since we believe it diminishes the academic implications of a learning disabilities diagnosis.

On the other hand, it is obvious from our preliminary definitions that we concur with the NACHC's exclusion from the classification of learning disabled children those who have learning problems that are primarily the result of visual, hearing, or motor handicaps, or of mental retardation, emotional disturbance, or environmental disadvantage. But we suggest that emotional disturbance be expanded to include behavioral problems from any source, and that the exclusion of motor problems be narrowed to gross motor disturbances since visual/motor dysfunction is frequently implicated in learning disabilities and fine motor problems of a subtle nature may express themselves in a variety of cognitive problems of potential importance to learning disabilities.

DETERMINING SECONDARY LEARNING
DISABILITIES

Let us now proceed in formulating a definition of secondary-level learning disabilities. The reader will remember the exclusionary criteria that we (and the National Advisory Council for Handicapped Children) have already established to distinguish the learning disabled from other handicapped children.

The determination of learning disabilities at the secondary level, we believe, must emphasize four diagnostic components: (1) identification of significant academic deficit, (2) determination of average mental ability, (3) determination of process disorder, and (4) determination of neurological dysfunction.

These components establish the necessary inclusionary criteria by which secondary-level learning disabled youth are to be identified; they hold, as well, for the elementary learning disabled. They help to prescribe the steps that should be followed in identifying the learning disabled pupil.

We shall examine each of these components further in this book. For diagnostic and theoretical clarification, we shall deal first with those components that are relatively easy to manage, i.e., intellectual status and neurological dysfunction, leaving the more difficult components of learning disabilities identification, i.e., those of process disorder and educational disability, for later consideration.

Average Mental Ability

Let us first of all look at the identification-diagnostic component of average mental ability. We say "average" rather than "normal" since, by definition, the learning disabled pupil has abnormal mental ability, i.e., disabilities, that impair his functioning in skills required for academic learning. Two considerations for evaluation are (1) the psychometric instruments chosen for assessing intellectual ability, and (2) the designation of limits for average mental ability.

Should we use a *Peabody Picture Vocabulary Test* (PPVT) or the *Slosson Intelligence Test for Children and Adults* (SIT) to determine ability since these tests are so easy to administer. What about the group tests that are available for this purpose, such as the *Lorge Thorndike* or the *Otis Lennon?* No. We insist upon the administration of the most valid of individual intelligence tests: the *Stanford-Binet* and *Wechsler* scales. Intellectual assessment, particularly when decisions are to be made regarding educational placement of individual students, must be based on the best technology available. We doubt that many will disagree that the Stanford-Binet and Wechsler scales offer the best assessments of individual global mental ability.

There is no point in arguing about the legitimacy of any or all available intelligence tests as vehicles for assessing mental abilities. We know, as does the reader, about the fallibility of such instruments and the intellectual measures they yield. We recognize, too, the tests' unfairness for many ghetto and Hispanic children. Arguments and dissension and contentions have gone on ever since Binet and Simon introduced their original scale in 1905. But these tests are the best we've got, and we insist that they are better than the variety of substitutes currently available to provide other estimates of mental ability. If we wish to discard our best traditional mental tests, we should perhaps consider discarding the entire concept of learning disabilities, or, for that matter, most of our efforts at assessing intellectual ability in handicapped children. We are all interested in better instruments in the future, such as those which are being developed from Piagetian inspiration. But, until better tests are available, please accept no substitutes—insist on the Binet or Wechsler scales.

We eschew the use of short forms of these tests and brief intelligence tests, such as the Slosson, the PPVT, or group-administered intelligence tests, such as the Lorge Thorndike or Otis Lennon for intellectual assessment of pupils referred for learning disabilities placement (except for confirmatory or follow-up purposes). Although these tests have many legitimate uses, they are inappropriately used for identifying and diagnosing learning disabled pupils because they tap less of the pupils' cognitive skill repertoires, and they are less accurate in what they do assess.

Our second consideration in intellectual assessment is concerned with the definition of average mental ability. What constitutes average mental ability? Shall we base our decision on a parent's doting comments or a teacher's more pessimistic view? We, of course, hold to a psychometric definition. But here, too, the temptations are many. We may insist firmly on a 100 IQ or above. We may accept the range of 90 to 110, the usual range of average mental ability. Or we may extend our range down the lower half of the normal curve to 85 or 80, while some have even accepted IQs of 75 or 70 as normal.

All of this is becoming increasingly arbitrary as anxious parents, concerned school teachers, and politicized public groups are reluctant to classify youth who are failing by traditional academic means as mentally retarded or some other negative label yet demand educational services for them. *Learning disabled* has not yet become a pejorative term, and many prefer it because of the benignity of its implications.

We suggest that the lower limits of average intellectual ability accepted for a diagnosis of secondary learning disabilities be a full scale intellectual quotient of 90 on the Binet or the Wechsler test. We believe that accepting as learning disabled those pupils whose intellectual quotient falls below traditional average ability waters down the definition of learning disabilities so as to make it far less manageable and productive for all concerned. If we regard the IQ as a purely pragmatic index, which provides a prognosis of academic achievement rather than a direct measure of intelligence, it is obvious that the individual with a higher IQ has a better prognosis academically then a low-functioning individual. The minimum criterion of 90 insures that pupils who are placed in the learning disabilities program have a good chance of adequate academic achievement. Having higher ability learning disabled youth in our programs gives us an opportunity to test our developing technology in learning disabilities remediation against a fair standard.

Nevertheless, the learning disability specialist is confronted with repeated attempts to breech the lower limits of the average psychometric definition that we have recommended. Usually, it is inferred that the pupil's true ability is higher than that indicated by his IQ score and is either in or above the average range of intellectual functioning. The psychologist or special educator usually supports such claims with information from test scatter on the Standard-Binet, i.e., the student passes certain subtests at or beyond his chronological age, despite his subnormal IQ, or from the intersubtest scatter on the Weschler with various subtests falling in or beyond the average range, despite overall depression of the global IQ scores. Certain limited-focus tests, like the PPVT, the format of which can result in lucky runs, can also provide good IQs when the Binet and Wechsler would tell us otherwise.

We will not argue the fallibilities of the concept of *true* intellectual potential any more than we would argue those of the IQ. There is adequate evidence supporting the IQ as one of the best predictors of school success and academically related achievement; hence we recommend continued reliance on it for the present.

To repeat, we insist upon the criterion of average or better IQ—90 or above—in our learning disabilities definition on purely pragmatic grounds, based on the use of the IQ as a predictive index rather than in terms of some ill-defined etiological conception of intelligence. The average IQ is predictive of average achievement, the subaverage IQ of subachievement, the high IQ of higher achievement. And implicit in our hypothesis of learning disabilities is the expectation of at least average achievement by the learning disabled pupil.

Other intellectual criteria are suggested in the literature (Wiederholt, 1975). We have selected our intellectual standard because it appears logical and consistent with accepted conceptions of learning disabilities, and because it has demonstrated its viability and utility in our secondary classroom programs. Our Pennsylvania state guidelines for operating the special education program establish or specify an IQ of 80 as the lower limit of normalcy; pupils whose intellectual quotients are below this level are considered retarded, those with an intellectual quotient above this are considered normal. The demarcation between retardation and normalcy, of course, varies from one state to another, and in some states the cutoff for retardation is even lower than it is in Pennsylvania.

Our criterion of a 90 IQ for the learning disabled creates a gap between the upper limit of the ability range that defines mental retardation and the lower limit of the normal intellectual range within which a pupil must achieve to be considered a learning disabilities class candidate. The students between the two standards—who achieve too high for placement in an educable mentally retarded class and too low for placement in a learning disabled class—constitute slow learners or dull normals. Of all those excluded from the learning disabled classification (the retarded, the emotionally disturbed, etc.), the slow learner is the most difficult to justify. However, we believe that the learning disabled student and the slow learning student are not identical, and that their academic failure problems are quite different.

We have several reasons for concern about the possible confusion of learning disabilities and slow learning populations. First, slow learners are essentially normal individuals who are inappropriately labeled as handicapped and placed in special education programs. Then there is the issue of false expectancies. In a much needed article, Shepard (1975) explored the problems resulting from the misdiagnosis of slow learning children as learning disabled. Although she studied elementary school children, her arguments apply equally well to the secondary school pupils. We agree with Shepard that the designation of the truly slow learning children "whose performance is consistent with their own abilities" but below the expected standard as learning disabled "constitutes a misdiagnosis and misplacement." If placed in a learning disability program, a slow learning student is likely to be subjected to undue pressure to perform beyond his capabilities, if the teacher attempts to fulfill the expectations for academic achievement which we hold for learning disabled students. A general deficit and specific deficits are indeed different. The misplacement of the slow learning child in a learning disabilities classroom is a disservice to both the slow learning child and the learning disabilities program; the learning disabled pupil is difficult enough to manage effectively without adding the additional burden of intellectual lag.

Given the present situation in most secondary schools, excluding the slow learner or dull normal student from consideration for learning disabilities placement may place such pupils in an educational limbo since many schools provide few or no programs to meet their needs. However, this does not justify their being labeled as learning disabled. Slow learners are still appropriately the responsibility of general education; and their inclusion as learning disabled would mean an overburdening of limited special education resources.

Of course, some slow learning youth also have learning disabilities. When we have developed appropriate technologies for the learning disabled student of average mental ability, programs may hopefully be developed for slow learner–learning disabled pupils that also take into account these students' limited potential. Our book, however, is concerned with the learning disabled pupil of average mental ability.

Some readers may object that errors of measurement possibly result in a pupil of average ability scoring below our lower average limit on an intelligence test. We recommend erring on the side of overqualification. If we are ever to develop a technology for learning disabilities, we must load the dice in favor of our expectations.

Neurological Dysfunction

Implicit in almost all definitions of learning disabilities is the hypothesis of neurological dysfunction (McCarthy and McCarthy, 1969). Like it or not, reject the medical model as much as they desire, special educators are forced to live with the fact that the children they deal with are defined (with the exception of the gifted) by medical, as well as psychological and educational criteria. So the diagnosis of learning disabilities implies some nervous system (conceptual nervous system, some wags would call it) dysfunction. And although psychologists' instruments are relied on heavily by physician and educator alike in such a diagnosis, neurologists must make the final decision of neurological disability. We wish that their instruments could distinguish and diagnose the relatively subtle neurological problems that we presume underlie many learning disabilities, as opposed to the clearly delineated and observed ones that we so rarely find.

Neurological assessment poses a considerable problem for the learning disability specialist. The first diagnosis of presumptive neurological dysfunctioning is usually made by the school psychologists, who constitute the first line of extraeducational diagnosis for the school system. These diagnoses often are not confirmed by subsequent neurological examinations. This is not to fault the psychologist who bases his diagnoses on certain types of tests or otherwise observed behaviors that may reveal disorganized cognitive functioning, which from his inferential standpoint indicates a neurological disorder. He may be correct. However, the distance from his inferences to the physical symptomatology that the neurologist requires to confirm the diagnosis of neurological dysfunction is often a long one fraught with problems; and the neurologists' assessments of neurological dysfunction are often negative despite the original positive psychological diagnoses. But should they be expected to be positive unless the learning disability was the result of or was accompanied by gross neurological disorders. Whereas in fact, the typical secondary learning disability student described here has been diagnosed and distinguished from those secondary school pupils who are suffering from severe neurological disorders, e.g., brain injured youth with behavioral disturbances? The subtle central nervous system disorders that may underlie secondary learning disabilities can defy diagnosis by the neurologist.

And yet with all the schools' reliance upon the tools of psychological and educational diagnosis, the diagnosis of learning disabilities in most states, and in some cases by regulation or law, requires confirmation of a neurological disorder by a neurologist. In practice, this dilemma often is resolved by the neurologist's utilization of the psychologist's data, rather than his own, to make a positive diagnosis in the face of his own negative findings. Or the neurologist may temper his negative diagnoses stating that his negative results do not necessarily exclude a condition of subtle neurological disorder. Problems of neurological diagnosis must be resolved by individual practitioners, rather than by some general rule, and in accordance with the state and local standards under which learning disabilities programs operate.

CONCLUSION

We have considered first the easier diagnostic issues in secondary learning disability: identifying normal mental ability and neurological dysfunctioning. We have left for later consideration the issues as to what the learning disabled secondary-level pupil is learning disabled in, with, or by, and the type of educational problems that he or she presents that are distinctive for a diagnosis of learning disability. These latter problems are the most difficult to resolve satisfactorily, and by their nature they create the most controversy and dissension among learning disability specialists. But they, too, require our attention.

We shall deal with *processes* in Chapter 3, and the educational component of our secondary learning disabilities definition in Chapter 4.

REFERENCES

Budoff M: Studies in learning potential. Cambridge, Mass, Research Institute for Educational Problems, vol 3, no 39 (undated)

Budoff M, Meskin J, Harrison RH: Educational test of the learning-potential hypothesis. Am J Mental Deficiency 76:159–169, 1971

McCarthy JJ, McCarthy JF: *Learning Disabilities.* Boston, Allyn & Bacon, 1969

Myers PI, Hammill DD: *Methods for Learning Disorders.* New York, John Wiley & Sons, 1969

National Advisory Committee for Handicapped Children. Federal register. Washington, D.C., Department of Health, Education & Welfare, US Office of Education. US Government Printing Office, vol 38, no 196, October 11, 1973

Sattler JM: *Assessment of Child Intelligence: With Individually Administered Tests.* Philadelphia, WB Saunders, 1974

Shepard MJ: Learning disabled or slow learner? Teacher 92:29–31, 1975

Wiederholt JL: A report on secondary school programs for the learning disabled. Tucson, University of Arizona, Leadership Training Institute in Learning Disabilities, 1975

CHAPTER 3

The Process of Determining Process

Let us turn now to consider *process*. In Chapter 1 we stated that some type of process disability definition is required for a diagnosis of learning disabilities. In fact, this decision was reached at a recent conference of learning disability specialists dealing with problems of secondary-level learning disability pupils (Mann, Goodman, Wiederholt, 1977). Even those who disagreed violently with the conception of process as it is usually employed agreed that a process definition is required for the diagnosis of learning disabilities.

The *process* definition was included in the NACHC definition of learning disability, which emphasizes a "disorder in one or more of the *basic processes* involved in understanding or in using language 'spoken or written'." We will begin our deliberations about process disorders by discussing that definition.

The NACHC definition clearly establishes language as the primary area of focus in learning disabilities. Yet as we know, at least as many learning disabled children are diagnosed as learning disabled on the basis of so-called visual perception and perceptual motor tests as through language tests.

The NACHC definition includes perceptual handicap, brain injury, minimal cerebral palsy, brain dysfunction, dyslexia, as well as

23

developmental aphasia as causative of disorders in the "basic processes" presumed to be involved in learning disabilities. However, neither "perceptual" handicap, brain injury, nor minimal brain dysfunction is necessarily associated with or caused by problems with understanding and using language.

Further, the NACHC's conceptualization of the process difficulties a learning disabled pupil manifests in "listening, thinking, speaking, reading, writing, spelling and mathematical calculations" appears to provide simply a catalog of the problems generally encountered in children with learning problems, rather than a systematically researched determination of what truly constitutes a learning disability. We thus find the NACHC definition ambiguous, in places contradictory, and too broadly pathological. We do accept from the NACHC definition the indication that there is in learning disabilities "a disorder in one or more of the basic psychological processes," and we agree that critical to any definition of learning disability as a handicapping condition are disabilities of "basic psychological processes."

Having accepted a process disorder criterion to establish a diagnosis of learning disabilities, we must reduce the types of processes that may be legitimately dealt with at the secondary level from those that are appropriate to the specialist at the elementary level.

We believe that the "processes" of concern for education programming for secondary learning disabilities should be those directly affecting academic achievement, i.e., as manifested in the basic skill areas of reading, spelling, arithmetic, writing, or other academic areas. To believe that the field of learning disabilities has or will have anything of substance to offer to preadolescent or adolescent youth who cannot comprehend or express spoken language in a utilitarian fashion (we do not mean subtle language usage problems) or are otherwise grossly language impaired is presumptuous. Although the management of communicative and receptive oral language problems may be reasonably within the operating domain of the elementary learning disabilities specialist, the secondary level is too late for such management. An aphasic simply doesn't belong in a secondary learning disabilities program. Incidentally, if we adhere to our definition of average mental ability as a criterion for a secondary learning disability diagnosis, few severely language impaired youth would possibly meet our screening criteria.

The process disabilities with which we are concerned at the secondary level are those that cause academic failure in a reasonably well-motivated, well-adjusted, and otherwise unhandicapped preadolescent or adolescent. Such a youth has received sufficient environmental support for his learning experiences and has been exposed to appropriate and sufficient instruction. But because of dysfunctional cognitive processes resulting from neurological dysfunction, he cannot profit from instruction at the level anticipated on the basis of his general mental ability.

The diagnosis of "process" variables is the most problematic diagnostic issue we face at the secondary level. After having taken the diagnostic positions that are reasonably forthright, e.g., regarding intelligence and neurological dysfunctioning, we become tentative and somewhat evasive because we know little about cognitive processes, and yet we are forced to diagnose cognitive dysfunctions if we are to identify the learning disabled. This issue of knowing the unknowable, which is critical to the diagnosis of learning disabilities, requires elaboration.

A CLOSER LOOK AT PROCESS

The term *process* has become more popular than the term *ability*—for which process is by and large synonymous in most of the literature—possibly because the former is a more dynamic term. We use both expressions interchangeably in the book. The term *skill* usually refers to some specific performance that is immediately manifest (unlike the process which is inferred), such as decoding skills or two-column addition skills.

The critical component in the diagnosis of learning disabilities is *the specific cognitive disability.* (We include under cognitive all perceptual, language, and intellective capacities.) To diagnose learning disabilities in a problem pupil, we must be able to point to limitations or impairments in specific components of the pupil's cognitive makeup, i.e., to deficiencies in his cognitive "processes" that cause his academic failure. This reasoning is opposed to the explanation of those failures in terms of gross global intellectual limitations or impairments (such as would be suggested by low IQ).

Before we proceed on this point, let us consider what a cognitive process is. A useful definition has been provided by Kagan and Kogan:

. . . cognition stands for those hypothetical psychological processes invoked to explain overt verbal and motor behavior as well as certain physiological reactions. Cognitive process is a superordinate term subsuming the more familiar titles of imagery, perception, free association, thought, mediation, proliferation of hypotheses, reasoning, reflection, and problem solving. All verbal behavior must be a product of cognitive processes, as are dreams and intelligence test performances. But skeletal muscle movements of visceral reactions are not necessarily linked to cognition. [1970, p. 1275]

As may be seen from this definition, an enormous variety of inner activities or events may be subsumed under the rubric of cognitive processes. However, workers in the field of learning disabilities are used to dealing with processes that have been defined by various psycho-educational tests. Of these tests, the most popular and certainly the most influential in determining practices in learning disabilities are the *Illinois Test of Psycholinguistic Abilities* and the *Marianne Frostig Developmental Test of Visual Perception, Third Edition.* Other popular instruments include the *Bender Visual Motor Gestalt Test,* the *Wepman Auditory Discrimination Test,* the *Southern California Perceptual Motor Tests,* the *Ayres Space Test,* and the *Developmental Test of Visual Motor Integration.*

Such instruments are used to evaluate specific processes and to determine strengths, weaknesses, and impairments in these processes.

Several major problems confront us when we use such tests to evaluate processes, as when we conceptually employ processes in any form. This book is not intended to provide a battleground for the controversies in the field of learning disabilities, but we must confront these problems if we are to diagnose learning disabilities intelligently at the secondary level.

PRESUMPTIONS AND ASSUMPTIONS ABOUT PROCESSES

First, let us examine some assumptions underlying the current use of the term *process.* Some workers assume that causative of the various behaviors we engage in (and school work is included here) are underlying "inner organismic" activities or structures (as Guilford would have it)—i.e., processes.

Relative to academic achievement, the term *process* presumes that underlying performance and achievement in various academic areas are some "things" that create and direct them. Further, deficiencies, or deficits or impairments in these processes, are held to be directly responsible for failures in academic performance. Thus, the disability of an ability, so to speak, is responsible for school failure. If a pupil has a global ability deficit and low intelligence [which may also be construed as a process as defined by Spearman (1927)], he is expected to have problems with academic work. However, if that pupil suffers from weaknesses or impairments of specific processes, e.g., figure ground perception or verbal encoding, we still anticipate academic failures, even though he might have average or better general intelligence. (These activities or structures, i.e., processes, presumably have a neurological basis.) Specific disabilities may be just as deleterious to academic performance as the global deficits associated with low mental ability, because the specific academic deficiencies the former cause disturb the global structures of academic achievement, just as failure in one component of a car's engine will halt it despite the soundness of its other components.

Education's answer to global deficits usually has been to program for the children for lower expectancies or to seclude them in special classes. More recently, rather global, usually academically oriented efforts have been made to raise the children's levels of general ability or improve the gross process areas associated with academic performance, such as language. These approaches have been used in Head Start programs.

Education's answer, on the other hand, to the deficits of the specific variety as defined on psychoeducational tests, such as the ITPA and the DTVP, has been to attempt to remediate the impaired processes directly in programs such as *The Frostig Program for Development of Visual Perception* (Frostig and Horne, 1964), *Developing Learning Readiness* (Getman, Kane, Halgren, and McKee, 1968), and the *MWM Program for Developing Language Abilities* (Minskoff, Wiseman, and Minskoff, 1973). Also educational programs have been established which capitalize on the pupil's unimpaired or strong processes. For example, when auditory processes are weak or deficient, visual learning is emphasized.

Teachers of the learning disabled surely are familiar with this, and we apologize for oversimplifying the issues involved. We believe that oversimplification is required to clarify the problems that confront us when we attempt to define and diagnose learning disabilities.

The field of learning disabilities is predicated on the assumption of specific process deficits. And certainly it is a reasonable assumption that the academic failure of a student with good general ability, who has had adequate exposure to a reasonable environment, is free of other handicaps, and has been reasonably taught is due to some process difficulty; something is wrong with his specific learning abilities. However, we encounter problems when we attempt to determine what that process difficulty is.

From the Kagan–Kogan definition, it is clear that processes are "hypothetical," meaning presumed. [For an interesting discussion of the relationship of test measures to processes, see Messick's article (1975).] In short, we cannot directly identify a process, we must guess at what it is, and guesses are by definition most uncertain propositions.

One would never assume that the processes that so many professionals talk about are hypothetical. These processes are discussed, diagnosed, and treated with aplomb and surety. But such casual acceptance of the unproven is born of an age-old cognitive warp, reification (Mann, 1969), or the confusion of words, labels, and names with realities. It is ironic that when so many special educators criticize labels such as IQ and mental retardation as being inaccurate and poorly representative *of their real* referents, these educators are willing to accept far less substantial labels as accurately identifying specific processes. The processes that special educators in learning disabilities discuss so freely are guesses that are labeled according to some theorist's or test maker's hypotheses (guesses—nothing more), despite the air of scientific precision, indeed rectitude, that they are often associated with.

Thus, Ebel wrote:

> . . . part of the difficulty with the term higher mental processes is seeing the difference between higher and lower mental processes. Is recall a lower mental process? When I leave the office and try to recall where my car was parked the last time I left it, in Lot D, H, M, or P, and where in the lot, it seems that I am using about all the mental processes, high and low, that I possess. Further because we do not really know what a mental process is, may it not be premature to try to differentiate higher and lower mental processes? [1974, p. 487]

Let us play devil's advocate *against* the hypothetical status of processes and abilities. Assume that some internal cognitive structures are identifiable by specific names, such as *figure ground perception* or *grammatic closure*. The next question concerns how we identify, measure, and quantify these. Easy enough, some reader replies, we have tests for this purpose; tell me the process you are interested in, and I will requisition the test blanks to measure it for you. If it were only so easy. We have no real knowledge as to what tests assess, beyond correct and incorrect responses to their items. We must guess or have the test makers guess for us (which has usually been the case) what inner processes the tests have measured. Certainly, test makers have responded to the "process" challenge by providing us with tests that measure any number of processes, and they are eager to produce still more tests when we find new processes to be measured. It would be very nice if we could trust tests to measure what the test makers say they are measuring. However, the promise of most test makers that their instruments measure this or that process is usually based on face appearances, and tests and test names are too quickly confused with processes. Sober measurement specialists over the years have been concerned about this.

Thus, Brigham wrote over 45 years ago:

Most psychologists working in the test field have been guilty of a *naming fallacy* which easily enables them to slide mysteriously from the score in the test to the hypothetical faculty suggested by the name given to the test. Thus, they speak of . . . perception, memory, intelligence, and the like, while the reference is to a certain objective test situation. [1930, p. 159-160]

When an evaluator assumes that various perceptual tests measure various specified perceptual functions, he is making a gross leap from what is known to what he assumes. He cannot be sure what his tests measure, and neither can we. Such lack of knowledge, unfortunately, has not stopped many people from proceeding, as if the subtests of the DTVP, for example, properly and accurately define such areas as figure ground perception and identify perceptual areas requiring training.

Various testmakers have attempted to operationalize their definitions or assess construct validity to support their claims. But, at best, the names assigned to processes are "guesses," or, more scientifically, hypothetic constructs.[1] It is extremely naive in any case to assume that any particular test, no matter how precisely developed, measures a single process. Test responses are multidetermined. It is more logical and more legitimate to presume that underlying any given test score are a variety of processes; that a digit test, for example, measures (among others) processes identifiable with attention, concentration, perceptual discrimination, figure ground perception, encoding, and

---

[1]The reader can choose his own list from some of those processes that Neisser (1967) has described. In the visual area: transient iconic memory, verbal coding, perceptual set, span of apprehension, displacement and rotation iñ pattern recognition, backward masking, template matching, decision time, visual search, feature analysis, focal attention, preattention control figural synthesis, search, analysis by synthesis, and perceptual defense. In the auditory area: segmentation, echoic memory, filtering, auditory synthesis, recoding, slotting, decay, linguistics, Gestalts, and grammatical structure. This is indeed a challenging number, and we have not even reviewed Neisser's "higher" cognitive processes.

short- and long-term memory, rather than any one of the above. In assessing the results, one must also consider motivational factors, energy level, and other parameters. These may explain test result deficiencies better than any deficiencies in process or processes. Distinctions of separate processes, such as Guilford (1967) has attempted, are artificial and justifiable so far on research, rather than on practical grounds. Guilford's processes, too, are hypothetical inferences drawn from correlations of sets of measurements with other sets of measurements, and the nature of the underlying processes they represent cannot be fully understood.

Once again, we assume, like a good devil's advocate—for the sake of understanding other problems inherent in the diagnosis of learning disabilities—that process tests' names are synonymous with the processes they profess to assess and measure. Thus, for argument's sake, accept that the figure ground test of the DTVP produces results that are somewhat identifiable as figure ground perception. What then? Under the best circumstances, how accurately can we measure such a process using this test? All tests are unreliable to varying degrees, and the more specific and intensive the test in measuring a single area of functioning, the more inaccurate the test usually is in predicting some utilitarian behavior. For example, if we wish to predict reading achievement in high school, a global reading test at elementary levels is more accurate than a test of single letter discrimination.

It is true that we have had some success in assessing specific, reasonably gross areas of cognitive functioning. For example, we have been able to distinguish and contrast verbal and performance test results from the Wechsler for some modestly precise predictions and diagnoses. However, more precise discriminations than those implied by verbal-nonverbal performances have been less successful. As we attempt to become more precise, our predictions weaken in validity and reliability. We are talking now about the area of everyday life, school, and academic performance, not about results obtained under carefully controlled artificial experimental conditions or from contrived correlational studies.

However, if we are dealing with specific learning disabilities, we must discriminate specifically between abilities and disabilities. Assuming, as we have for the purposes of argument, that our process tests measure what they say they measure, and that process test names are generally identifiable with specific processes, we still cannot use these tests to diagnose specific learning disabilities. The individual subtests of the DTVP are for the most part unreliable. The subtests of the ITPA are considerably better. But all such subtests are rarely sufficiently precise to make reliable discriminations in individual disability for any child. The issues involved are rather abstruse and are best pursued in other articles (Ysseldyke and Salvia, 1974 for one).

Even if we accept the claim that tests of specific processes measure specific processes accurately for sufficiently diagnosing individual children, we still must determine the strengths and weaknesses of these processes. After all, if we are to teach to strengths, we must find strong processes. If we are to correct weaknesses, we must first identify them. But are the processes that we are measuring with tests such as the DTVP measurable as to strength? Such tests are normative measurement instruments intended to discriminate individuals and place them on a continuum. The tests were not designed to measure amounts of deficits in the processes they are assessing. Yet we usually assume that high scores on one of these tests represent strong processes, and low scores represent weak processes. Given the wrong kind of norming population, a process test could identify truly strong processes as weak, and truly weak processes as strong. Another dilemma among many dilemmas, leaving the learning disabilities specialists using tests that measure processes which cannot be identified, or identifying the processes inaccurately at best, and then providing questionable information about the strengths and weaknesses. Yet we in the field of learning disabilities are committed to the diagnosis of processes and their disabilities.

A SLIGHTLY DIFFERENT APPROACH
TO PROCESSES

The answers to the questions we have raised cannot be truly satisfying to anyone. All of us recognize that individual differences distinguish pupils in their performance of academic tasks. We see nothing wrong with assuming that some definable activities, call them processes, going on inside of those individuals create such individual differences; that, in fact, specific disabilities of these processes may cause specific problems in academic achievement. We do not agree, however, and we believe that the bulk of available research supports us, that we can identify and measure these processes precisely and determine their strengths and weaknesses accurately. Yet, in the face of our inability to identify and diagnose processes with any degree of assurance, we still must diagnose a process dysfunction if we are to identify pupils with learning problems as being learning disabled.

Our answer to this, and it is a tentative one justified only by pragmatic considerations, is to rely on significant deviations in functions on cognitive (process) measures as provided by cognitive test instruments; and to assume that these deviations are manifestations or at least performance reflections of process disabilities.

Even though we have no fully satisfactory instruments for determining processes and their disabilities, we recommend that we continue to use existing cognitive assessment instruments to establish process difficulties. These include instruments intended to assess specific processes directly and others of a more global nature, such as the Stanford-Binet and Wechsler scales, which assess them secondarily, if our tests meet legitimate criteria (see APA standards).[2] Specific failures on cognitive tests are to be used to imply that something is specifically wrong with the individual, to assume, if one is willing to accept hypothetical cognitive constructs (as opposed to remaining with behavioral definitions), that he or she has or is suffering from some process disability or weakness.

The reader at this point asks as to what benefits or improvement have been yielded by our tortuous definitions beyond that offered by typical process advocates. Let us continue!

Our assessment of process difficulties or deficits calls for a determination of significant specific failures or weaknesses in performance on cognitive tests, in the context of otherwise average or better than average achievement on these instruments. We are willing to presume that these "deficits" represent some type of process(es) dysfunction without making a commitment as to the specific process(es) that they represent. To paraphrase: we recommend that specific failures or weaknesses in the performance on general or specific tests of cognitive processes be interpreted as indicating specific process dysfunction without a commitment being made as to what particular process(es) is impaired. Thus, poor functioning on a subtest of the Frostig test in a child of normal mental ability may be interpreted as meaning that something is awry with a specific area of that child's cognitive functioning. But we do not have to identify that specific area

---

[2]One may protest that the Binet was not intended to assess specific process difficulties. Wechsler has never claimed that his tests measures specific processes either. But of course they both do, as in fact does every instrument, meaning almost every type of behavior (see Kagan and Kogan, 1970).

as necessarily perceptual.[3] Rather, the deficit is to be understood as a specific deficit identified by the Frostig test and related to specific dysfunctional behavior on that test. Dysfunctioning on a Frostig subtest may be caused by difficulties in attention, memory, or a variety of perceptual areas other than those intended for measurement by the subtest. We cannot be sure which process or processes are involved. We maintain our diagnostic integrity by limiting ourselves to minimal assumptions concerning process dysfunction on the basis of our cognitive measurements, by identifying process difficulties as related to specific dysfunctional test performances rather than as directly revealed. This is an operational approach but not an operational definition.

Let us clarify this rather confusing but most important point: specific problems on cognitive tests may be assumed to represent underlying specific process dysfunction, but all we can assume on their basis is that there are specific process difficulties. We cannot directly know the nature of that process(es) or its dysfunctional characteristics.

For example, we can identify poor scorers on intelligence tests. Their achievement on these tests is lower than that of their chronological peers. But have we in fact measured their intelligence? Do we know what intelligence is? No. We have measured behaviors on cognitive tasks (those on the IQ test) that are related to other particular behaviors we are interested in, usually academic variables. So-called mentally retarded individuals achieve scores on IQ tests that are unsatisfactory compared to normative standards. But we have not directly measured their intelligence nor do we know what their true intellectual capacities are, although we usually hypothesize that a global process called intelligence is involved. Their mentally retarded state is an inference. Yet we do not believe that even the most hardened opponent of intelligence testing would disagree that consistently poor performance on an intelligence test may mean that something is wrong with the pupil. The test may be a poor test for that child. It may have been culturally unfair; he may not have understood its instructions; he may have been poorly motivated. However, something went wrong! Limited cognitive competency, i.e., mental retardation, may account for the pupil's low IQ scores if other explanations of his poor achievement can be ruled out. The experienced diagnostician must discriminate one possible explanation from the other and make accurate

---

[3]We are ignoring issues of unreliability in this example.

inferences about what caused the low scores. We never validate a test; we validate inferences from a test (Messick, 1975).

    We are faced with much the same problem in assessing learning disabilities when we attempt to make specific determinations of process disabilities. Our process testing tells us that something is wrong—something specifically is wrong. We must judge what that "something" is, and if we can rule out other explanations, we can hypothesize that a process disability causes the defect. However, we recommend again, based on the serious problems we have had in the past with IQ and other labels, that we avoid a definitive application of specific labels to those processes. For if intelligence is a questionable construct, those of specific processes are even more suspect, and we should not commit ourselves blindly to them. To say that a pupil has difficulties on a test of figure ground perception or grammatic closure is not the same as committing ourselves to a position in which we claim that we have assessed the processes akin to those names and that we are able to make determinations of there being this or that much of a deficit in these processes. It will be presumptive enough if we attribute the child's cognitive difficulties to processes at all, which, to belabor our earlier point, are hypothetical constructs. Then let the examiner say that he found failure on a test of figure ground relationships, not that the pupil is suffering from difficulties in figure ground perception. It may be argued that this is a terribly stilted way of communicating, and that difficulties in figure ground perception or figure ground problems are the same as failures on a figure ground test. But surely we know by now that once we turn verbs into nouns, those nouns become reified and regarded as "things." By loose communication, we invite the belief that we know the specific processes, e.g., identified with the test, and we are back to where we hope to take you from. If one persists in talking about impaired perceptual problems or defective auditory decoding, he must at least make sure that those to whom he communicates such information understand the real referents of such interpretations and help them to recognize the highly inferential nature of their communications.

SOME PROCESS RECOMMENDATIONS

    To sum up our major recommendations: the usual accepted standardized tests of cognitive functioning may continue to be used to determine the presence of process difficulties. These include specific process instruments, such as the ITPA and the DTVP, but also the more global instruments, such as the Binet and the Wechsler. Scores indicating specific deficits in performance on these tests may be interpreted as indicative of some type of process difficulty providing simpler explanations are ruled out. However, we recommend that the inferred process deficit not be directly identified with the name on the particular test or subtest which identified it; we prefer to speak of difficulties on a particular test of processes, rather than of a specific process difficulty.

A failure or poor performance on the DTVP of figure ground perception should be interpreted on the basis of that test as suggesting process difficulties, but not necessarily as indicating specific problems or deficits in figure ground perception.

The restrictions in inferences that we are suggesting should eventually result in a more intelligent and sober diagnosis of learning disabilities. Admittedly, these restrictions deprive us of many of the diagnostic satisfactions that traditional process interpretations have given us in the past, which made us feel that we had at last discovered a child's problems. Nevertheless, it is time to kick the habit.

PROCESSES AT THE SECONDARY LEVEL

Another major issue in determining process difficulties is determining them for the secondary-level learning disabled pupil. It is obviously foolish to expect that such tests as the ITPA or the DTVP can be used effectively at the secondary level. A teenager who fails the DTVP or the ITPA is likely to be a seriously impaired student and one we would expect to show general cognitive deficiencies, as well as specific defects. This student would not be a secondary learning disabilities candidate. Unfortunately, there are not too many choices of specific process tests at the secondary level. Table 3-1 summarizes some of the popular instruments used and provides some identifying data.

We urge diagnosticians who make process diagnoses of learning disabilities at the secondary level not to limit themselves to using specific process tests—DTVP, ITPA, Bender, Gestalt, and the like. Process deficiencies are also represented in failures of attention, concentration, and memory, and cognitive controls (if we use these common labels with a full recognition of their fallibilities), which are best measured through traditional global intelligence tests such as the Binet

Table 3-1
Process Tests for Evaluation of Learning Disabilities for
Secondary Students

Name	Publisher Copyright	Level	Contents
Detroit Tests of Learning Aptitude	Bobbs-Merrill 1968	Children and adults	Pictorial absurdities; verbal absurdities; pictorial opposites; verbal opposites; motor speed and precision, auditory attention span; oral commissions; social adjustment; visual attention span; orientation; free association, memory for designs; number ability; social adjustment; broken pictures; oral directions; likenesses and differences
Developmental Test of Visual-Motor Integration	Follett Educational Corporation 1967	Ages 2–15	Figures and designs to be reproduced
Visual Motor Gestalt Test	American Orthopsychiatric Association 1946	Ages 4 and over	Designs to be copied
Memory-for-Designs Test	Psychological Test Specialists 1960	Ages 8.5 to adult	Simple straight line designs to be reproduced from memory
Benton Test of Visual Retention	Psychological Corporation 1955	Ages 8 and over	Memory for designs and sequence of designs
Elizur Test of Psychoorganicity— Children and Adults	Western Psychological Services 1969	Children and adults	Drawings, digits, blocks
Minnesota Percepto-Diagnostic Test	Clinical Psychology Publishing 1962	Ages 5–20	Gestalt designs to be copied

Table 3-1 *(Continued)*

Name	Publisher Copyright	Level	Contents
The Minnesota MAST (Motor Accuracy and Speech Test)	Special Education Materials	Preschool to adult	Motor tasks
Wechsler Memory Scale for Adults	Psychological Corporation 1945	Adults	Personal and current information; orientation; mental control; logical memory; memory span; visual reproduction; associate learning

and Wechsler. Erratic and unstable intellectual functioning and a variety of other deficiencies in cognitive organization and stability are also manifested on such tests, which may serve as bases from which to infer process difficulties. Scatter analysis on the Binet and subtest variation on the Wechsler assist us in such determinations, and they were used even before the modern learning disability movement for making inferences about process. However, we hope that the examiner or the diagnostician uses appropriate clinical judgments in making his guesses about process disability in evaluating performances on these tests as on others. We have had too many unfortunate experiences with examiners who relied excessively on such mechanical procedures as scatter analysis and subtest variation not to have learned from their mistakes.

We have chosen not to recommend academic and diagnostic achievement tests for assessing process disabilities for several reasons. Process difficulties are expressed in the performances on such tests, as they are on the cognitive ones that we have recommended. There is no reason why the school diagnostician could not use educational tests for this purpose. Spelling and writing tests in particular may be especially sensitive to learning disabilities.

However, at the present, it is difficult for most diagnosticians to discriminate school achievement or failure on academic achievement tests from the cognitive capacities and incapacities that are responsible for them.

Thus, we are probably better off relying on tests that are specifically intended for cognitive evaluation, as opposed to those developed for academic diagnostic and achievement assessments in our process determinations. Cognitive tests, even the Binet, also attempt to tap different cognitive processes, whereas academic tests are directly concerned with school performance. Finally, the convergence of dysfunctional cognitive test results with poor achievement test results may give us more confidence in our hypotheses about the learning disabilities that cause both.

In short, we do not recommend academic assessment instruments for determining process disabilities. Those who wish to use them for this purpose must demonstrate that their tests discriminate the learning disabled pupil from those who are poor academic performers for other reasons.

SUMMARY AND CONCLUSIONS

We are committed to process dysfunction in determining learning disabilities at the secondary level, no less than at the elementary. Educational tests should not be used for this purpose unless the diagnostician feels that he can distinguish failures on these tests that result from learning disabilities as opposed to those caused by other types of learning problems. We recommend using traditional process instruments for process assessment when applicable to the secondary pupil. We also suggest that global intelligence tests, particularly the Wechsler and Binet, have much to offer for process diagnoses, particularly since few process tests are legitimate at the secondary level, and the information provided by such instruments as the Bender and the Wepman, which are appropriate, are too restrictive in the information they provide. Interpretation of process difficulties on tests like the Wechsler and the Binet should be aided by such techniques as scatter analysis and subtest variation. But the final judgment of process involvement should rest on clinical judgment and substantiation. Hence, skilled cognitive diagnosticians are still needed. Clinical or school psychologists are best suited for this role by the nature of their broad psychometric training.

Without the diagnosis of process difficulties, the field of learning disabilities really does not exist. However, when we accept the need to evaluate processes, we are faced with the problem of making valid diagnoses with fallible instruments based on even more fallible assumptions. The diagnostician should refer his results to the tests he has used to make his process distinctions and diagnoses; he should be able to justify his process decisions; and he should clarify the inferential basis of the processes he identifies to the consumers of his information. This is surely not too much to ask.

Our process recommendations, we hope, may at least serve as a guide for the field of secondary learning disabilities even if they do not fully settle the question of what process is and how to measure it.

REFERENCES

Ayres AJ: Ayres Space Test. Los Angeles, Western Psychological Services, 1962

Ayres AJ: Southern California Perceptual-Motor Tests. Los Angeles, Western Psychological Services, 1969

Baker HJ, Leland B: Detroit Tests of Learning Aptitude. Indianapolis, Bobbs-Merrill, 1968

Beery KE, Buktenica NA: Developmental Test of Visual–Motor Integration. Chicago, Follett Educational Corporation, 1967

Bender L: Visual Motor Gestalt Test. New York, American Orthopsychiatric Association, 1946

Benton AL: Test of Visual Retention New York, Psychological Corporation, 1955

Briggs PF, Tellegan A: The Minnesota MAST (Motor Accuracy and Speed Test). Yonkers, New York, Special Education Materials, (undated)

Brigham CC: Intelligence tests of immigrant groups. Psychol Rev 37:1958–1965, 1930

Ebel RL: And still the dryads linger. Am Psychol 29:485–492, 1974

Elizur A: Elizur Test of Psycho-organicity: Children and Adults. Los Angeles, Western Psychological Services, 1969

Frostig M, Horne D: The Frostig Program for Development of Visual Perception. Chicago, Follett, 1964

Frostig M, Lefever DW, Whittlesey JRB, Maslow P: *Marianne Frostig Developmental Test of Visual Perception, ed 3.* Palo Alto, California, Consulting Psychologists Press, 1966

Fuller GB: Minnesota Percepto-diagnostic Test. Brandon, Vermont, Clinical Psychology Publishing, 1962

Getman GN, Kane ER, Halgren MR, McKee GW: Developing Learning Readiness. Manchester, Missouri, Webster Division, McGraw-Hill, 1968

Graham FK, Kendall BS: Memory-for-designs Test. Missoula, Montana, Psychological Test Specialists, 1960

Guilford JP: Nature of Human Intelligence. New York, McGraw-Hill, 1967

Kagan J, Kogan N: Individual variation in cognitive processes, in Mussen PH (ed): Carmichael's Manual of Child Psychology, ed 3. New York, John Wiley & Sons, 1970

Kirk SA, McCarthy JJ, Kirk WD: Illinois Test of Psycholinguistic Abilities, rev ed. Urbana, University of Illinois Press, 1968.

Mann L: The training of reifications: its significance in the education of teachers of the emotionally disturbed. International Council for Exceptional Children, Denver, April 1969. Council for Exceptional Children Proceedings, p 57, 1969

Mann L, Goodman L: Perceptual training: a critical retrospect. In Schopler E, Reichler RJ (eds): Psychopathology and Child Development: Research and Treatment. New York, Plenum, 1976, pp 271–289

Mann L, Goodman L, Wiederholt JL: The Learning Disabled Adolescent: A Book of Readings. Boston, Houghton-Mifflin (in press)

Messick S: The standard problem: meaning and values in measurement and evaluation. Am Psychol 30:955–966, 1975

Minskoff E, Wiseman D, Minskoff JG: MWM Program for Developing Language Abilities. Ridgefield, New Jersey, Education Performance Associates, 1973

Neisser U: Cognitive Psychology. New York, Appleton-Century-Crofts, 1967

Spearman C: The Abilities of Man. New York, The Macmillan Co, 1927

Wechsler D: Wechsler Memory Scale for Adults. New York, Psychological Corporation, 1945

Wepman JM: Auditory Discrimination Test. Chicago, Language Research Associates, 1973

Ysseldyke JE, Salvia J: Diagnostic-prescriptive teaching: two models. Except Child 41:181–185, 1974

CHAPTER 4
Identification of Academic Deficits

THE TWO TYPES OF ACADEMIC EVALUATION

We believe that two types of academic assessment are required for learning disabilities programs: (1) evaluation for placement; and (2) evaluation for instruction.

Evaluation for placement is the starting point of the total assessment procedure. It is concerned with substantiating the existence of disability, rather than defining in any great detail the nature of the pupil's academic difficulties. This type of evaluation must be clearly distinguished from the more comprehensive evaluation required for instructional purposes, which occurs after the actual placement of the student in a learning disabilities program and is intended to examine all facets of that pupil's academic performance. The two types of evaluation are, of course, related parts of a total assessment process. Let us briefly examine their how's and why's.

The referral of a student for learning disability services raises the immediate question of the student's eligibility for such services. This question must be answered on the grounds that we have stipulated in Chapter 2: (1) academic disability, (2) average intellectual ability, (3) process disorder, and (4) neurological dysfunction.

Regarding academics, the topic of this chapter, a pupil's consideration as a learning disabled pupil must depend upon whether there is a significant disparity between that pupil's actual achievement and the achievement that we would anticipate on the basis of his general cognitive capacity. When we assess for placement, we are concerned with evaluating both the anticipated achievement and the actual achievement. The degree of disparity between the two is critical in our determinations. If the student in question meets the criterion of significant disparity between anticipated and actual academic achievement, as well as all the other criteria we have listed, he may be legitimately enrolled in a learning disabilities program. Further evaluation, this time for instructional purposes, is now indicated.

The preplacement evaluation is intended solely for determining the existence of a significant academic retardation for the learning disabilities candidate. It is thus restricted to certain subject areas and the determination of gross, overall achievement levels. In contrast, evaluation for instructional purposes is comprehensive. It should include an in-depth examination of the student's performance in a variety of academic areas and the nature of the pupil's specific academic skills, strengths, and deficits. It is also advisable to assess motivation, self-concept, interests, and specific aptitudes in both academic and vocational spheres.

To recapitulate, evaluation for placement is for the purpose of determining whether the pupil's academic deficits are sufficiently severe to qualify him as a learning disabilities candidate. Evaluation for instruction should result in a detailed picture of his academic abilities—one that will serve as a basis for his subsequent educational programming. These two types of evaluation are obviously complimentary, sequential steps in the assessment process. Evaluation for placement will be discussed in detail in this chapter, since it is a component of the identification process. Instructional evaluation will be discussed in a later chapter devoted to educational programming for the learning disabled.

EVALUATION FOR PLACEMENT

In evaluating for placement in secondary learning disability classes, we are concerned with determining the degree, not the nature, of a student's disability in basic school subjects. A significant disparity between general ability and academic achievement should, obviously, be a prominent characteristic of a learning disabled pupil and the reason that prompts the student's referral initially. It is explicit in any definition of learning disabilities.

However, there is little clear agreement as to how much of a disparity should be considered educationally significant for a learning disabilities diagnosis. For example, Thompson (1970) feels that it is indefensible to classify a developmental lag of even 3 years in reading as a learning problem, whereas Bryan and Bryan (1975) report that the general practice in the field is to consider a 6-month delay at the primary level and a 1½-year delay at third grade or beyond as a significant achievement discrepancy. There are no definitive guidelines presently available as to the areas of achievement that are relevant to the diagnosis of learning disabilities, or as to how to proceed to evaluate achievement in the secondary-level potentially learning disabled candidate. While developing our own secondary-level learning disabilities programs, we reached some of our own tentative answers to these questions.

THE REFERRAL

Identification and placement of learning disabled students begin with the classroom teacher. Gradewide screening for learning disabilities is rare, even at the elementary level (Senf and Comrey, 1975). It is virtually nonexistent at the secondary level; we know of only our own attempt, which is still quite experimental (Goodman and Mann, 1975). The teacher must initiate the learning disabilities identification process identifying a student as having a learning problem.

It is unrealistic to expect teachers to identify children with learning disabilities among their students, unless the teachers have had special preparation for this task. This is particularly true at the secondary level, where learning problems are associated with any number of other affective, social, or behavioral difficulties. In-service training concerning learning disabilities is, therefore, essential if a school system wants its teachers to be knowledgeable about learning problems and attuned to the distress signals raised by such disabilities. A school's investment of time and money in such training can yield many dividends. It will very likely result in a change in the number of referrals. The volume of learning disabilities referrals might rise as teachers become more sensitive to learning disabilities; conversely, it might decrease as teachers become more discriminating in assessing their pupils' academic difficulties. Whatever the case may be, as teachers' judgments improve, they will refer more appropriate candidates for learning disabilities evaluation.

If we may also assume that knowledge breeds acceptance and understanding, in-service training in learning disabilities should prepare teachers to help learning handicapped individuals more effectively within their own classrooms—both those learning disabled students who are being maintained therein, and others who are returning from special class placements.

Referral procedures, of course, vary from one school district to another. At the secondary level, a learning disabilities referral ordinarily passes from the classroom teacher to the school counselor and/or school principal and eventually is brought to the attention of the school psychologist and other psychoeducational specialists. These specialists must then conduct a comprehensive formal evaluation of the child referred.

It is unlikely that the older student with a learning disability will be discovered for the first time in the junior high or high school setting, but some teachers may be more reluctant to refer an older student. One characteristic of a secondary learning disability is its chronicity; a pupil's learning disabilities are usually apparent early in the child's school career and tend to persist, particularly if remediation is not provided, as the student proceeds through the grades. Or the learning disabled student may have learned to compensate for his learning disabilities, e.g., by relying on the use of concrete objects or a hand calculator to manage number facts, or by using a good memory for sight words to master early reading despite poor decoding skills. But usually he has just been passed on. Perhaps he was referred at an earlier time but for one reason or another did not receive assistance. No learning disabilities program may have been available, his learning problem may have been attributed to a different cause, or perhaps he was promoted on the basis of age.

In instances such as these, we urge the teacher and school administrators not to adopt a "what good will it do" attitude about referring candidates for learning disabilities evaluation and possible programming. The school's professional staff should make every effort to identify those students who need help.

ACADEMIC EVALUATION FOR PLACEMENT

The educational evaluation of a student referred for learning disabilities placement raises the following questions: (1) What areas of academic achievement need to be tested? (2) How should the test results be interpreted in keeping with the strictures of our learning disabilities definition?

We recommend that the academic placement evaluation be directed toward achievement in the areas of mathematics and language. We suggest extensive assessment of the language area—reading, handwriting, written composition, and spelling. Often assessment of learning disabilities at the secondary level emphasizes reading to the exclusion of other language skills. Exclusive concern with reading is restrictive, even at the elementary level. It seriously diminishes an understanding of the secondary-level student's language ability. Language abilities other than reading become increasingly important at the secondary level, when expression through written communication (preparation of reports and term papers, essay questions on tests, and taking notes in lecture) is required. Even individuals who can read competently at the secondary level may have learning disabilities that affect their performance in such other language areas as spelling, grammar, and syntax. For these reasons, we recommend the extension of academic assessment at the secondary level to reading and essential written communication skills.

We do not, however, recommend that the evaluation of oral language be part of the academic assessment. As discussed in Chapter 3, it is highly unlikely that students with severe expressive or receptive language problems, such as deafness or aphasia, will attend regular junior and senior high school programs. Language disorders of this type are so severe and their effects so damaging to normal growth and development that they are usually identified at an early age and the pupil is channeled into special schools or classes. If the pupil has somehow avoided identification or succeeded despite his disabilities, learning disabilities services will rarely have anything to offer him.

Therefore, we recommend that if language training at the secondary learning disabilities level is to be provided, it should be restricted to helping the student in understanding and expressing through written communication, i.e., the traditional language arts. Significant oral deficiencies or deviances should serve as criteria for referral to other than learning disabilities programs.

For assessing secondary learning disabilities for placement, we emphasize assessing basic math skills generally taught at the elementary level. Algebra, geometry, or other secondary-level mathematics are not included, since we believe competency at secondary levels precludes considering a pupil for learning disabilities class services, which brings us to a most important recommendation.

For placement in a secondary learning disabilities program, we recommend that an upper limit of end of sixth grade be applied to achievement test results. Students whose performance exceeds this level in critical skill areas and who, even though they may not be achieving up to age in general ability expectations, have met other criteria for learning disabilities placement are not to be considered for learning disabilities program placement at the secondary level. We are then insisting that secondary learning disability programming focus on basic education. The end of sixth grade achievement cutoff will insure that the secondary-level learning disabilities programs will deal with academic problems in fundamental skill areas and that learning disability services will be limited to those students with basic academic deficiencies. This academic achievement standard evolves from our belief that learning disability programs should be primarily developmental and focus on the acquisition and mastery of basic skills—skills encompassed in academic work grade levels one through six.

The student who demonstrates sixth-grade proficiency in basic school subjects—reading, writing, spelling, math—can function independently within both the school and community environments. Most daily living activities, such as reading the newspaper, filling out employment forms, making purchases in a store, or maintaining savings or checking accounts, can be accomplished by individuals who have reached this academic level. A student who can read typical sixth-grade materials, although not likely to be college bound, can by current standards (Robinson, 1963) be considered a functionally literate adult. We, of course, recognize that many learning handicapped students experience difficulty with secondary-level content subjects despite their mastery of basic skills, but regrettably we do not consider them candidates for a secondary learning disabilities program. We suggest that their problems be dealt with in ways similar to those approved for other types of students with learning difficulties—tutoring, alternative education, vocational education. Learning disabilities specialists rarely have much to offer for problems in secondary school content areas. Let them shy away from areas where their training and skills are not relevant.

To reiterate, learning disabilities programs at the secondary level should be reserved for learning disability students who have failed to master academic (elementary school) fundamentals. Restricting the instructional scope of secondary-level learning disability programs to elementary school-level skills provides a reasonable basis for rational and realistic learning disability programming into our secondary schools.

SELECTING TESTS FOR SCREENING SECONDARY-LEVEL LEARNING DISABLED STUDENTS

Many commercial tests can be used to evaluate pupil performance in math and language skills. To assist the reader, we have compiled a list of test instruments along with some identifying information in Table 4-1. A variety of general achievement tests and tests of specific skill areas are included, though we have by no means provided an exhaustive listing, we do provide the examiner with a range of test instruments from which to choose the test(s) most suited to his purpose. (The most comprehensive library of test materials that we know of is the test collection of the Educational Testing Service in Princeton, New Jersey, which currently contains over 10,000 published tests. This facility, available for professional use, is an invaluable resource.) We have reviewed all of the tests included in Table 4-1 and they are, in our opinion, appropriate in terms of appearance, contents, and format for use with the older academically deficit student.

Achievement tests such as the *Metropolitan Achievement Tests* or *Stanford Achievement Tests* evaluate skill development in both math and reading. Most of these tests are widely used in both regular and special education. The reader is probably acquainted with most of them, with the possible exception of the *Adult Basic Learning Evaluation* and the *Tests of Adult Basic Education*. Both of these instruments were designed for use with educationally handicapped adults, and they lend themselves well to use with older learning disabled students.

The *Adult Basic Learning Examination* (ABLE), available at three levels of difficulty (ABLE I, II, III), includes subtests of reading, vocabulary, spelling, arithmetic computation, and problem solving; the test assesses skills from grades 1 through 12. The test items employ adult-oriented material, and the test format is pleasantly uncluttered with only a few questions, printed in large type, appearing on each

Table 4-1

Academic Assessment Tests for Secondary Learning
Disabled Students

| | General Achievement Batteries | | |
Name	Publisher Copyright	Level	Contents
Adult Basic Learning Examination	Harcourt Brace Jovanovich		
Level I	1967	Grades 1-4	Dictated vocabulary; reading; spelling; arithmetic problem solving and computation
Level II	1967	Grades 5-8	Vocabulary; reading; spelling; arithmetic
Level III	1970-1971	Grades 9-12	Vocabulary; reading; spelling; arithmetic.
California Achievement Tests*	CTB/McGraw-Hill, 1970		
Level II		Grades 2-4	Reading (vocabulary, comprehension); mathematics (computation, concepts, problems); language (mechanics, usage, structure spelling)
Level III		Grades 4-6	Reading (vocabulary, comprehension); mathematics (computation, concepts, problems); language (mechanics, usage, structure, spelling)
Level IV		Grades 6-9	Reading (vocabulary, comprehension); mathematics (computation, concepts, problems); language (mechanics, usage, structure, spelling)

Table 4-1 *(continued)*

| | General Achievement Batteries | | |
Name	Publisher Copyright	Level	Contents
Level V		Grades 9-12	Reading (vocabulary, comprehension); mathematics (computation, concepts, problems); language (mechanics, usage, structure, spelling)
Iowa Tests of Basic Skills*	Houghton-Mifflin, 1972		
Levels edition		Grades 3-9	Vocabulary; reading comprehension; language (spelling, capitalization, punctuation, usage); work study skills (map reading, graphs); table skills (problem solving, concepts)
Metropolitan Achievement Tests*	Harcourt Brace Jovanovich, 1971		
Primary II		Grades 2.5-3.4	Reading (word knowledge); word analysis; spelling; mathematics (computation, concepts, problem solving)
Elementary		Grades 3.5-4.9	Reading (word knowledge); language; spelling; mathematics (computation, concepts, problem solving)
Intermediate		Grades 5-6.9	Reading (word knowledge); language; spelling; mathematics (computation, concepts, problem solving); science; social studies
Advanced		Grades 7-9.5	Same as intermediate

Table 4-1 *(continued)*

General Achievement Batteries

Name	Publisher Copyright	Level	Contents
Stanford Achievement Test*	Harcourt Brace Jovanovich, 1968		
Primary II battery		Grades 2.5– 3.9	Word meaning; paragraph meaning; science and social studies concepts; spelling; word study skills; language; arithmetic computation and concepts
Intermediate I battery		Grades 4–5.4	Word meaning; paragraph meaning; spelling; word study skills; language; arithmetic computation, concepts, and applications; social studies; science
Intermediate II battery		Grades 5.5– 6.9	Same as Intermediate I except for omission of word study skills
Advanced Battery		Grades 7–9.9	Same as Intermediate I except for omission of word study skills and word meaning
Peabody Individual Achievement Test	American Guidance Service, 1970	Grades K–12	Mathematics; reading recognition; reading comprehension; spelling; general information
Tests of Adult Basic Education	CTB/McGraw-Hill, 1967		
Level E		Grades 2–4	Reading (vocabulary, comprehension); arithmetic (reasoning, fundamentals)

Table 4-1 *(continued)*

| General Achievement Batteries | | | |
Name	Publisher Copyright	Level	Contents
Level M		Grades 4–6	Same as level E but with addition of language (mechanics, spelling)
Level D		Grades 7–9	Same as level M
Wide Range Achievement Test*	Guidance Associates, 1965		
Level 2		Ages 12 and over	Spelling, arithmetic, reading

| Reading | | | |
Name	Publisher Copyright	Level	Contents
Adult Basic Reading Inventory	Scholastic Testing Service, 1966	Functionally illiterate adolescents and adults	Sight words; sound and letter discrimination; word meaning-reading; word meaning-listening; context reading
Iowa Silent Reading Tests	Harcourt Brace Jovanovich, 1942 and 1973		
1942 Edition Elementary Test		Grades 4–8	Rate; comprehension; directed reading; word meaning; paragraph comprehension; sentence meaning; alphabetizing; use of index
Advanced Test		Grades 9–14	Rate; comprehension; directed reading; poetry comprehension, word meaning; sentence meaning; paragraph comprehension; use of index, selection of key words.

Table 4-1 *(continued)*

Name	Publisher Copyright	Reading Level	Contents
1973 Edition Level I		Grades 6–9	Vocabulary; reading comprehension; directed reading; reading efficiency
Level II		Grades 9–14	Same as Level I
Level III		Grades 11–16	Vocabulary; reading comprehension; reading efficiency
Metropolitan Achievement Tests: Reading Tests	Harcourt Brace Jovanovich, 1970–1971		
Primary 2 Reading Tests		Grades 2.5– 3.4	Word knowledge; reading
Elementary Reading Tests		Grades 3.5– 4.9	Same as Primary 2
Intermediate Reading Tests		Grades 5–6.9	Same as Primary 2
Advanced Reading Tests		Grades 7–9.5	Same as Primary 2
Monroe's Standardized Silent Reading Test	Public School Publishing Co., Bobbs-Merrill, 1959	Grades 3–5	Rate; comprehension
		Grades 6–8	Same as for grades 3–5
		Grades 9–12	Same as for grades 3–5

Table 4-1 *(continued)*

Name	Publisher Copyright	Reading Level	Contents
Diagnostic Reading Tests*	Committee on Diagnostic Reading Tests, 1972		
K-4—booklet 3		Grades 3-4	Word recognition, comprehension, word attack (oral)
K-4—section 4		Grades 1-8	Word attack (oral)
Lower level—survey section (available through SRA)		Grades 4-8	Booklet 1: word recognition, comprehension Booklet 2: vocabulary, story reading; rate of reading; comprehension
Lower level—section 4 (available through SRA)		Grades 1-8	Word attack
Upper level—survey section (available through SRA)		Grades 7-13	Section 1: vocabulary; section 2: comprehension; section 3: rate of reading; section 4: word attack
RBH Basic Reading and Word Test	Richardson, Bellows, Henry and Co., 1969	Disadvantaged adults	Vocabulary; comprehension
Woodcock Reading Mastery Tests	American Guidance Service	K-12	Letter identification, word identification; word comprehension; passage comprehension

Table 4-1 *(continued)*

Name	Math Publisher Copyright	Level	Contents
Contemporary Mathematics Test	CTB/McGraw-Hill, 1966	Grades 3-4, 5-6, 7-9	Supplement to arithmetic tests of the California Achievement Tests
Mathematics Inventory Test III	American Testing Co., 1970	Grades 4-12	Problem solving
Diagnostic Arithmetic Tests	Human Sciences Research Council, 1966	Ages 9-12	Addition; subtraction; multiplication; division; money; weights; measures; fractions; decimals; percents
SRA Arithmetic Index	SRA, 1968	Ages 14 and over	Addition and subtraction of whole numbers; multiplication and division of whole numbers; basic operations involving fractions; decimals and percentages
Key Math Diagnostic Arithmetic Test	American Guidance Service, 1971	Grades 1-9	Numeration; fractions; geometry and symbols; addition; subtraction; multiplication; division; mental computation; numerical reasoning; word problems; missing elements; money; measurement; time

Name	Spelling Publisher Copyright	Level
Lincoln Diagnostic Spelling Test	Educational Records Bureau, 1956	Grades 2-4, 2-5, 4-8, 8-12, 9-12

Table 4-1 *(continued)*

Name	Publisher Copyright	Spelling Level
Spelling Inventory With Sentences— Form A	The Reading Clinic, Temple University	Grades 1–8
Iowa Test of Basic Skills— Spelling Subtest	Houghton-Mifflin, 1973	Grades 1.7–3.5
Gates-McKillop Reading Diagnostic Tests— Spelling Subtest	Teachers College Press, Columbia University, 1962	Grades 1–6
Metropolitan Achievement Tests—Spelling Subtest	Bureau of Educational Research and Service, University of Iowa, 1971	Grades K–9.5
California Achievement Test—Spelling Subtest	California Test Bureau, 1970	Grades 1.5–12
Durrell Analysis of Reading Difficulty— Spelling Subtest	Harcourt Brace Jovanovich, 1955	Grades 1–6
The New Iowa Spelling Scale	Bureau of Educational Research and Service, University of Iowa, 1954	Grades 2–8

*Levels not suitable for adolescent use have been omitted.

page. The mature appearance of the test stands in positive contrast to that of many other widely accepted instruments. It is also likely to seem more manageable and less threatening to the testee of limited skill than are many other test instruments.

The format of the *Tests of Adult Basic Education* (TABE), published by CTB/McGraw-Hill, is similar to that of the *Adult Basic Learning Examination* just described. (Cohen (1969) has reviewed the *Tests of Adult Basic Education* and found many serious structural flaws. He concludes that the TABE might be better used as a clinical rather than as a statistical instrument and for groups rather than for individual assessment; but we feel the reader should be aware of the instrument.) The series of three tests at different difficulty levels of the TABE, are adaptations of various levels of the *California Achievement Test (1957) Edition.* Level E of the tests includes four subtests: reading vocabulary, reading comprehension, arithmetic reasoning, and arithmetic fundamentals. Levels M and D include these subtests plus two more, mechanics of English and spelling. The tests are easily administered and yield grade-equivalent scores.

Table 4-1 also includes achievement/diagnostic instruments restricted to assessment of specific subjects, e.g., reading, mathematics, or spelling. Many of these instruments fulfill the dual purposes of diagnostic evaluation and achievement assessment.

We have entered a number of spelling subtests from various achievement or diagnostic instruments in Table 4-1 so that the examiner can supplement a general achievement test lacking a spelling subtest with the selection of a spelling subtest from another instrument. On occasion, the examiner might also want to replace a spelling subtest that is not fully appropriate for the student being evaluated, e.g., in format or difficulty level, with another more appropriate one.

Spelling tests in many standardized achievement batteries embody a multiple choice answer format in which the student selects the correct answer to the question from among a limited number of alternative choices. In such a situation it is presumed that a testee can demonstrate spelling competency by selecting the words spelled correctly rather than by actually spelling the desired words on command. However, identifying a misspelled word and spelling a word correctly from dictation are clearly not equal tasks, the latter more closely resembles the traditional spelling behavior teachers expect of their students. Tests that evaluate the student's ability to spell from memory are, we believe, preferable to the contrived formats of multiple choice spelling tests. In Table 4-1, the tests of spelling that require direct production of words by the student are the *Lincoln Diagnostic Spelling Test*, and spelling tests of the *Gates-McKillop Reading Diagnostic Tests* and the *Durrell Analysis of Reading Difficulty*, the *Spelling Inventory with Sentences*, and *The New Iowa Spelling Scales;* the others employ multiple choice questions. The examiner should be aware of these two types of spelling tests when he selects an instrument for use with a particular student.

Also, two silent reading tests are included in Table 4-1, the *Iowa Silent Reading Test* and *The Monroe's Standardized Silent Reading Test*. Although many teachers view silent and oral reading as identical processes, these two reading skills are quite dissimilar and are not of equal difficulty. Silent reading is by far the more important, particularly for the adult reader. It might be worthwhile for the reader to stop and try to recall the last time that he or she (elementary school teachers excepted) was required to "read out loud." Unfortunately, too many teachers have overrated the importance of oral reading, assuming that it is an accurate reflection of reading ability. (Maria Montessori (1965) pointed out the persistent confusion in teachers' minds of the two quite distinct processes of oral and silent reading early in the 20th century; her observation is still timely today.) We suggest that for the purpose of establishing levels of reading competency, silent tests will often be the most appropriate choice as they offer good evidence of the level of material the student can handle efficiently and competently. In addition, silent tests have the added advantage of avoiding oral recitation, which may very well turn off the older student.

Although we have urged that composition and handwriting be part of the initial student assessment, no tests of composition or handwriting are included in Table 4-1; useful tests of this variety (for secondary students) are just not available at this time. In lieu of standardized evaluative instruments, the evaluator will have to settle for subjective and clinical evaluations of the quality of students' composition and handwriting, rather than specific grade-equivalent scores. However, the information derived from samples of written work, along with the other test results, will be helpful in diagnosing language problems.

Whatever tests are ultimately chosen for use (and inclusion in Table 4-1 should not be interpreted as our endorsement of the instrument), some general guidelines for test usage apply. The American Psychological Association in its publication *Standards for Educational and Psychological Tests* (1974) provides a comprehensive exposition of issues related to test development and use. We recommend the selection "Standards for the Use of Tests" for any "test user" defined as the "one who chooses tests, interprets scores, or makes decisions based on test scores." Adherence to sound principles of test administration, scoring, and interpretation will increase the likelihood of valid and accurate assessment of pupil performance. (It is important to remember, too, that the closer a norm-based test is administered to the time of year of its norming, the more conclusive and valid the inferences made from it are. Otherwise, we work on the basis of extrapolated scores—and these are risky!)

INTERPRETING TEST RESULTS:
THE DISPARITY CONCEPT

The concept of disparity is central to definition and identification of the learning disabled. Having determined the achievement levels of the potential secondary learning disabilities candidate, the examiner must next compare these levels with the expectations that we would have for the student. This is done by contrasting the student's actual academic performance with academic expectations that we would ordinarily hold for him, and by determining if the differences between the two are significant. Once again, it is necessary to make an arbitrary decision, this time regarding the term "significant" as it applies to expectancy-achievement disparity. There are different methods for determining the expectancy–achievement disparity, yet no single method can be offered as the ultimate one. Let us look at some methods that have been used.

One approach is to express test results (from both achievement and mental ability tests) in similar terms or units, e.g., grade equivalents or standard scores, and subtracting to determine the difference between the pupil's performance on the two tests.

Student score on an intelligence test (expressed as mental age)	9-3
Student score on achievement test	−4-2
difference (deficit)	5-1

This approach underlies many of the operational definitions for learning disabilities given in the literature. For example, in a multidisciplinary study of learning disabilities, Rice (1970) defines "significant deficit" as a standard achievement score (WRAT) of 15 or more points below the full scale IQ (WISC).

Another approach to quantifying the discrepancy between achievement and ability involves applying a formula that yields a numerical index of the disability. Myklebusts Learning Quotient (1968) is an example of such a procedure. His calculations are based on mental age (MA), chronological age (CA), and grade age (GA). These three units of information are used in the two-step calculation. The first step yields an expectancy age (EA)[7]:

$$EA = \frac{MA + CA + GA}{3}$$

The learning quotient is then derived by dividing the achievement age (AA) by the expectancy age:

$$IQ = \frac{AA}{EA}$$

A learning quotient of 89 or below is indicative of a learning disability.

Another numerical index of learning disability, reading disability, is offered by Kline et al. (undated). His dyslexia quotient (DQ) is "designed to specify the degree of reading disability in a given child, irrespective of age, grade level, or intra-school factors." The first step in calculating the DQ is to determine the difference between reading performance (as expressed in the grade-equivalent scores on the Iota test of reading) and exact grade level in school. The difference is preceded by a plus if the reading score is higher than grade placement and a minus if the reading score is lower than grade placement. The difference is then divided by the grade placement level and multiplied by 100 to convert the quotient to a percentage. An example taken from the paper of Kline et al. is given below:

If John has an Iota reading grade equivalent of 3.8 and a grade placement level of 7.3,

$$\begin{array}{l} 7.3 \text{ Grade placement level} \\ \underline{-3.8} \text{ Iowa grade equivalent} \\ -3.5 \text{ Difference} \end{array}$$

$$\frac{3.5}{7.3} = .48 \times 100 = 48$$

$$DQ = 0.48$$

[7]There are many different formulas for the calculating expectancy ages. A number of them are reviewed and the shortcomings inherent in this approach are discussed by Bruinincks, Glaman, and Clark (1973).

A DQ of zero means that the student is scoring exactly on grade level; a high positive score means advancement, and a low negative score suggests a handicap.

Weaknesses of the Approach

These approaches commonly used to quantify and contrast achievement and ability scores for learning disabled prospects rely heavily on test scores and, as a consequence, have serious shortcomings. Salvia and Clark (1973) have discussed the statistical weaknesses inherent in using test scores for the identification of the learning disabled. In particular, they point out that "as a general rule, difference scores are less reliable than the scores on which the difference scores are based." The examiner should, therefore, be aware that the achievement and ability measures he used in the initial evaluation of the student possess varying degrees of error, and the difference between the two test scores is even more unreliable.

If test scores must be used, and they are almost inevitable in our diagnosis of learning disabilities, one easy and practical alteration (suggested by Salvia and Clark) is merely to substitute actual grade placement for the MA or IQ estimates; the examiner can then determine the disparity between achievement and grade placement, rather than that between achievement and an estimate of achievement expectancy or potential. This approach reduces the error factor (grade placement being an absolute fact without any error component) and also eliminates the awkward situation of having an underachieving child whose performance, even if on grade level, may be significantly below the expectancy based on his or her ability. We recommend this approach even though we recognize that there are problems in applying it.

One grade-level approach to dealing with the disparity concept has recently been suggested by Wiederholt (1975), who avoids the difficulty of determining the degree of disparity between performance and potential by setting an extremely stringent and unvarying achievement standard for learning disabilities selection. According to Wiederholt, only students whose achievement falls at the first, second, and, in some instances, third grade level are to be considered for learning disabilities placement. Secondary students whose achievement reaches the fourth grade level would not be candidates for learning disabilities programs by his definition. This approach does not do away with the disparity criterion, but it limits the secondary learning disabilities category to those students who are so severely educationally handicapped that the degree of disparity simply is not an issue. At the very least, a secondary learning disabled student would have to be four or more years behind in academic achievement to qualify for special services according to Wiederholt's criterion. For older students the minimal achievement lag, based on this criterion, would be even greater, e.g., 5 years for an eighth grader, 6 years for a ninth grader, 7 for a tenth grader. Clearly, this amount of disparity between achievement and ability, when achievement is expressed as either a grade placement per Salvia and Clark or a grade expectancy, would indicate critical disability by anyone's standard. However, the imposition of an achievement cutoff at such a low level would deny special services to many students with severe learning problems who have a better prognosis for progress. The secondary student who cannot read beyond the beginning of fourth grade must be regarded as very handicapped academically. If he meets the other criteria for learning disabilities services, we believe we should not deny him services.

The grade level criterion that we recommended as an alternate to Wiederholt's standard—and we believe it is a realistic one—is an academic lag of at least 2 years with performance levels not to exceed the end of sixth grade. The discrepancy score we recommend is the difference between achievement scores and actual grade placement (Salvia and Clark) at the time of testing. For example, if an eighth-grade youngster was given math and reading achievement tests in January and scored at the third year, fourth month level in reading and the fifth year, seventh month level in math, the deficits between the achievement levels and actual grade placement would be calculated as follows:

Grade placement	8-5	Grade placement	8-5
Reading achievement score	−3-4	Math achievement score	−5-7
Deficit	5-1	Deficit	2-8

Since January represents the fifth month of a 10-month school year, grade placement at the time of testing would be 8-5—eighth year, fifth month. By subtracting the achievement grade-equivalent scores for reading and math 3-4 and 5-7, respectively, from the grade placement, we can see that the student is more than 5 years behind in reading and is almost 3 years behind in math. The deficits in both math and reading are significant according to the criteria stated above.

Another example further illustrates the application of our criterion. Given a tenth-grade student who scored at the 7-3 level in reading and the 4-2 level in mathematics when tested during May of the school year, the deficits between achievement and grade placement would be:

Grade placement	10-9	Grade placement	10-9
Reading achievement score	−7-3	Math achievement score	−4-2
Deficit	3-6	Deficit	6-7

For this student, a substantial discrepancy exists in both primary academic subject areas. However, only the deficit in math performance is significant by our definition. Since the tested reading performance exceeds the maximal level of end of sixth grade proficiency, it would not be considered as indicating a severe and significant instructional deficit. Yes, the student has room for improvement, but additional progress beyond the current level is as much, if not more, a matter of the student's initiative and application as of special educational intervention. (At any rate, even if further growth does not occur, the student possesses essentially enough skill for successful adult living). The math deficit, however, requires remediation as the math disparity far exceeds our criterion, and the student's functional level is well below the sixth-grade level.

We anticipate objections to the criteria and procedures outlined above; the most probable ones are that test scores are unreliable, that the grade placement is a fallible concept, and that the 2-year differential is too small (Thompson, 1970).

We are well aware that achievement test scores are subject to considerable degrees of error. However, the error factor can be minimized by the selection and appropriate use of quality test instruments. Second, we believe that Salvia and Clark's procedure of using grade placement to assess "expectancy" achievement is the best of a variety of poor choices. As to the third objection, we have found that achievement tests' scores typically are inflated estimates of the student's performance and that the scores represent the upper limits, or frustration level, of the student's true performance ability. The level at which the student can function with teacher assistance is lower, often considerably lower, than the achievement score indicates. The student's independent functional level is even farther removed from the achievement level attained in the testing situation.

For these reasons, we have found that a 2-year difference between achievement and placement is cause for concern. The 2-year criterion will, we know, allow some false positives (non–learning disabled students) to slip by, but we prefer to evaluate some inappropriate candidates initially rather than exclude any truly handicapped individuals. Also, achievement is only one of the four LD screening criteria, and we suggest the educational lag in and of itself is not sufficient for diagnosis and placement; non–learning disabled students who pass the initial academic screening are very likely to be screened out later on.

REFERENCES

Bruinincks RH, Glaman GM, Clark CR: Issues in determining prevalence of reading retardation. The Reading Teacher 27:177–185, 1973

Bryan TH, Bryan JH: Understanding Learning Disabilities. Port Washington, New York, Alfred Publishing, 1975

Burnett RW: Adult Basic Reading Inventory. Bensenville, Illinois, Scholastic Testing Service, 1966

Cohen SA: Review. J Counsel Psychol 16:281–282, 1969

Connolly AJ, Nachtman W, Pritchett EM: KeyMath Diagnostic Arithmetic Test. Circle Pines, Minnesota, American Guidance Service, 1971

Contemporary Mathematics Test: Elementary and Junior High. Monterey, California, CTB/McGraw-Hill, 1966

Diagnostic Arithmetic Tests. Pretoria, South Africa, Human Sciences Research Council, 1966

Dunn LM, Markwardt FC Jr: Peabody Individual Achievement Test. Circle Pines, Minnesota, American Guidance Service, 1970

Durost WN, Bixler HH, Wrightstone JW, Prescott GA, Balow IH: Metropolitan Achievement Tests. New York, Harcourt Brace Jovanovich, 1971

Durrell D: Durrell Analysis of Reading Difficulty. New York, Harcourt Brace Jovanovich, 1955

Farr R: Iowa Silent Reading Tests. New York, Harcourt Brace Jovanovich, 1973

Gates AI, McKillop AS: Gates-McKillop Reading Diagnostic Tests. New York, Teachers College Press, Columbia University, 1962

Goodman L, Mann L: Needs Assessment Survey: Final Report. Blue Bell, Pennsylvania, Montgomery County Intermediate Unit, 1975

Jastak JF, Jastak SR, Bijou SW: Wide Range Achievement Test, rev ed. Austin, Texas, Guidance Testing Associates, 1965

Johnson M: Spelling Inventory with Sentences—Form A. Philadelphia, Reading Clinic, Temple University (undated)

Karlsen B, Madden R, Gardner EF: Adult Basic Learning Examination. New York, Harcourt Brace Jovanovich, 1971

Kelley TL, Madden R, Gardner EF, Rudman HC: Stanford Achievement Test. New York, Harcourt Brace Jovanovich, 1968

Kline CL, Ashbrenner M, Barrington B, Reimer L: Dyslexia Quotient: an index of reading ability. Pomfret, Connecticut, The Orton Society, reprint No. 22 (undated)

Lincoln AC: Lincoln Diagnostic Spelling Test. Princeton, New Jersey, Education Records Bureau, 1956

Lindquist EF, Hieronymus AN: Iowa Tests of Basic Skills. Boston, Houghton-Mifflin, 1972

Mathematics Inventory Test, III: Basic Skills of Problem Solving. Fort Lauderdale, American Testing Company, 1970.

Monroe M, Sherman EE: Group Diagnostic Reading and Achievement Tests. Brandenton, Florida, C H Nevins, 1939

Monroe WS: Monroe's Standardized Silent Reading Test. Indianapolis, Bobbs-Merrill, 1959

Montessori M: The Montessori Elementary Materials. Cambridge, Mass, Bentley, 1965

Myklebust HR: Learning disabilities: definition and overview, in Myklebust HR (ed): *Progress in Learning Disabilities,* vol I. New York, Grune & Stratton, 1968

New Iowa Spelling Scale. Iowa City, Bureau of Educational Research and Service, University of Iowa, 1954

RBH Basic Reading and Word Test. Washington, D.C., Richardson, Bellows, Henry & Co, 1969

Rice D: Learning disabilities: An investigation in two parts. J Learning Disabil 3:149–155, 1970

Robinson HA: Libraries: active agents in adult reading improvement. Am Library Assoc Bull 416–421, 1963

Salvia J, Clark J: Use of deficits to identify the learning disabled. Except Child 39:305–308, 1973

Senf G, Comrey A: State initiative in learning disabilities: Illinois project screen, report 1: The SCREEN early identification procedure. J Learning Disabil 8:451–457, 1975

Seville EW: Diagnostic Number Tests 1–2 (formerly Diagnostic Arithmetic Tests). Hawthorn, Vic., Australia, Australian Council for Educational Research, 1966

SRA Reading and Arithmetic Indexes. Chicago, Science Research Associates, 1968

Standards for Educational and Psychological Tests. Washington, D.C., American Psychological Association, 1974

Thompson A: Moving toward adulthood, in Anderson L (ed): Helping the Adolescent with the Hidden Handicap. Los Angeles, California Association for Neurologically Handicapped Children, 1970

Tiegs EW, Clark WW: California Achievement Tests. Monterey, California, CTB/McGraw-Hill, 1970

Wiederholt JL: A report on secondary school programs for the learning disabled. Final report, Leadership Training Institute in Learning Disabilties, Tucson, University of Arizona, 1975

CHAPTER 5
Guidelines for Identifying the Secondary-Level Learning Disabled Pupil

OVERVIEW

In this concluding chapter of the first part of this book, we will summarize the discussion of the preceding chapters and highlight key issues regarding the definition of secondary learning disabilities. Second, we will set forth guidelines for identifying these secondary-level learning disabled pupils. Presented in a step-by-step sequence, these guidelines should assist the practitioner in making the decisions of placement or nonplacement for individual students. Third, we will illustrate the application of our identification schema through actual case histories.

DEFINING THE SECONDARY LEARNING
DISABLED STUDENT—AGAIN!

Who are the learning disabled adolescents in our secondary schools? They are a select group of students, relatively few in number, if we hold to the specific intellectual, academic, and behavioral criteria that we have suggested in earlier chapters.

The junior or senior high school student, who, by our standards, qualifies for the label "learning disabled" is a preteenage or teenage youth who is experiencing serious academic difficulties despite adequate intellectual endowment and the absence of academically significant sensory impairments or physical disabilities. Test results suggest that although such a student's overall intellectual ability is average, sometimes superior, he may be suffering from specific weaknesses, deficiencies, or deficits in cognitive functioning. Though the exact nature of these "disabilities" cannot be elucidated, we make the assumption that they are responsible for impeding the student's school achievement. The student may also exhibit some emotional difficulties, which would not be unexpected considering a long history of school failure, but these are definitely secondary to his learning problems and are not severe enough to make him difficult to manage. The secondary-level learning disabled student is by definition learning disabled because of neurological dysfunctioning; however, this "dysfunctioning" has not resulted in any significant behavioral problems, though it has contributed significantly to his learning problems.

Further, *culturally disadvantaged* and *learning disabled* are not synonymous terms, although some individuals certainly merit both labels, and it is also quite possible for severe cultural deprivation to cause neurological dysfunctioning, which in turn could result in learning disabilities.

In the realm of academics, achievement testing will show that the secondary school LD student performs significantly below the academic levels that are commensurate with his age, general ability and years of schooling. Regardless of the degree of disparity between his achievement and expectancies, to justify formal LD programs he should be functioning below seventh-grade levels in math and/or language areas—indicating a failure to acquire basic school skills. Because of his educational deficiencies, he cannot be expected to succeed at the secondary level without a significant amount of help.

Having briefly described the secondary LD student, let us be more specific about the criteria that define members of that group. The criteria for the diagnosis and selection of secondary level learning disabled students in operational terms are as follows:

1. The student must demonstrate a full scale intellectual quotient of 90 or better on the Wechsler or Stanford-Binet scales.
2. There must be indications that the student is deficient in specific cognitive areas (i.e., in his processes or abilities) on the basis of evaluations of specific cognitive abilities.
3. The student's academic performance must lag 2 or more years be-

hind his actual grade placement in basic math and language skills and in all cases fall below the beginning seventh-grade level.

4. The student must not suffer from sensory deficiencies, physical impairments, emotional disturbances, organically induced behavioral problems, or sociocultural problems that take priority in explaining his significant school failures.

5. The student suffers some degree of neurological dysfunction.

In the following section of this chapter, we will apply our criteria to the selection of secondary-level LD pupils.

**IDENTIFYING THE SECONDARY LEARNING
DISABLED STUDENT**

In the step-by-step procedure outlined below, we have applied our criteria to identifying the secondary-level learning disabled pupil. The procedure has evolved from work within our programs; it "works" for us. We hope that the procedure may be of benefit to our readers as well.

Step 1: *Decision point:* Is the student free of problems of a sensory, physical, or behavioral-emotional variety that are current major determinants of his learning problems? *Determination:* (1) sensory disabilities, (2) physical handicaps, (3) behavior problems, (4) emotional problems.

If the answers to these four questions are positive, referral for services to other than learning disabilities resources is advised. If the answers to all four are negative, we proceed with our learning disabilities evaluation.

Step 2: *Decision point:* Does the student possess average intellectual ability? *Determination:* If the student's full scale intellectual quotient is 90 or above on Binet or Wechsler scales, the student should be considered a learning disability candidate and the evaluation should continue. If the intellectual quotient is below 90, the student should—with very few exceptions—no longer be considered a learning disability candidate.

Step 3: *Decision point:* Is there evidence of specific process or cognitive disabilities. *Determination:* Clinical judgments based on evaluations must establish the possible existence of "process" deficits. Since these are essential to the diagnosis of a learning disability (or disabilities) the grounds for the clinician's decision making must be explicit. If there is no evidence of process dysfunction, the pupil is no longer considered a learning disabilities candidate.

Step 4: *Decision point:* Is the student's academic performance significantly below standard? *Determination:* If the student has not achieved full sixth-grade competency in the academic areas of language and mathematics and is at least 2 years below grade expectancy in math, reading, spelling, handwriting, or/and written composition (refer to Chapter 4, page 61 for calculations) at the time of evaluation, he is considered significantly educationally handicapped from the standpoint of secondary-level LD programming and qualifies for learning disabilities services. If the student is less than 2 years behind his grade placement, or if he performs adequately at or beyond the seventh-grade levels in basic skill areas, the student should not be placed in a learning disabilities program, even though he may still have learning problems. Academic assistance, as needed, should be provided through some other means—tutorial, small group instruction, mastery learning approach.

Step 5: *Decision point:* Is there evidence of neurological dysfunction? *Determination:* This is the last procedure to be implemented because it is the most vexing for the parent and pupil. The postponement of the neurological examination until all other LD criteria have been satisfied eliminates needless alarm and expense for those parents whose children ultimately do not qualify for learning disabilities programs. If the neurological examination reveals clear-cut evidence of central nervous system involvement or if the neurologist's clinical judgment supports the possibility of neurological dysfunction, the diagnosis of learning disability is confirmed medically.

Step 6: *Decision point:* Is the student learning disabled? *Determination:* If the determinations made at the five previous decision points are positive, the answer is yes and secondary LD programming should be begun. See Table 5-1 for a review of the procedures.

CASE STUDIES

Case Study A: Sally

Sally was 12 years old when she was evaluated for possible learning disabilities class placement. Her referral was prompted by her teacher's concern about her poor academic performance and her parents' concern regarding her seventh-grade class placement.

Table 5-1

Secondary LD Preplacement Evaluation: Summary
of Steps

Evaluation Sequence	Criteria	LD	Non-LD
Step 1	Absence of sensory impairment, physical disability, or emotional disturbance relevant to academic failures	These conditions not present, or sensory disability is within normal limits after correction	Any of the above conditions
Step 2	Average intellectual ability	Full scale intellectual quotient of 90 or above on Binet or Wechsler scales	Full scale intellectual quotient below 90
Step 3	Specific process or cognitive disabilities	Evidence of specific "process" deficits through appropriate evaluation	No evidence of process deficits
Step 4	Significant academic difficulties	2 years or more disparity between language and/or math performance and grade placement with achievement below 7th grade level	Less than 2 years disparity between language and math performance and grade placement with achievement at or above 7th-grade level
Step 5	Evidence of CNS dysfunction	Neurological examination confirms or suggests possibility of CNS involvement	Neurological examination provides no evidence of CNS dysfunction
Step 6	Meets criteria 1–5	Assignment of pupil to secondary LD programs and services	Alternate means of helping pupil are sought

INTELLECTUAL AND PROCESS ASSESSMENT

WISC
Full Scale IQ   93
Verbal IQ   85
Performance IQ   105

Comments: Considerable subtest variability with severe depression of digit
    span subtest scores.
Bender Gestalt
    Koppitz Error Score   0
    Developmental Age   Age appropriate
Detroit Test of Learning Aptitude   Age equivalents
    (selected subtests)
    Auditory Attention Span for Unrelated Words   6 yr., 2 mo.
    Visual Attention Span for Objects   13 yr., 8 mo.
    Auditory Attention Span for Related Syllables   8 yr., 3 mo.
    Visual Attention Span for Letters   15 yr., 9 mo.
    Oral Directions   11 yr., 3 mo.
    Sally's WISC full scale intellectual quotient of 93 exceeds the minimal
level stipulated in our LD criteria; in terms of intellectual capacity, she qualified for a secondary level learning disabilities program. The marked and statis-
tically significant disparity between vocabulary and digit span scores on the
WISC together with deficient auditory attention subtest scores on the Detroit
test also suggest "process" difficulties.

ACADEMIC ACHIEVEMENT

Wide Range Achievement Test   Grade equivalent
    Reading   6.2
    Spelling   6.7
    Arithmetic   6.3
Woodcock Reading Mastery Test   Reading grade score
    Letter Identification   6.2
    Word Identification   5.1
    Word Comprehension   3.7
    Word Attack   12.9
    Passage Comprehension   5.7
    Total Reading   5.4
Handwriting—informal evaluation   Adequate performance
Composition—informal evaluation   Adequate performance
    The academic criterion which we apply in the screening of learning dis-
abilities candidates states that there must be an achievement lag of 2 years or
more with performance not to exceed the upper sixth-grade level. Sally's
performances in math, reading, and spelling on the *Wide Range Achievement
Tests* (WRATs) were 6.2, 6.7, and 6.3, respectively; her scores approach the
upper limit of sixth-grade achievement. Sally's reading scores on the
Woodcock Reading Mastery Test were generally lower, however, with only
one particularly strong subtest. The *Woodcock Reading Mastery Test*
provides five reading subtest scores and a total reading performance score, all
expressed as grade equivalents. However, only the total reading score need
concern us at this point; Sally's total score was 5.4. Using the three WRAT

scores and the total reading score from the Woodcock test, we would determine her degree of achievement deficiencies in the following manner:

Grade placement at time of testing	6-9
WRAT Reading score	6-2
Achievement deficit	7 months
Grade placement at time of testing	6-9
WRAT Spelling score	6-7
Achievement deficit	2 months
Grade placement at time of testing	6-9
WRAT Arithmetic score	6-3
Achievement deficit	6 months

Grade placement at the time of testing was determined by converting the date of testing (5-75) to a grade equivalent. The fifth month of the year, May, is the ninth month of the school year. Therefore, Sally's grade placement at the time that the WRAT was given was sixth year, ninth month. The three WRAT scores were also expressed as grade equivalents and were subtracted from the grade placement; the differences, 7 months for reading, 2 months for spelling, and 6 months for arithmetic, fall far short of the 2-year achievement discrepancy needed to satisfy the academic criterion.

We also determined the degree of Sally's achievement lag in the area of reading using her total reading score on the Woodcock test:

Grade placement at time of testing	6-9
Woodcock total reading score	5-4
Achievement deficit	1-5

The reading deficit that emerges from comparing Sally's Woodcock reading test score and her grade placement at time of testing is substantially greater than that indicated by her WRAT scores. However, Sally's "deficit" of $1\frac{1}{2}$ years still does not meet our academic criteria for secondary LD services. Although there is definitely an achievement lag, it is not of sufficient magnitude to warrant a learning disabilities class placement.

On a continuum of disability ranging from severe to mild, Sally's academic difficulty would merit a rating of "mild." Sally appears to be able, with the help of her parents who work with her in the evenings, and with the additional support of a private tutor, to maintain herself in the regular school program. We did not feel that placement in learning disabilities class would be beneficial or appropriate for this youngster. Rather, we recommended that she remain in her regular class program and that the parents continue to provide her with the academic support she needs. Neurological evaluation was not recommended because Sally did not meet the academic criteria for secondary LD programming. A summary of this case study is presented in Table 5-2.

Table 5-2
Summation, Case Study A (Sally; 12 years old)

Pupil Characteristics	Instruments Used	Results	
		LD	Non-LD
Intellectual	WISC	Full scale IQ = 93	Age appropriate
Process/cognitive deficits	Bender Gestalt Detroit Test of Learning Aptitude WISC	Deficits on auditory and attention tests; Deficits in several subtest performances	Age appropriate
Significant sensory impairment	Pupil's health and school records	Not present	
Physical disability	Pupil's health records	Not present	
Behavioral/ emotional disturbance	Pupil's school records	Not indicated	
Environmental problems	Pupil's school records	Not indicated	
Academic achievement	WRAT		Mild education lag; 6th-grade level performance in math, reading, spelling
	Woodcock Reading Mastery Test Handwriting sample Composition sample		Mild lag in reading Adequate performance Adequate performance
Neurological evaluation			Not required since pupil did not meet academic criteria for LD placement

Case Study B: Charles

Charles an eighth-grade student, was 14 years and 4 months old at the time of his evaluation. He had experienced academic difficulties even in his early elementary school years. At one time Charles showed much anxiety and avoidance behavior regarding school attendance, but this lessened once Charles was transferred from parochial to public school. Outside of school, Charles was active and well integrated, enjoying many friends and a warm family relationship.

INTELLECTUAL AND PROCESS ASSESSMENT

WISC
Full Scale IQ	85
Verbal IQ	88
Performance IQ	84

Charles' full scale intellectual quotient of 85 eliminates him from consideration for a learning disabilities class. Subtest score profiles were flat with one exception favoring picture completion. The results on the Bender-Gestalt test provide no evidence of a disability in visual motor functioning.

ACADEMIC ASSESSMENT

Wide Range Achievement Test	Grade Equivalents
Spelling	5.5
Arithmetic	5.3
Woodcock Reading Mastery Test	Reading grade score
Letter Identification	6.2
Word Identification	5.7
Word Attack	2.9
Word Comprehension	8.0
Passage Comprehension	6.0
Total Reading	5.1

Charles' scores on the WRAT and the *Woodcock Reading Mastery Test* are considerably below his grade placement. The degree of his educational lag was determined in the follow manner:

Grade placement at time of testing	8-10
WRAT Arithmetic score	5-3
Achievement deficit	3-7
Grade placement at time of testing	8-10
WRAT Spelling score	5-5
Achievement deficit	3-5

Table 5-3
Summation, Case Study B (Charles; 14 years, 4 months old)

Pupil Characteristics	Instruments Used	Results	
		LD	Non-LD
Intellectual	WISC		Full scale IQ = 85; flat profile of subtest scores
Process/cognitive deficits	WISC Subtests		Little subtest reliability
Significant sensory impairments	Pupil's health and school records	Not present	
Physical disability	Pupil's health records	Not present	
Behavioral/ emotional disturbance	Pupil's health records	Not indicated	
Environmental problems	Pupil's school records	Not indicated	
Academic achievement	WRAT	Significant educational lag in math and spelling	
	Woodcock Reading Mastery Test	Significant educational lag in reading	
	Handwriting sample		Adequate performance
	Composition sample	Poor performance	
Neurological evaluation			Not required since pupil did not meet intellectual or processing dysfunction criteria

Grade placement at time of testing	8-10
Woodcock Total Reading score	5-1
	3-9
Grade placement of time of testing	8-10
Woodcock Passage Comprehension score	6-0
	2-10

Charles' overall achievement is significantly below the eighth-grade level; he appears to have reached an achievement plateau at the fifth- to sixth-grade level of performance. However, his 5-1 total reading score on the Woodcock is somewhat misleading because results on the word comprehension and passage comprehension tests (the most important subtests) are considerably higher than the overall test score; one extremely low test score depressed Charles' total reading grade. If one evaluates Charles' achievement deficit using the reading passage comprehension subtest score, the resulting discrepancy between achievement and grade placement is 2 years and 10 months—well beyond the 2-year standard disparity we have established for secondary learning disabilities programming. However, lower achievement scores may be quite appropriate for a student of dull-normal, borderline intellectual ability (as is the case for Charles), particularly in the absence of any strong evidence of specific process or cognitive disability. We should add that Charles' handwriting was adequate, and his composition ability was generally poor, even though it was on a par with his general performance level. Charles was not placed in the learning disabilities program, but was retained in the regular class with a modified program. A summary of this case study is presented in Table 5-3.

Case Study C: David

David was 12 years, 4 months of age when he was evaluated. Although he had attended a private school for much of his elementary program, his academic difficulties persisted. David displayed a defeatist attitude and responded to new or challenging tasks with reluctance. His referral was initiated by his teacher because of his poor achievement in reading and math.

INTELLECTUAL AND PROCESS ASSESSMENT

WISC
Full Scale IQ	90
Verbal IQ	95
Performance IQ	86

WISC Subtests
Performance Subtests	Scale Score
Picture Completion	5
Picture Arrangement	11

Block Design	11
Objective Assembly	5
Coding	8
Verbal Subtests	Scale Score
Information	8
Comprehension	10
Arithmetic	11
Similarities	11
Vocabulary	6
Bender Gestalt	
Koppitz error score	6
Developmental age	6–11

Subtest discrepancies within both verbal and performance scales are suggestive of process difficulty. The subtest variations are somewhat unusual and do not suggest a consistent interpretation of deficits. David's WISC full scale intellectual quotient of 90 satisfies our intellectual criterion for learning disabilities class placement.

ACADEMIC ASSESSMENT

Wide Range Achievement Test	Grade Equivalents
Reading	2.4
Spelling	2.2
Arithmetic	6.1
Woodcock Reading Mastery Test	Grade Equivalents
Letter Identification	4.6
Word Identification	3.9
Word Attack	2.7
Word Comprehension	2.6
Passage Comprehension	2.9
Total Reading	2.9
Handwriting—informal evaluation	Inadequate performance
Composition—informal evaluation	Inadequate performance

David's academic deficiencies, particularly in reading skills, were reflected in the scores he achieved on both the WRAT and Woodcock tests. David's grade placement at the time of testing was eighth grade, eighth month; his actual achievement deficiencies were determined as follows:

Grade placement at time of testing	8.8
WRAT Reading score	2.2
Achievement deficit	6-6

Grade placement at time of testing	8.8
WRAT Arithmetic score	6.1
Achievement deficit	2-7

Table 5-4
Summation: Case Study C (David; 12 years old)

Pupil Characteristics	Instrument Used	Results LD	Non-LD
Intellectual	WISC	Full Scale IQ = 90	
Process/cognitive deficits	Bender Gestalt	Development age = 6–11	
	WISC Subtests	Subtest variation	
Significant sensory impairment	Pupil's health and school record	Not present	
Physical disability	Pupil's health records	Not indicated	
Behavioral/ emotional disturbance	Pupil's school records	Not indicated	
Environmental problems		Not present	
Academic achievement	WRAT	Severe educational lag in reading, math, spelling	
	Woodcock Reading Mastery Test	Severe educational lag in reading	
	Handwriting sample	Poor performance	
	Composition sample	Poor performance	
Neurological evaluation		Soft signs	

Grade placement at time of testing	8.8
WRAT Spelling score	2.2
Achievement deficit	6-6
Grade placement at time of testing	8.8
Woodcock Total Reading score	2.9
Achievement deficit	5-9

David's academic performance as reflected by the results of the WRAT and Woodcock tests is far below his current (at time of evaluation) grade placement. Reading scores are particularly low with most scores falling below the third-grade level. Achievement deficits range from 5 years, 9 months to 6 years, 6 months. For instructional purposes, David's reading performance is on par with that of a second grader. Spelling skill is also extremely weak. Math is the stronger of the two prime subject area; David's math score (on the WRAT) places him at the beginning sixth-grade level, 2-7 years below his grade placement and below our end of sixth grade achievement limit.

According to intellectual, process, and academic tests, David appeared to be a good candidate for learning disabilities placement. There were no physical or sensory impairments, and contributing emotional factors were minimal. There were soft signs of neurological involvement. David was placed in a learning disabilities class (Table 5-4).

PART II

Programming and Instructional Concerns

CHAPTER 6
Educational Programs for Learning Disabled Adolescents

INCIDENCE OF SECONDARY-LEVEL
LEARNING DISABILITIES

The second part of this text is devoted to discussion of educational programming for the learning disabled adolescent. Before we become immersed in this topic, let us reflect for a moment on the phenomenal development of the field of learning disabilities.

On April 6, 1973, Dr. Samuel Kirk, in a speech at a conference sponsored by the Fund for the Perceptually Handicapped, Inc., introduced the term *learning disabilities*. As a result, the Fund for the Perceptually Handicapped reorganized to form the Association for Children with Learning Disabilities. Although this date is generally accepted as the starting point of the learning disabilities movement, the antecedents of learning disabilities can be traced centuries back into history. The historical background of the field has been explored and discussed in the works of Wiederholt (1974) and Mann and Proger (in press). From its inception, the field of learning disabilities has grown faster than any other area of exceptionality (Hallahan and Cruickshank, 1973). As recently as the 1950s and early 1960s, the parent concerned about his learning disabled child of any age had little choice but private school placement, if such a school could be found. Public school programs for the children we today refer to as learning disabled were almost nonexistent. In the past 12 years, however, a combination of parent activism, professional concern, and federal fiscal support and legislation has spurred the development of educational programs for this newest area of exceptionality. The growth of programs for the learning disabled was such that by 1969 two-thirds of the states had enacted legislation that either directly or indirectly mandated services for learning disabled children (Kass, Hall, and Simches, 1969); today that number is even greater.

However, despite the growth rate of learning disabilities programs, it is readily apparent that such programs begun during the 1960s and early 1970s were, almost without exception, established in elementary schools to serve the young handicapped child. We have already discussed this elementary bias of the learning disabilities movement. The preponderance of elementary classes that we see today (Scranton and Downs, 1975), in contrast to the still limited services available to older learning disabled students, is evidence of the continuing strength of the elementary focus. We believe, however, that others feel as we do. Thus, Hammill states that the withholding of educational services from the secondary learning disabled students can no longer be justified.

From the beginning [of the learning disabilities movement] there was a relatively small number of parents and professionals who felt that the movement was ignoring the needs of their older children . . . and all too often they had to sit back and watch with resignation as programs were initiated at the elementary levels. Of course, time was on their side, for children in elementary schools eventually do grow up and become adolescents in junior and senior high schools. With each passing year, therefore, the ranks of those who are interested in adolescents with specific learning disabilities have become larger and increasingly more vocal . . . now twelve years after the founding of the learning disabilities movement, the problems of young adults who have specific learning disabilities are beginning to receive a fair proportion of attention. [Hammill, 1975, p. 291–292]

Similarly, Kline (1972) admonished the educational community for its treatment of adolescents with learning disabilities who are "grossly misunderstood and even more grossly neglected" (p. 266). His query, "How long must they wait?" is a much needed prod to the professional conscience of the learning disabilities field to begin to come to grips with the problems of the older disabled individual.

Fortunately, there are strong indications that as the first wave of program development for elementary learning disabled children reaches its peak, a second wave of program development at the secondary level is likely to follow in its wake. In May 1974, a symposium titled "Youth in trouble" was held in Dallas; the topic of that conference was the learning disabled adolescent (Kratoville, 1974). Another conference entitled "Learning Disabilities in the Secondary School" was sponsored by the Montgomery County Intermediate Unit (Pennsylvania). At that conference, 12 panelists, well-known professionals in the learning disabilities field, gathered to discuss and debate the problem of secondary-level learning disabled students (Goodman and Mann, 1975).

Additionally, the First Invitational Caucus on Learning Disabilities, hosted by the Division for Children with Learning Disabilities of the National Association of Children with Learning Disabilities, was held in New Orleans on November 10th and 11th, 1975. At the meeting 105 representatives from parents' associations, governmental and state agencies, and the educational sector focused on important issues relevant to education for the learning disabled; programming for the secondary-level learning disabled was one of the key issues. In addition to these recent symposia, which both reflect the emergence of the cause and encourage its support, the increase in the number of publications dealing specifically with the topic of secondary learning disabilities is a particularly encouraging sign of the mounting interest in this area.

However, having conducted an extensive search during the past year, we know that the literature on secondary learning disabilities still comprises only a small portion of an extensive body of literature on the general topic of learning disabilities. Few references to secondary learning disabilities predate 1970. On the positive side, our correspondence with various state education officials and project directors has revealed that a considerable number of secondary-level programs are currently in operation or are planned for implementation in the near future.

Two questions that are likely to be asked at this point are: (1) How great is the gap between elementary and secondary services? (2) How many programs will be needed to serve the secondary learning disabled population in the future?

For the first question we have a partial answer, but the second question is, at present, completely open to speculation. Let us explain. In a recent nationwide survey undertaken to determine the levels of development of secondary and elementary programs for the learning disabled, Scranton and Downs (1975) found a preponderance of elementary as compared to secondary programs; this finding is not unexpected—it merely documents what we have found in our own work and what we would expect to hold true for the country at large. [As a result of a countywide needs assessment (Montgomery County, Pa.) for secondary learning disabilities carried out during the 1974–1975 school year, we found that public school programs for learning disabled elementary students outnumber programs for learning disabled adolescents by more than 2 to 1.] More interesting and revealing was the result of a secondary part of the survey in which Scranton and Downs solicited the opinions of state education department officials which might explain the observed differences in levels of program development. Many of the proffered explanations, in one way or another, referred to a general unpreparedness—e.g., lack of background information, shortage of trained personnel, materials, and fiscal support for secondary programming. The elementary bias, already discussed, was reiterated many times. For example, they were told that elementary intervention would eliminate the need for secondary school programs. Finally, many of the comments led one to believe that nothing short of parental action and/or specific legislative mandate will be needed to spur the development of secondary-level programs for the learning disabled.

The second question, how many classes will be needed for the secondary learning disabled, presupposes that one knows how many secondary learning disabled there are. However, at the present time, the extent of the learning disability problem in our secondary schools is anyone's guess; indeed, the incidence figures we find in the literature are probably just that—somebody's guess. Despite an exhaustive search through the literature, we were unable to find even one empirical investigation (but many secondhand references to someone else's opinion) that established incidence statistics for learning disabilities at the secondary level. In the absence of empirical data on the prevalence of learning-disabled secondary students, special educators seem all too ready to apply the same standard generally accepted for elementary programming to the secondary school, even though the validity of these prevalence figures, generally accepted for the elementary learning disabled population, are, we feel, poorly substantiated.

In an effort to uncover the substantiating evidence on which elementary learning disability evidence figures are based, we consulted eight current and authoritative texts that dealt with learning disabilities and found that six of them included some discussion of the prevalence issue (Dunn 1963; Lerner, 1971; Hammill and Bartel, 1971; Kirk, 1972; Bryan and Bryan, 1975; Hewett and Forness, 1974). In all the discussions we found reference to only one report in which the evidence of learning disability among a designated population of children was determined by empirical investigation. In this study, Myklebust & Boshes (1969) found 7–8 percent incidence of learning disabilities within a third- and fourth-grade student population.

For the purposes of future programming, we have undertaken our own needs assessment in an effort to determine the scope of the learning disabilities problem at the secondary level. The needs assessment survey involved the screening of over 800 sixth-grade students from Montgomery County, Pennsylvania during the 1974–1975 school year. The procedure permitted us to determine the extent and degree of underachievement among these soon-to-be secondary students. A substantial number of these students, the exact number varying with the stringency of the achievement criteria (too many to be ignored in any event and more than one would expect to find in a rather well-to-do suburban area), were found to be performing far below grade placement despite normal intellectual ability. The criterion of 1 year or more below grade placement yielded an incidence figure of 23 percent for academic underachievement; a more rigorous criterion of 2 or more year below grade placement reduced the incidence of underachievement to 10 percent. Tolor (1969), in another survey of underachievement, also found similarly high levels of underachievement—26 percent (excluding the mentally deficient) in an affluent, suburban, middle-class community.

Recognizing the need for more empirical evidence concerning the incidence of secondary learning disabilities problems, and in accordance with our own insistence on evidence of process or cognitive disabilities as a criterion for learning disabilities, we are currently carrying out a second needs assessment in which process/cognitive abilities as well as achievement and intellectual abilities will be assessed. The results will be published at a later date. In the meantime, we just do not know how many secondary learning disabled students there are—and we don't think anyone else really knows either. Until we have data on which to base a definitive figure, it is probably safe to assume that the problem is as great and possibly greater than that of the elementary level. Without realistic data, we should avoid citing incidence figures by concensus, as this would lead to the provision of services by quota rather than by need. We do not recommend arbitrarily presenting maximal allowable incidence figures which artificially restrict the growth of secondary learning disability programs. The alternative we propose is the establishment of firm and stringent but also appropriate and responsible criteria by which secondary learning disabled students can be identified for special education services.

SECONDARY SCHOOL PROGRAMS: A SURVEY

In the following section we present brief descriptions of selected secondary learning disabilities programs. This review is by no means inclusive of all secondary-level programs currently in operation; such an undertaking would have been impossible. Rather, we have focused our attention on current programs operating under Title III and Title VI, Part G. Despite our omissions, the programs summarized do, we believe, offer sufficient breadth and variety to illustrate current programming trends. Uniform information on the objectives and operations of current programs is quite difficult to obtain because secondary programs are new and are not yet well publicized; final project reports are in many instances not yet available. The problem of information retrieval has been compounded by the absence of a central clearinghouse for information on federally funded projects in the secondary learning disability area. The National Learning Disabilities Assistance Project (NaLDAP) is a promising model for the future.

Title VI, Part G

WEST VIRGINIA CHILD SERVICE
DEMONSTRATION CENTER

The West Virginia project provides educational assistance to learning disabled and potentially learning disabled children through regular class instruction. The target population includes children in grades K through 12. Four alternative educational interventions are available (levels 1, 2, 3, and 4) once a child has been identified as handicapped or potentially handicapped: (1) short-term placement in a school that has a special education or reading teacher who can determine appropriate instructional methodology and communicate it to the child's home school teacher; (2) instruction in a resource room operated on an itinerant basis by the reading or language arts teacher who in turn is supported by an itinerant center clinician; (3) a diagnostic/prescriptive program provided by the child's teacher with the assistance of a center clinician or trained staff members, such as the language or reading teacher; and (4) a diagnostic/prescriptive program provided independently by a teacher who has received prior training in diagnostic/prescriptive teaching.

Clearly, the West Virginia program embodies a strong bias toward mainstreaming in that a child is never dismissed from the regular class and the responsibility for his instruction rests primarily with the regular classroom teacher or with other regular school personnel. A group of learning disabilities center clinicians, who provide in-service training and field services, are the demonstration center's back-up support for the regular teachers. Their services are facilitated by the use of mobile clinic laboratories.

OHIO CHILD SERVICE DEMONSTRATION CENTER

The purposes of the Ohio project are threefold: (1) development of an in-service training program model for teachers, tutors, and program consultants who assist learning or behaviorally disordered children, (2) development of a model secondary program, and (3) extension and refinement of identification and selection procedures for learning disabled students in both elementary and secondary schools. Exportable products currently being developed include learning disability identification instruments for both primary and secondary school use, multimedia in-service training packets, and assessment procedures and materials to be used in secondary classes. Five classroom programs for adolescent students are planned.

MICHIGAN CHILD SERVICE DEMONSTRATION CENTER

The objective of the Michigan project is to serve learning disabled students better by means of regional learning disabilities centers to be established in rural and urban sections of the state. The centers will provide services to children with learning disabilities from kindergarten through senior high school. Activities of the center include in-service training for teachers, consultants, and administrative personnel, consultative services provided by a staff of itinerant learning disabilities specialists, and diagnostic/prescriptive services. If she desires to do so, a teacher may bring a child to the center for evaluation. Within a day, a thorough evaluative diagnostic work-up will be completed and an individualized prescription prepared. Eventually, regular class teachers should be able to do their own evaluation and programming for handicapped students if the in-service and consultative services are effective. Lastly, in-service counseling for administrators and programs for parents will be provided to help foster a better understanding of the learning and behavior patterns of learning disabled children at home and at school.

TEXAS CHILD SERVICE
DEMONSTRATION CENTER

The goal of the Texas project is to develop a replicable instructional management system consisting of a diagnostic system and task specification systems in three curricular areas. The development of a series of exportable minimodule instructional packets is a second major project endeavor. Each minimodule will include explanations of diagnostic techniques, instructional strategies and materials, and a measurement instrument. The modules are intended to be used for 5–10 days, for approximately 30 minutes each day. The curricular packets emphasize instruction for process deficits.

OKLAHOMA CHILD SERVICE
DEMONSTRATION CENTER

In Oklahoma, a secondary-level resource room program has been developed to serve students in grades 7 through 12 who have "major learning dysfunctions." Learning disabled students are defined in accordance with Oklahoma state guidelines, which emphasize: (1) normal or potentially normal intelligence, (2) evidence of neuropsychological involvement, (3) learning disabilities of perceptual, conceptual, or integrative functioning, and (4) exclusion of students with emotional disturbance, sensory deficit, mental retardation, or severe organic insult with accompanying motor dysfunction.

The intervention model employs the diagnostic/prescriptive teaching strategy with the resulting individualized prescriptive programs being prepared by the intervention team composed of the school psychologist and learning disabilities teachers. The developmental areas included in the educational programs are visual motor and visual processing, auditory processing, language, social behavior, and emotional development. The project's staff believes that the student's regular program should be modified as little as possible. Therefore, in programming, the least disruptive alternatives are tried first; e.g., modification of regular classroom procedures rather than special placement if at all feasible. The extent and duration of special services in the modified program are determined by the degree of the pupil's disabilities and the rate of their amelioration. The resource rooms are substituted for those classes in which the student is experiencing failure and frustration. A student is never removed from a class in which he is succeeding. Although the program's major objective is "normal academic growth," the project staff is particularly sensitive to the unique social and emotional pressures secondary students face. The project staff attempts to come to grips with those special aspects, including the influence of adolescent peer pressures, as well as the overall goal of developing the student's academic skills and abilities.

Title III

In addition to the Title VI projects just described, many innovative projects have been initiated through Title III, ESEA. Some of these projects are described.

ALTERNATIVE TO FAILURE (IOWA)

A learning disabilities program for junior and senior high school is in progress in the Des Moines public school system. The Alternatives to Failure program is the most recently implemented part of a comprehensive continuum of school programming (K–12) for learning disabled students in the Des Moines schools. The program, which services secondary students, can appropriately be termed a community rather than a school-based program since pupil, peer, staff, parent, and community involvement are integral components of the total project structure.

The project's classroom model—the resource room— has become quite familiar to us by now. The instructional orientation is decidedly remedial and uses the diagnostic/prescriptive approach. Assessment of each student's areas of weakness is followed by individualized programming to "help the child with his problem areas in learning." The basic instructional strategy, "remediation of deficits," is apparently adhered to at all levels with the teachers substituting tests and materials appropriate to the student's age.

The project's secondary classrooms were first opened in July 1973. By November 1974, three senior high schools and seven junior high schools had learning disabilities programs. The goal was to have the program operational in all twenty Des Moines' secondary schools by the fall of 1975.

In each school the learning disabilities program is backed up by a learning disabilities team composed of a learning disabilities specialist, a resource teacher, 4 regular teachers (1 from each content area), the principal or his representative, and, when requested, the nurse, psychologist, speech therapist, or social worker. The involvement of teachers with both special education and regular education backgrounds has facilitated the acceptance of the program and the adapting of curriculum in content subjects to meet the needs of learning disabled students.

PROJECT CROSSOVER ASSISTANCE TO
CHILDREN WITH HANDICAPS (COACH)

COACH is a Pennsylvania Title III project currently operating in the Central Dauphin School District (Hines, 1974). The program is designed to provide assistance to seventh and eighth graders who are unable to cope with the scholastic demands of junior high school. The students included in the program are identified as low achievers and/or learning disabled. A low achiever is defined as a student whose academic performance is 1 or more years below his actual grade placement. The learning disabled are identified by their classroom teachers and receive help from a learning therapist assigned to their school.

The experimental program focuses on math and social studies and is based on a multimedia instructional approach and a philosophy of continuous progress from the student's own baseline of achievement (the unrealistic, and often harmful, standard of grade-level performance has been avoided). In comparison to their peers, underachieving adolescents are constantly losing academic ground, falling further and further behind. Through Project COACH the school personnel hope to reverse the trend toward academic deterioration among these students. Just "holding the line" in math or social studies represents progress; gains are doubly rewarding to both the students and project staff.

As a result of the project, many significant changes have occurred in regular classroom procedures, e.g., a shift from traditional lecture and textbook approaches to small group instruction using a variety of approaches (audiovisuals, manipulatives, simulations). Other noted effects include a marked decrease in discipline problems and improvement in student attitudes toward school reported by both teachers and parents. Many of the students made impressive academic gains. During the project's second year (1973–1974), the number of seventh graders who gained academically in math and social studies was 73 percent and 83 percent, respectively. Among eighth graders, 85 percent and 65 percent demonstrated improvement in math and social studies. In math, 27 percent of the seventh graders and 11 percent of the eighth graders made no gains or lost ground; in social studies, the percentage of students who regressed was 17 percent at the seventh-grade level and 35 percent at the eighth-grade level. Although the project did have a designated control group, statistical comparisons between experimental and control subjects were not available.

CHESTERFIELD COUNTY JUNIOR HIGH
SCHOOL LEARNING DISABILITY PROGRAM

Junior high school students are also the primary concern of the Chesterfield County Junior High School Learning Disability Program. The project established junior high school resource room programs in eight junior high school buildings to help "prepare adolescent learning disabled students for functioning in mainstream environments." The program is seen as part of, not separate from, the regular school setting. Two modifications in regular programming structure facilitate the accommodation of the special program; a learning disabilities resource room, complete with observation room, and a learning laboratory were established in each participating school (mobile labs were constructed for use in schools lacking sufficient space for a permanent laboratory classroom).

The student participants are selected in accordance with the NACHC learning disabilities definition endorsed by the U.S. Department of Health, Education and Welfare. The service model stresses the diagnostic-prescriptive-remedial model. The initial screening is done by the learning disabilities teacher. A Title III team was established to review referral and screening information in order to plan appropriate individualized education encompassing remediation, compensation, counseling, and home involvement. The prescription from the team is implemented by the learning disabilities teacher within the learning lab, and, if possible, through modifications within regular classroom programs.

The learning disabilities teacher is an important link between the special and regular school programs. Several areas of student performance are evaluated: self-esteem, school attendance, growth-performance average, academic achievement (paragraphing, comprehension, word recognition, arithmetic computation, and spelling). After participating for 2 years, the students had made significant improvements in four academic areas: paragraph comprehension, word recognition, arithmetic computation, and spelling. Significant improvements in grade-point averages and school attendance were also demonstrated for the second year. And there were general carry-over effects from special classes to the regular programs in that students began to respond more positively to the mainstream school environment, or their classroom teachers began responding more positively to them.

LANDIS CURRICULAR MODIFICATION PROJECT

Another Title III effort that resembles Project COACH and the Chesterfield County Junior High School Learning Disability Program is described by Landis et al. (1973). The Landis Curricular Modification Project is intended to meet both the "subject matter needs and remedial needs of the learning disabled student" by extensive modification of the existing reading curriculum. Teachers of English I, mathematics I, and science I were urged to substitute a multisensory learning approach for traditional textbook-oriented instruction. The teachers also had to structure course content in terms of behavioral objectives, prepared appropriate auditory, visual, and kinesthetic learning aids, and materials to facilitate the student's acquisition of skill and knowledge in the content areas.

A basic remedial program parallels the new, modified instructional program. Removed from the demands and pressures of the standard reading situation, students can profit from reading instruction in basic skills, word recognition, comprehension, and study skills as stressed in the remedial instruction program.

As a result of the program, learning disabled students are passing their academic courses, which the author insists were not "watered down"; the courses differed in method of presentation, not content. There has also been marked improvement in attitudes and behavior, as well as academics. Success in content subjects and the self-respect it engendered seem to have been the impetus for improvement in both remedial and general reading.

The four projects described above—Project COACH, Chesterfield County Junior High School Learning Disability Program, Alternatives to Failure, and the Landis Curricular Modification Project—have at least one important element in common: the involvement of secondary content area teachers. Each project was able to stimulate alterations and modifications of methods and materials in regular classes to bring academic instruction more in line with the needs of learning disabled adolescents. Experimental programs designed to achieve this kind of effect are particularly promising.

Secondary students have two needs, remedial or compensatory aids and "school survival therapy" (Ansara, 1972). We have to help adolescents to achieve not only in separate special programs but also in regular courses, the mainstream, with their nonhandicapped peers. Unfortunately, this task is not going to be easy. Too few secondary teachers outside the realm of special education view themselves as responsible for teaching basic skills, particularly reading skills, along with the subject matter of their discipline (Herbert, 1974). Their attitudes will have to change; Project COACH, Alternatives to Failure, The Chesterfield County Junior High School Learning Disability Program, and the Landis Curricular Modification Projects are worthwhile efforts headed in the right direction.

AREA LEARNING CENTER

The last Title III project involves the establishment of a regional diagnostic learning center offering comprehensive social, medical, and educational services to children with learning disabilities. The Area Learning Center (Huizinga and Smalligan, 1968) is a multidisciplinary team service for children and adolescents with classroom learning problems. The center staff includes reading experts, psychologists, and psychiatric, pediatric, and academic professionals. After a student is referred from a local school system, a center consultant observes the child in his own classroom and completes some preliminary testing. Thereafter, two courses of action are possible: an educational plan can be developed by the consultant working cooperatively with the teacher and school principal, or the child may receive further diagnostic testing in an evaluation at the Area Learning Center. An assessment of intellectual, perceptual, academic, and personality factors will be done. After the evaluation, a joint conference is held between the center and school personnel, which results in the formulation of an educational plan. The plan is then implemented in the school with backup support provided by the center's consultant.

By the end of the center's first year in operation, some secondary benefits of the center concept came to light. During evaluations for learning disabilities, numerous health problems were detected and appropriate medical treatment given. The interdisciplinary team approach made it possible to coordinate the services of many organizations avoiding wasteful duplication of services. Finally, the project staff found that the center concept was very well accepted by parents and school personnel.

SUMMARY

The field of learning disabilities has benefited greatly from the infusion of funds through Title VI, Part G and Title III (now changed to Title IV, Part C) educational assistance acts. Although federal support has encouraged the development of innovative secondary learning disabilities programs, new program development is by no means restricted to federally funded operations. However, title projects are unique in that they are designed to be exemplary, innovative models for the rest of the field. As a group, they are indicative of current trends and future directions of the field. The emphasis in title projects is definitely on exportability and replication of proven, validated practices and products.

Certain key trends are apparent in the projects we have reviewed. By far the most appealing service model is the resource room coupled with modification of the regular classroom programs, as opposed to the self-contained classroom which is now out of vogue. The overriding instructional approach is diagnostic/prescriptive teaching, which emphasizes the intensive and extensive evaluation of the learner's strengths and weaknesses and the development of an individualized educational plan. From our reading of program reports it is often difficult to determine whether disabilities refers to curriculum, i.e., specific academic skill deficits, or specific process/cognitive dysfunctions within the learner, i.e., visual perception, memory, spatial orientation. The difference is important. The problems of psychoeducational process testing and training have to be documented, discussed, and argued repeatedly by ourselves and others (Wepman, Cruickshank, Deutsch, Morency, Strother, 1975; Hammill and Larsen, 1975, Minskoff, 1975; Newcomer, Larsen, & Hammill, 1975). We will not belabor the issue at this point. Suffice it to say that the evidence overwhelmingly argues against the validity or utility of this approach for educating the learning disabled. We support the correction of academic deficits and emphasize such in our own program but definitely avoid the training of "processes." We will explore instructional alternatives to process training in the following chapter.

Another programmatic trend is in-service. In-service, and occasionally preservice training are important components of some of the projects reviewed. In-service training may be offered to both regular and special personnel; teachers, learning specialists, and consultants in diagnostic prescriptive teaching are most frequently involved. And finally, the development of exportable prepackaged learning materials specifically designed for learning disabled students is a major objective of some of the current projects.

REFERENCES

Ansara A: Language therapy to salvage the college potential of dyslexic adolescents. 22:123–139, 1972

Bryan TH, Bryan JH: *Understanding Learning Disabilities.* Port Washington, NY, Alfred Publishing, 1975

Dunn LM (ed): *Exceptional Children in the Schools.* New York, Holt, Rinehart and Winston, 1963

Goodman L, Mann L: *Learning Disabilities in the Secondary School: Title III: Curricular Development for Secondary Learning Disability.* Blue Bell, Pa, Montgomery County Intermediate Unit, 1975

Hallahan DP, Cruickshank, WM: *Psychoeducational Foundations of Learning Disabilities.* Englewood Cliffs, New Jersey, Prentice-Hall, 1973

Hammill DD: Adolescents with learning disability: definition, identification, and incidence, in Goodman L, Mann L: (eds): *Learning Disabilities in the Secondary School: Title III: Curricular Development for Secondary Learning Disability.* Blue Bell, Pa, Montgomery County Intermediate Unit, 1975

Hammill DD, Bartel NR (eds): *Educational Perspectives in Learning Disabilities.* New York, John Wiley & Sons, 1971

Hammill DD, Larsen SC: The effectiveness of psycholinguistic training. Exceptional Children 41:5–16, 1974

Herbert JR: Specific language disability in secondary schools. Bull Orton Soc 24:135–140, 1974

Hewett FM, Forness, SR: *Education of Exceptional Learners.* Boston, Allyn and Bacon, 1974

Hines JD: Personal communication, 1974

Huizinga RJ, Smalligan DH: The area learning center—a regional program for school children with learning disabilities. J Learning Disabil 1:502–506, 1968

Kass CE, Hall RE, Simches RF: Legislation in minimal brain dysfunction in children, phase two: educational, medical, and health-related services. Public Health Service Publications no. 2015, 44–50, 1969

Kirk SA: *Educating Exceptional Children.* Boston, Houghton-Mifflin, 1972

Kline CL: The adolescents with learning problems: How long must they wait? J Learning Disabil 5:262–284, 1972

Kratoville BL (ed): *Youth in Trouble.* San Rafael, California, Academic Therapy Publications, 1974

Landis J, Jones RW, Kennedy LD: Curricular modification for secondary school reading. J Reading 16:374–378, 1973

Lerner JW: *Children with Learning Disabilities: Theories, Diagnosis, and Teaching Strategies.* Boston, Houghton-Mifflin, 1971

Mann L, Proger BB: *Historical Perspectives of Childhood Exceptionalities.* New York, Grune & Stratton (in press)

Minskoff EH: Research on psycholinguistic training: Critique and guidelines. Exceptional Children 42:136–144, 1975

Myklebust HR, Boshes B: Minimal brain damage in children. Washington, DC, US Department of Health, Education and Welfare, Final report USPHS Contract 108-65-142, 1969

Newcomer PL, Larsen SC, Hammill DD: A response to "Research on psycholinguistic training." Exceptional Children 42:144–147, 1975

Scranton TR, Downs MC. Elementary and secondary learning disabilities programs in the U. S.: a survey. J Learning Disabil 8:394–399, 1975

Tolor A: Incidence of underachievement at the high school level. J Education Res 63:63–65, 1969

Wepman JM, Cruickshank WM, Deutsch CD, Morency A, Strother CR: Learning disabilities. *In* Hobbs N (ed): Issues in the Classification of Children, Vol. 1. San Francisco: Jossey–Bass, 1975

Wiederholt JL: Historical perspectives on the education of learning disabled, in Mann L, Sabatino DA (eds): *The Second Review of Special Education.* Philadelphia, JSE Press, 1974

CHAPTER 7
Programming for the Secondary Learning Disabled Student: A Model of Service

INTRODUCTION

In this chapter we will present our rationale for educational programming for the secondary-level learning disabled student. We provide it from two perspectives—the philosophical and the practical. Our attention in all of this will be on the classroom unit rather than on the total school structure. Our formulation is that of an effective and efficient classroom model, under the teacher's control, serving learning disabled students in the secondary school.

RATIONALE

The basic premises of the secondary learning disabilities program model which we espouse are as follows:

1. A secondary learning disabilities program is a basic education program.
2. The secondary learning disabilities instructional program does not include process-based training.
3. A secondary learning disabilities program embodies the concept of mastery learning.
4. A secondary learning disabilities program emphasizes curriculum and curricular management.

5. A secondary learning disabilities program achieves a balance between academic and career education.
6. A secondary learning disabilities program is an integrated program, operating somewhere between the poles of total containment and total integration.

A Basic Education Program

We firmly believe that the primary instructional responsibility of the learning disabilities teacher at the secondary level is the teaching of basics in the areas of mathematics and language arts. This position is consistent with the academic criterion that we have suggested for identifying learning disabilities candidates, namely, that enrollment in secondary learning disabilities programs be restricted to students who are performing below the seventh-grade competency level, i.e., lacking full sixth-grade competency. This academic criterion limits secondary-level learning disabilities program placement to those students who are still functioning at the elementary level and excludes students who have passed beyond this level, even if their academic achievement is still below academic expectancies held for them as per grade, age, or IQ.

The student population to be served at the secondary level should be one with severe learning problems. The term "severe" requires some explanation. We conceive of the academic deficiencies of secondary students whose performance ranks below the seventh-grade level as severe because we feel that students functioning below this level are inadequately equipped to cope with the demands of adult living. What level of skill development is needed to enable students to assume the role of independent adults in our society? The performance criteria which we selected, emphasize the mastery of full sixth-grade elementary school curricula in the areas of mathematics and language arts. They are realistic in view of the actual demands to be faced by a student once he leaves school.

Apropos of our position, Robinson (1963) has delineated levels of literacy and their corresponding school grade equivalents. The levels of literacy, extending from low to high, are complete illiteracy, low-level literacy, partial literacy, variable literacy, and complete literacy. In Robinson's schema, sixth-grade competency corresponds to partial literacy, described as the level at which individuals are "just able to read essential information for daily living and working at low levels" [p. 417]. An individual with skills below the level of partial literacy to the level of low literacy ("barely able to contend with the adult reading material available") is likely to "disintegrate to complete illiteracy because of lack of use and practice" [p. 417].

Some educators may object to our criteria on the basis that our standards are too stringent (Thompson, 1970) or too loose (Wiederholt, 1975). Not infrequently, too, we encounter the notion that functional literacy corresponds to the end of third grade proficiency in reading. This belief probably stems from the fact that by the end of the third grade the student has, in most reading programs, been exposed to all word attack and word analysis skills and has developed a relatively extensive vocabulary. He thus has a foundation of skills for independent reading. Nevertheless he is not yet an expert or proficient reader, merely a marginally functional one. As Robinson and others who work with undereducated adults have discovered, if reading is arrested at this level, the individual probably will not possess sufficient literacy to contend with daily living, and further, he may avoid reading as much as possible in the future, thereby losing whatever reading skills he has. Sixth-grade proficiency, the goal we are suggesting for secondary-level learning disabilities programming is really a very minimal one.

Our goal is to help students achieve reading and mathematical skills to a level at which these skills are practically usable and to assist the students to carry on meaningful and independent lives. Some learning disabled students may never reach this goal; many will surpass it.

We do not want to mislead any reader, however, into thinking that the student's participation in a secondary-level learning disabilities program should end abruptly when he scores at the upper sixth-grade level on a standardized reading or math achievement test. We are suggesting that candidates for the learning disabilities program should have entry level skills below this level. Once they are enrolled they should continue to receive help as long as progress is accomplished. However after a secondary-level learning disabilities pupil achieves full sixth-grade competency he should receive further help within the mainstream of regular education.

If a student can be helped to reach beginning seventh-grade level performance, integration in the regular program is possible. Generally speaking, within the secondary-level mainstream, one is likely to find pupils whose ability and performance levels fall below this level coping with the scope of regular programs. The student functioning at or slightly beyond a beginning seventh-grade level has a good chance of holding his own in some regular secondary school programs.

The validity of these last statements regarding integration, of course, depends heavily on the character of the particular secondary school the learning disabled pupil attends. Does the school attend primarily to the needs of the college bound, to the exclusion of the other less able students? Are there alternative academic programs for the not so academically oriented? Is a reading laboratory or a remedial reading specialist available in the school? Is reading an integral part of all content subject instruction? Is there a tutoring program? What are the attitudes of the staff toward the reintegration of handicapped students? Individual schools vary in their receptiveness toward the integration and maintenance of handicapped students, and the secondary learning disabled pupil is handicapped. He cannot be expected to achieve normal performance unless some unique maturational or biological restorative process occurs. A school that is elitist in orientation may mean failure for even previously successfully taught learning disabled pupils. A school that accepts a pupil's limitations may make the school career of even a poorly corrected learning disabled pupil successful.

One last point in defense of our basic education program. From a practical standpoint, if the instructional programs for the learning disabilities secondary class have no curricular limits—i.e., are not limited in subject area to math and language arts between grade levels one and six as we have done or in some other way—the demands placed on the L. D. teacher may become so great that they are unrealizable. Can we expect a teacher to be proficient in teaching basic skills and content subject areas as well for all subject areas from grades one through twelve? Consider the number of subjects included in a typical comprehensive high school or junior high school curriculum. It is unlikely that one teacher would be able to cover all of them effectively unless, of course, the program was reduced to a limited tutorial model in which learning disabilities teacher merely assisted students to meet the assignments of their regular classes—study for tests, prepare homework papers, etc. Although tutorial services are legitimate, particularly during the integration of students in regular programs, we feel that they should not be the primary responsibility of the learning disabilities teacher. Teams of learning disabilities teachers, consisting of specialists competent in specific subject areas are of course conceivable. They are, however, not a practical solution at the present time.

Process Training at the Secondary Level

We dealt with the problem of establishing the presence of process dysfunction in secondary-level learning disabled pupils at considerable length in Chapter 3. The diagnosis of process dysfunction still constitutes a most problematic issue for the field of learning disabilities, and our solutions to date are controversial and tentative.

What, then, is the state of affairs relative to process training? Although heated argument still rages between those who espouse process training at the elementary level and those (like ourselves) who regard it largely as misinterpretation of data and a general waste of time, both process training enthusiasts and nay sayers generally agree that it is rarely relevant at the secondary level. The student has, so to speak, matured away from the possibilities that the training of perceptual functions or the remediation of specific language skills will make anything more than the most peripheral contribution. Even hardened process enthusiasts will probably agree that by the age of 12 or thereabouts it is probably too late to direct remedial efforts to training perceptual functions qua perceptual functions. The student, by this age, is operating within high cognitive realms, even if defectively, so that the tools of the process-oriented learning disabilities specialist—which have been designed for simple "lower" processes and for younger children—no longer apply. The improvement of "processes" for the secondary learning disabled pupil in any case is best approached by training through formal academic and vocational training which, if successful, should have a generally positive effect on cognitive functioning (see Mann, 1974).

To repeat, we find no place for formal process training at the secondary level.

The Concept of Mastery Learning

The idea of learning for mastery is not new. In the first half of the 20th century Carleton Washburne (1922) introduced the Winnetka Plan and an approach was developed by Henry C. Morrison at the University of Chicago's Laboratory School (1926). The most important approach to the problem in recent years was formulated by Benjamin Bloom.

Bloom (1968) has defined mastery for a subject area in terms of specific major instructional objectives that students are expected to achieve by the course's completion. The subject is broken down into a number of smaller learning units, and objectives are defined for those units whose mastery is essential for mastery of the subject's major objectives. The units, taught by usual classroom procedures, are supplemented with feedback/correction procedures and brief diagnostic tests administered at each unit's completion. Each test covers all of a particular unit's objectives and thus reveals what a student has learned from instruction for that unit. Supplementary instructional correctives are then applied to help the student overcome a given unit's learning problems before proceeding further.

We are told for college students that:

> Mastery learning [Bloom, 1968] offers a powerful new approach to student learning which can provide almost all students with the successful and rewarding learning experiences now allowed to only a few. It proposes that all or almost all students can master what they are taught. Further, it suggests procedures whereby each student's instruction and learning can be so managed, *within the context of ordinary group-based classroom instruction,* as to promote his fullest development. Mastery learning enables 75 to 90 per cent of the students to achieve to the same instructional methods. It also makes student learning more efficient than conventional approaches. Students learn more material in less time. Finally, mastery learning produces markedly greater student interest in and attitude toward the subject learned than usual classroom methods. [Block, 1971, p. 3]

Reports are not likely to be as glowing for the learning disabled pupils, but we believe that the mastery approach has much to recommend it. We have used a variant of this procedure called *Individual Achievement Monitoring* (Proger and Mann, 1973), which provides for a continuing recycling of the pupil through the same instructional curricular sequence until mastery is achieved, with indications being additionally provided for intervention with specific remedial academic techniques when the curricular approach proves unsuccessful. The technique, which is an adaptation of *Comprehensive Achievement Monitoring* of Gorth et al. (1972), also provides for pre-, as well as post-, unit evaluation to identify areas of instruction that require more (or less) attention depending on the student's previous mastery level.

We have used the mastery approach at both secondary and elementary levels. We have found it to be more successful than any other method we have used, provided that appropriate curricula are taught. We believe it is the method of choice for most learning disabled pupils. We refer the reader to Block's *Mastery Learning* (1971) for the theoretical and research supports of the approach.

Curriculum Selection and Management

The fourth basic underlying premise of our learning disabilities program is that managed curricula are essential components of a classroom secondary-level learning disabilities program. By curriculum, we mean a cohesive and comprehensive approach to instruction in a given content area as opposed to the teaching of splinter skills. Curriculum, of course, includes a specific program's materials and the modes of presentation used to impart a given subject matter and a philosophy of instruction. Curricula help establish comprehensive frameworks to control, direct, and provide purpose to learning disabilities programming. The burden for instructional decision making—what the student will actually do while he is in the learning disabilities class—will be greatly simplified by reliance on "curriculum," and we believe, in light of our own experience over 5 years of public school programming, that carefully selected (modified or adjusted, to be sure) commercial curricular materials offer the best approach to the curricular plan we are recommending.

We are, of course, concerned with the hows and whys of curriculum selection and its use in secondary learning disabilities classrooms. For purposes of this book, we have reviewed commercial curricular materials and have selected what we feel are the best for secondary-level learning disabilities purposes. The reader's immediate reaction to this statement may be that few commercial curricula are appropriate for secondary learning disabled students. Nevertheless, the shelf is not completely bare. Some curricula seem to have potential for the secondary-level learning disabilities program, and we will have to make do with others until better ones materialize.

Good curricula in any case are not sufficient by themselves to meet the needs of the secondary-level learning disabled student. They must be used correctly.[1] After selecting the core and supplemental curricula to be used, the teacher must manage them effectively.

[1] We have too often responded to a teacher's request for more materials, only to find that many potentially good materials were already available in the class or school building; they just were not being used, or were being used incorrectly.

CURRICULUM MANAGEMENT SYSTEMS

A curriculum management system generally includes a combination of instructional objectives, usually behaviorally stated, and a series of criterion-referenced evaluative tests assessing mastery of the objectives at each level of the curriculum. Many of the new curriculum programs in reading and math come with management components, e.g., Developmental Reading (Los Angeles Unified School District; 1975). If a management system is part of a curriculum package, it is a strong selling point as regards its applicability to learning disabilities programs. However, if a particular curriculum lacks such a system, it may still be selected for use if a management system can be locally devised to go along with it.

A number of instructional management systems also are available that are not directly tied to any specific curriculum (e.g., Fountain Valley Teacher Support System in Reading; Fountain Valley Teacher Support System in Mathematics; Houghton-Mifflin's Instructional Pupil Monitoring, CTB/McGraw-Hill Prescriptive Inventory). These systems generally include instructional objectives and evaluative tests for specific subject areas, but they are independent of any specific curricula for these areas and are designed to be used in many different teaching situations. Since they are indexed to various commercial materials, they have considerable flexibility. However, having developed and worked with both types of management systems, we can say that those that are developed for specific curricula have a decided advantage. They directly and intimately "match" the objectives of those curricula and help teach "organically" organized contents, whereas the independent systems tend to teach isolated objectives and foster "splinter" skill development.

The management of the curriculum is essential for the following reasons:

1. We need to be able to place the student appropriately in an institutional sequence in any given subject area.

2. We need to evaluate student progress in an ongoing, continuous fashion for instructional purposes. Although pre-post assessment at the beginning and end of the year may be sufficient for total program evaluation or to gauge student growth over a long period of time, evaluation at frequent and regular intervals is necessary for effective daily educational programming. A criterion-referenced, instructional, objective-based management system gives us the information we need to adjust our instructional pace and techniques (repeat, speed up, slow down, supplement, etc.).

3. Management systems permit us to identify specific areas of educational difficulty or handicap to which we can bring additional help; they also allow us to recognize a pupil's strengths and capitalize on these.

4. We need to be accountable for the educational planning and progress for each student. It has become increasingly important that teachers be able to document what the course of study for a particular student entails. A management system simplifies this task by helping the teacher specify to administrators, evaluators, and parents the instructional goals of training, the materials and techniques to be used, and the outcomes expected.

Curriculum management approaches are particularly feasible within the scope of the basic education approach we have described because generally accepted sequences and ranges of content and skills are found in the basic math and language curricula for grades one through six.

Thus far in our discussion of instruction we have stressed the importance of instruction in the basic skill areas. However, many authors writing about learning disabled adolescents emphasize the social, emotional, and psychological needs of this age group (Weber, 1974; Kronick, 1975; Gordon, 1966, 1970; Giffin, 1971), as well as their persistent academic needs. We recognize that the adolescent years are indeed a difficult time for any student and particularly for the student with a handicap. And we believe that any adult who has chosen to work with handicapped adolescents must be sensitive and perceptive to their social and emotional needs, as well as to their academic deficiencies, but we maintain that social and emotional factors are not appropriate "direct" concerns of secondary learning disabilities programs. We emphasize that the primary responsibility of the secondary-level learning disabilities teacher is an instructional one. Classroom teachers are not psychologists, counselors, or social workers, and we believe that they should refrain from assuming these roles or becoming too involved in areas in which they lack credentials and competency. Teachers can assist the students most by helping them, despite their handicaps, achieve reasonable amounts of academic and career success (we have found that few things help damaged self-concepts more than success). A classroom teacher's preoccupation with socioemotional factors and the home situation often serves as an excuse for not pressing too hard on the adademic front. Teachers must always remember that their primary responsibility is to teach. If they do not provide this service to the learning disabled pupil, no one else is likely to.

Social skills may be legitimately and necessarily emphasized in the learning disabled student's program, particularly if they relate to job success. But if students have social or emotional problems of such magnitude that they are unable to participate in or profit from academic-career education programs, their placement in the learning disabilities program is questionable. A learning disabilities program should not become the last stop for emotionally disturbed or socially maladjusted youths; neither the students nor the program will be benefited. Other educational and/or supportive services should be sought for these handicapped individuals.

Career Education

Any program for adolescent students with learning disabilities would be incomplete if it did not provide for both the academic and career training needs of the student. Whereas remediation of specific deficiencies and academic instruction are the foremost goals of elementary learning disabilities programs, the teacher at the secondary level must strive for a realistic balance between continued academic instruction and the pupil's preparation for post–high school pursuits. We prefer to use the term career education or training in place of vocational training which evokes the image of the student preparing for a specific job or occupation (generally one that involves technical and/or manual training) rather than academic training. Career education, on the other hand, is a much less restrictive term. It does not carry with it narrow vocational connotations and may refer to a broad range of occupational pursuits.

To be effective for the learning disabled student, career education must to be adjusted to meet his needs. Williamson (1974) calls attention to three basic issues that can affect the success of secondary handicapped students in career education programs. First, career education programs for the disabled student must not replace basic academic skill training; rather, a combination of vocational and academic training should be given the student. She thus expresses the views of many teachers and particularly parents who fear that career education may deprive earning disabled students of important academic experiences. Many parents of learning disabled students are unwilling to abandon their academic aspirations for their children. We can appreciate their feelings. Nevertheless, time begins to run out in the upper grades; by the time the learning disabled adolescent reaches junior or senior high school, much of his academic training is behind him. At this point we must be prepared to make some realistic decisions about the future course of his remaining school years. Many factors should be considered: current levels of achievement in academic subjects, growth rate over the past years, career goals, and parents' aspirations. Ultimately, however, some final decision will have to be made concerning the learning disabled adolescent's remaining years of school. This decision hopefully will represent the shared feelings of the student, the parents, and the teacher.

The second issue Williamson discusses is that career education programs must offer a wide range of alternatives for the learning disabled student. The learning disabled by any definition are students with, at the very least, average intellectual ability. Anyone who has worked with the learning disabled realizes that many of the students so labeled do, in fact, possess above average and even superior intellectual abilities. The range of vocational options offered to the secondary learning disabled student must include a range of occupational pursuits commensurate with the levels of ability, accomplishments, and aspirations of these students. The scope of career education programs should be expansive enough to meet the legitimate needs of learning disabled adolescents. Every career avenue should be opened to them from technical, vocational training to college for those who are the most able. The existence of college programs for the learning disabled perhaps better than anything else underscores the untapped potential in this handicapped group.

Finally, Williamson suggests that career education programs must reach beyond the "narrow concept of occupational orientation" to deal with emotional problems and social relationships as well. We would add that vocational preparation for one specific job and no other is certainly outmoded in a technological society such as ours where jobs are both created and eliminated at an alarming rate. Ideally, career education programs will equip the soon-to-be-looking-for-a-job learning disabled student with marketable skills applicable to many occupations. Some professionals who work with the learning disabled adolescent suggest that career education should define the student's vocational strengths and then match these to requirements for specific jobs (Wiig, 1972; Brutten, 1966), thereby increasing the student's employability and his likelihood of job success.

Career education is an important aspect of the secondary learning disabilities program. We urge teachers to seek and work closely with vocational counselors and/or training programs that are ongoing within their school or district. We should willingly adjust our academic training, particularly for the senior high student, in order to introduce career orientation material into the classroom and to provide training in those skills that the individual requires for job success. As we progress from junior to senior high, the emphasis clearly should shift from an academic focus to one in favor of career preparation for the older student; academic instruction should continue of course, but in a secondary position. For students whose future life goals require a college education, career education and academic training coincide; for these students academic instruction retains its primary importance, even as they approach the limit of their high school education.

The Integrated Learning Disabilities Program

A good secondary learning disabilities program is best described as "integrated" in that every student spends part of the school day in both regular and special classes. Good programs offer a continuum of services ranging from the self-contained classroom to total main-streaming. We prefer to avoid the self-contained classroom versus resource room argument; the rigid and forced dichotomy between these two classroom models, which is so often portrayed in the litera-ture, is an exaggeration and distortion of the situation, and not a very productive one at that. (Readers who wish to delve into the con-troversy are referred to Hammill and Wiederholt, 1972; Dunn, 1968; Christopolos and Renz, 1969; Lilly, 1970; Chaffin, 1974; Iano, 1972; and Hayman, 1971.)

The label attached to a classroom operation, at any rate, often has very little to do with the type of service that is actually being provided by that classroom. The essential difference at the secondary level be-tween the resource room and self-contained programs, or any other program for that matter, really comes down to the amount of time that the student spends in one classroom for the purposes of academic instruction. At the secondary level, and at the elementary level as well, it would be difficult to find a total self-contained program, i.e., one in which students are completely shut off from contact with their non-handicapped peers. In elementary programs, learning disabled youngsters generally leave their classroom for instruction in art, music, and gym, and it would be unusual to find that elementary learn-ing disabilities youngsters are not having lunch and recess with nonhandicapped children. At the junior or senior high level, learning disabled students will partake of special activities and electives with the rest of the student body. The term self-contained is misleading. Every learning disabilities program that we know of involves some degree of integration. Containment is usually restricted to academic subjects; its degree, of course, varies depending upon the particular student and school.

In actual practice, we have found that we can provide service to students whose needs vary from total self-containment for academic instruction to minimal containment for instruction within the same classroom unit. The degree of instructional containment for each student should be based on the nature and extent of that student's disability, not a commitment to one or the other program model. This point will be illustrated further in the next section.

SETTING UP THE EDUCATIONAL PROGRAM

To begin a secondary learning disabilities program, the teacher must consider (1) class enrollment, (2) scheduling, (3) evaluation for instructional purposes, and (4) curriculum selection.

Enrollment

We need not repeat our rationale or procedures for the selection of students to participate in the secondary learning disabilities program—our criteria have appeared repeatedly throughout this text. Selection criteria for a program and the nature of that program should be closely aligned. For instance, having stipulated that our programs are only for those students who are achieving below full sixth-grade proficiency, we have predetermined that the program will be directed toward basic skill training.

However, at the classroom level, the issue of enrollment centers on the number of students that will be attending the class. State guidelines vary, of course, and the individual teacher must abide by the regulations enforced in her situation. The number of students attending resource rooms versus self-contained classrooms will vary greatly within a given school district; the number of students served in the same type of classroom program may vary across school districts. There is a limit, of course, to what can be accomplished if too many students are scheduled in the learning disabilities class regardless of the service model employed; both a resource room and a self-contained class can be overcrowded to the detriment of all involved.

Although the class enrollment must conform to state guidelines, the number of enrollees should also reflect the degree of disability among the students. For a group of very low functioning students, enrollment should be kept at or close to the allowable minimum, as such students will probably need self-contained programs for all or most of their academic instruction. On the other hand, less disabled students can be retained in regular classes for some of their academic instruction and may be less dependent on the learning disabilities teacher for direct and daily instruction; thus more of these students can be accommodated in a learning disabilities class.

Scheduling

Again, secondary learning disabilities classes should be able to accommodate students with varying degrees of educational handicap. This may be achieved through appropriate scheduling procedures.

The variety of schedule approaches that exist in most secondary schools is mind boggling. Nevertheless, learning disabilities classes must fit into and work around the schedule that exists in any given school situation. When trying to fit the pieces of the scheduling puzzle together, the learning disabilities teacher will quickly find that flexibility in scheduling, i.e., removing students from assigned courses and reassigning them to the learning disabilities class, is an absolute must. If the program is to have a significant impact on the performance of students, assignment to the learning disabilities class should have priority over regular class assignment for both major and minor subjects. For a student who is experiencing extreme difficulty in one of his regular courses, continuation in that course seems pointless. We recommend rescheduling such a student in the learning disabilities class and using this time for basic instruction.

Harking back to our position, if the criteria for enrollment that we have suggested are adhered to and the students identified fit the profile, then the question of scheduling is, for the most part, answered by the realities of the situation. For the nonreading student functioning at the first- or second-grade level, there will be little resistance to his removal from regular class programs. On the other hand, if the student's skills are relatively good, then the faculty are likely to protest the youngster's removal from the regular class program. The juggling of students' schedules may create some additional problems—crediting for course work, reporting student grades, and rescheduling students' classes. All of these minor problems can be overcome if the teacher has the cooperation of the school's administration. The principal, perhaps more than any other individual within the school building, can influence the acceptance or nonacceptance of the learning disabilities program.

Before we schedule students into the learning disabilities class, we do the following: (1) complete an extensive educational evaluation (which goes beyond the limited preplacement evaluation); (2) review the student's latest report card and talk with the teacher of each of his academic subjects; and (3) talk with the student about his preference regarding continuation in the regular program or attendance in the special class.

Having compiled all of the test results, explored the student's past record and current class performance, and probed the student's feelings and preferences about the proposed program as well as those of his teachers, we are ready to decide if the student's interest is best served by continuation in the regular program or by reassignment to the learning disabilities class. Sometimes the decisions are very clear-cut, and sometimes they are not. Generally, the more severe the handicap, the more likely that the student will do better to be put into the special learning disabilities class. Not infrequently, one encounters the special and commendable effort of a regular class teacher who will modify the program to meet the student's need. In these cases, we do not reschedule the student but instead put forth every effort to help the teacher help that youngster. These situations are still the exception, however.

Let us illustrate our scheduling procedure by referring to two of our students, Donald and Denise:

Student—Donald

Academic Subjects	Last Report Card	Teacher Preference	Student Preference	Decision
Reading	F	Student be removed	No preference	Reassigned to learning disabilities class
English	F	Student be removed	No preference	Reassigned to learning disabilities class

Mathematics	F	Student be removed	No preference	Reassigned to learning disabilities class
Social studies	F	Student be removed	No preference	Reassigned to learning disabilities class
Science	F	Student be removed	No preference	Reassigned to learning disabilities class

In Donald's case, the scheduling decisions were quite obvious; the student was removed from all academic subjects and rescheduled in the learning disabilities class during those periods. Special subjects and activities were not affected. Donald's program, as a result, was totally self-contained for academic instruction.

Denise's program was somewhat different:

Student—Denise

Academic Subjects	Last Report Card	Teacher Preference	Student Preference	Decision
Reading	D	Remain in class	Attend LD class	Reassigned to learning disabilities class
English	F	Student be removed	Attend LD class	Reassigned to learning disabilities class
Mathematics	F	Student be removed	Attend LD class	Reassigned to learning disabilities class
Social studies	C	Remain in class	Attend LD class	No change
Science	B	Remain in class	Attend LD class	No change

Denise was experiencing serious academic difficulty in three subject areas: reading, English, and math. Her grades in social studies and science were appropriate for her age and grade placement. Once informed of the opportunity to participate in the learning disabilities class, Denise expressed her desire to attend the special program for all academic instruction. However, as her performance in science and social studies was on par with that of her peers, she was not removed from either of those classes. For English and mathematics, Denise was reassigned to the learning disabilities class. Reading posed a problem.

Denise's performance was borderline, and she expressed a strong dislike for the class; her teacher, however, did not approve of her removal from the group. After weighing all of the factors, we decided to reassign the youngster to the learning disabilities program for reading instruction at least for a short time. As a result of the rescheduling Denise was, in effect, spending 60 percent of her academic instructional time in the learning disabilities program and the remaining 40 percent in regular classes. For this student the learning disabilities class was akin to a resource room.

Evaluation for Instruction

In Chapter 4 we made the distinction between evaluation for placement and evaluation for instructional programming. The evaluation of students before placement is really out of the teacher's hands and will have been completed before the student is entered on her roll. But the results of the preplacement evaluation should certainly be made available to the teacher; these results will be helpful in that they reflect the upper performance limits for math, reading, spelling, and other language skills. The teacher may be able to glean other useful information from the test results, depending on the type and number of test instruments used. For example, if an individual reading inventory was administered, the teacher will have a great deal of information not only about performance levels but also about specific patterns of errors and reading habits; if only a standardized reading achievement test was given, diagnostic information will be limited.

Additional testing will very likely be needed for one or more of the following reasons:

1. to determine instructional levels more accurately,
2. to collect more extensive and complete information on the student's specific skills and accomplishments,
3. to determine student entry levels for specific curriculum programs,
4. to establish performance base lines in order to.carry out a pre- and postplacement evaluation of student progress, or
5. to extend the preplacement evaluation to other important areas not included in the initial evaluation.

In our initial discussion of evaluation for placement, we purposely restricted the scope of the evaluation to specific subject areas and to the determination of grade-level performance scores. We place no such limits on the evaluation for instructional purposes; the teacher should probe in any direction or area relevant to the student's instructional program—academics, vocational interests, etc. Formal and informal devices can be used; work samples, classroom observations, checklists, and inventories all may be part of the evaluation carried out for instructional purposes. The specific assessment devices that will ultimately be used will be determined by the teacher's specific purposes.

At the very least, the teacher will want to evaluate the student's performance in those primary instructional areas in which she is to provide instruction—mathematics, reading, or language skills. The curricular management approach that we recommend is particularly useful for this purpose. By utilizing the evaluation component, the teacher can quickly assess the student's facility with a specific content material being taught and determine the appropriate entry level for the curriculum. In addition, the management systems' instructional objective sequence will reveal those objectives that the student has and has not mastered and provide a precise record of achievement as the student moves through the curriculum. Because the management approach is criterion rather than norm referenced, it also reflects student growth in terms of his own achievement against a preset standard of skill acquisition rather than that established by comparisons with his peers.

The curricular management approach may eliminate the need for much additional diagnostic evaluation, but when further testing is still indicated, or in the absence of a curricular management system, the teacher may find commercial instruments helpful. Some that we like are presented in Table 7-1.

Curriculum Selection

Before selecting curricula, the teacher will have to decide the nature of the curricula required for each student in each subject in the broad areas of instructional concern—mathematics, and language arts. Based on all of the evaluation results, we decide whether the student requires "remedial" or "developmental" assistance (these terms refer to the level of skill development). The distinction between developmental and remedial learners carries important implications for programming. Developmental learners are those who are functioning, in general terms, anywhere from rock bottom (complete non-readers) to fourth-grade level. A student who is functioning at ex-

Table 7-1
Diagnostic Instruments for Use in the Evaluation of
Secondary Learning Disabled Students

Test	Publisher and Date
Gates-McKillop Reading Diagnostic Tests	Teachers College Press, Columbia University, 1962
Diagnostic Chart for Individual Difficulties—Fundamental Processes in Arithmetic	Bobbs-Merrill, 1925
KeyMath Diagnostic Arithmetic Test	American Guidance Service, 1971
SRA Reading Index	Science Research Associates, 1968
SRA Arithmetic Index	Science Research Associates, 1968
Durrell Analysis of Reading Difficulty	Harcourt Brace Jovanovich, 1955
Classroom Reading Inventory	Wm. C. Brown Company, 1973
Standard Reading Inventory	Klamath Printing, 1966
Botel Reading Inventory Tests	Follett Publishing Company, 1970
Informal Reading Inventory	Temple University, undated
Reading Miscue Inventory	Macmillan, 1972

tremely low levels requires a highly structured sequential presentation of fundamental skills.

Remedial learners, as a group, have a higher level of skill development although their achievement records are often incomplete and punctuated with specific skill deficits. Some remedial learners totally lack certain skills, e.g., the ability to deal with the time problems or make change (skills introduced at the first-grade level).

The dichotomy between remedial and developmental students is admittedly a simplification, but a helpful one. The decision as to the student's status, remedial versus developmental, in the academic areas in which he needs assistance helps us to select one of two curricular approaches. The developmental learner still needs, even at this late date, to master the basic skills of the elementary curriculum. Unless we are willing to abandon basic academic instruction altogether—and some day this may be necessary—and train only the survival skills required for that rare secondary learning disabled student who will never master reading skills to any useful level, we must try to teach him by going through basic skill sequences again and again—albeit in ways

Table 7-2
Classifying Students for Instructional Purposes

Learner Classification	Functioning Level	Educational Strategy	Curriculum Selection
Developmental	Nonfunctional to low 4th grade level	Continued presentation of basic skills; mastery of basic math and language skills	Core curriculum for math and/or language skills
Remedial	Solid 4th to 6th grade level	Remediation of gaps in knowledge and skills while boosting achievement to the integration level	Core curriculum, particular attention to pretest information, supplementary material for specific skill development—tied to specific skill sequences

which the student will not find offensive. For this student, we recommend a core curriculum, one which embodies a clear structure and a sequential presentation of skill development; when possible, the curriculum should be in an adult-oriented, mature package. For the remedial learner we maintain a curricular "managed" approach using pretesting (see Proger and Mann, 1973) to identify specific deficit academic areas. We also use additional supplementary approaches to ameliorate specific gaps while seeking to raise overall performance levels.

The differences between the two curricular approaches in learning disabilities strategies and curriculum selection are presented in Table 7-2.

Let us demonstrate our approach by referring again to Donald and Denise. When Donald entered one of our junior high learning disabilities programs, his record revealed almost total academic failure. On his last report card Donald received *F*'s in all five academic areas. Donald was, in fact, a nonreader; test results indicated that his functional reading skill was at a primer level, and his math achievement level was placed somewhere near the end of first grade. Given Donald's extremely low performance levels in math and reading, we were not at all surprised by his failures in English, science, and social studies. In our frame of reference, Donald was definitely a developmental learner in both math and language skills: his achievement levels were so low that we realized Donald had never mastered the most basic and fundamental skills, and we planned his program accordingly.

Donald was placed in core curricula for math and reading instruction at an entry level commensurate with his performance. Other language arts instruction, e.g., spelling and composition, was built around the core reading program. Donald's need for instruction in language and math was so pressing that basic instruction in these areas superseded that in other areas of instruction, such as science, social studies, and history.

Denise, a classmate of Donald, presented a mixed profile of academic success and failure. Denise continued to participate in the regular science and social studies program; instruction in these subjects was not provided by the learning disabilities teacher. For reading, English, and spelling Denise began an instructional program consisting of core curricula and selected supplementary materials. Denise's curricular entry levels for the three instructional areas ranged from low third to mid fourth grade level. The core curriculum for each of these academic subjects was the primary instructional focus; supplementary materials for specific skill development in reading and English were also used.

REFERENCES

Block JH: *Mastery Learning Theory and Practice.* New York, Holt, Rinehart and Winston, 1971

Bloom BS: Learning for mastery. Evaluation Comments Vol. 1 (no 2), 1968

Brutten M: Vocational education for the brain injured adolescent and young adult at the Vanguard school, in *International Approach to Learning Disabilities of Children and Youth.* Proceedings of the Third Annual Conference, ACLD, Tulsa, 1966

Chaffin JD: Will the real "mainstreaming" program please stand up! (or . . . should Dunn have done it?). Focus on Exceptional Children, 6:1-18, 1974

Christopolos F, Renz P: A critical examination of special education programs. J Special Education 3:371-379, 1969

Dunn LM: Special education for the mildly retarded—is much of it justifiable? Exceptional Children 35:5-22, 1968

Fountain Valley Teacher Support System in Mathematics. Huntington Beach, California, Richard L Zweig, 1973

Giffin M: How does he feel?, in Schloss E (ed): *The Educator's Enigma: The Adolescent with Learning Disabilities.* San Rafael, California, Academic Therapy Publications, 1971

Goodman YM, Burke CL: *Reading Miscue Inventory.* New York, Macmillan, 1972

Gordon S: Reversing a negative self-image, in Anderson L (ed): *Helping the Adolescent with the Hidden Handicap.* Los Angeles, California Association for Neurologically Handicapped Children, 1970

Gordon S: *The Brain Injured Adolescent.* East Orange, New Jersey, New Jersey Association for Brain Injured Children, 1966

Gorth WP, Hambleton RK: Measurement considerations for criterion-referenced testing and special education. J Special Education 6:303–314, 1972

Hammill DD, Wiederholt JL: *The Resource Room: Rationale and Implementation.* Philadelphia, Buttonwood Farms, 1972

Hayman SJ: Special classes: helpful or harmful? The Crisis, January–February: 5–6, 1971

Iano RP: Shall we disband our special classes? J Special Education 6:167–177, 1972

Instructional Pupil Monitoring System—Reading. Pennington-Hopewell, New Jersey, Houghton-Mifflin, 1973

Kronick D: *What About Me? The LD Adolescent.* San Rafael, California, Academic Therapy Publications, 1975

Lilly SM: Special education: a teapot in a tempest. Exceptional Children 37:43–48, 1970

Los Angeles Unified School District: *Developmental Reading: Diagnostic Prescriptive.* Minneapolis, Minn, Paul S Amidon, 1975

Mann L: Cognitive training: a look at the past and some concerns about the present. A paper presented at the National Regional Resource Center Conference, Reston, Virginia, September 1974

Morrison HC: *The Practice of Teaching in the Secondary School.* Chicago, University of Chicago Press, 1926

Prescriptive Mathematics Inventory. Monterey, California, CTB/McGraw-Hill, 1972

Proger BB, Mann L: Criterion-referenced measurement: the world of gray versus the black and white. J Learning Disabil 6:72–84, 1973

Robinson HA: Libraries: active agents in adult reading improvement. Am Library Assoc Bull 416–421, 1963

Thompson A: Moving toward adulthood, in Anderson L (ed): *Helping the Adolescent with the Hidden Handicap.* Los Angeles, California Association for Neurologically Handicapped Children, 1970

Washburne CW: Educational measurements as a key to individualizing instruction and promotions. J Educational Res 5:195–205, 1922

Weber RE (ed): *Handbook on Learning Disabilities*. Englewood Cliffs, New Jersey, Prentice-Hall, 1974

Wiederholt JL: *A Report on Secondary School Programs for the Learning Disabled*. Tucson, University of Arizona, Leadership Training Institute in Learning Disabilities, 1975

Wiig E: The emerging LD crisis. Journal of Rehabilitation 38:15–17, 1972

Williamson AP: Career education: implications for secondary learning disabled students. Academic Ther 10:193–200, 1974–1975

CHAPTER 8
College Programs for Learning Disabled Youth

INTRODUCTION

Educational services for learning disabled youth do not necessarily end with high school graduation; for some, a college education is not an unrealistic goal. According to Ansara (1972), "If his primary problem is recognized and dealt with appropriately, the dyslexic adolescent becomes free to establish and pursue goals that can include college." Weber (1974) emphasizes that abilities among the learning disabled range from low normal to superior, and he counsels that these young people should pursue avenues commensurate with their abilities—including college for those who are able. College-level programs for the learning disabled are an acknowledgment of the abilities of many learning disabled young men and women. It is gratifying to know that the full gamut of life's opportunities are open to these handicapped youth.

Parents are, we are sure, elated at the prospect of college-level programs for their learning disabled children. A few words of caution, however. College-level programs for the learning disabled are at the present time very few in number,* and some of them are still in an ex-

*The reader may have heard of a program for learning disabled students at Parsons College or another at the American International College. At the present time, the American International College does not have a specific program for students with learning disabilities, although we were informed that they do have one student who

perimental stage. College enrollments for the learning disabled are often restricted—not only in number, but also by being limited to the more able learning disabled student. Many of the colleges still seek students from the upper range of ability, the gifted learning disabled student. Therefore, college programs are available for some, not all, learning disabled students. Finally, the cost of a college education for the handicapped student is by no means inexpensive. There may even be additional charges for learning disabled individuals; taken together with regular college fees, this adds up to a considerable amount of money. (The costs in this report reflect the 1975–1976 school year.)

AVAILABLE COLLEGE PROGRAMS

Six brief descriptions, little more than introductions, to college-level programs for the learning disabled individual are presented below. The information was gathered from college catalogs, pamphlets, personal conversations, and/or written communications with school personnel. Inclusion of a college program in this chapter in no way constitutes an endorsement of that program. We offer the information as a service to the interested reader and urge that he pursue it on his own.

College of the Ozarks

The College of the Ozarks is a private liberal arts college, affiliated with the United Presbyterian Church. It offers a program for "gifted" students with specific disabilities in learning as well as non-handicapped students. The gifted learning disabled are those students who, despite their handicaps, score one standard deviation above the norm on either the verbal or performance scale of the Wechsler Adult Intelligence Scale. The program does not admit the psychiatrically disturbed, the mentally subnormal, or dropouts from other universities or colleges. A 4-year program in 17 major areas of study leading to a bachelor of arts or science or general studies is offered. A commission as an officer in the U.S. Army may also be achieved through complet-

---

receives biweekly counseling, and that they would provide assistance for any student who needed it; there are no modified entrance requirements or special facilities. Parsons College did have a special program for learning disabled students; however, as of this writing, the college is no longer functioning.

ing an ROTC program. The college is accredited by the North Central Association of Colleges and Secondary Schools.

The learning disabled student attends classes with nonhandicapped peers, but special provisions are made so that he or she can succeed despite poor reading and/or writing skills. The program meets the needs of the learning disabled student through a closely supervised curriculum, regular counseling, compensatory techniques (use of tape recorders, self-evaluation, etc.) for specific disabilities, tutorial assistance, and specific instruction in study skills. Career preparation is stressed, and the college's Career Preparation Office offers many services to the learning disabled, as well as career information and counseling, practical work experiences, and placement services.

REQUIREMENTS FOR ADMISSION

1. The program is open to students 18 to 25 years of age.
2. A high school diploma is not required.
3. The student must score one standard deviation above the norm on either the verbal or performance scale of the Wechsler Adult Intelligence Scale.
4. The student and/or parents must give permission for the sharing of diagnostic information from previous clinics or agencies.
5. The student and his parents must be willing to sign a contract with the college.
6. The student must be willing to commit himself to 1 semester (minimum) of consistent effort.
7. The student must submit the results of a recent and complete physical examination.
8. The student must be free of serious physical handicaps including visual or hearing impairments.
9. The student must not have any serious personality disorders as determined by qualified professionals.
10. The student must undergo a current psychoeducational evaluation.
11. The student and/or parent must be willing and able to pay the tuition costs of $5000 per school year of 9 months. (The cost for the handicapped student differs considerably from the cost for the nonhandicapped student who pays $1750 yearly for tuition, room, and board.)
12. The student and parents must accept the college's right to refer any applicant for further psychoeducational appraisal.

13. Upon a tentative acceptance into the program, the student and his parents will be asked to come to the College of the Ozarks campus for an interview with the director and the admissions committee before the student can be officially accepted.

COSTS

$5000 per year.

CONTACT PERSON

For further information contact Tom Threlkeld, Ph.D., Director, Special Learning Center, College of the Ozarks, Clarksville, Arkansas 72830, Telephone: 1-501-754-3034.

University of Plano

The University of Plano is a private coeducational institution in a suburban area outside of Dallas. Admission to the university is open to students with reading problems and other learning disabilities. Programs for the learning disabled are available through the university's Middle College Program, the School of Developmental Education, located in Philadelphia. The purposes of the Middle College Program are to allow some students to begin earning college credits before completing high school, thereby reducing the total number of years needed to complete both a high school and college program, and to provide students who are deficient in some basic subjects with a combined program of neurological organization and remedial courses. This latter program strives to prepare the student to obtain a high school equivalency diploma and, hopefully, to enter a full-time college program at the University of Plano or Frisco College.

REQUIREMENTS FOR ADMISSION

1. The student must have completed the tenth grade of high school and be at least 16 years old (students who have completed high school but have some deficiencies in basic skills such as reading, English, or math may also attend).
2. The student must have average or above average intelligence.
3. Those students whose performance ranks in the lower percentile during their last academic year must submit a completed preadmission questionnaire, and must undergo testing, evaluation, and a personal interview.
4. Neurological evaluation is required.

COSTS

The fees for attending the University of Plano are approximately $2900 a year to cover tuition, room and board, and neurological evaluation.

CONTACT PERSON

For more information contact Mrs. Barbara Goostree, Director, Middle College Program, University of Plano, Drawer 418, Plano, Texas 75074, Telephone: 1-214-424-6541.

The School of Developmental Education, located in Philadelphia is an out-of-state affiliate of the University of Plano. The program is limited to neurologically disorganized men and women between the ages of 18 and 23. The students receive neurological training every day under the supervision of the staff, medical and paramedical, at the Institute for the Achievement of Human Potential. For each student, the program is designed to:

1. develop a sense of personal pride in work with increasing confidence that accompanies heightened neurological organization;
2. develop adequate self-discipline and emotional security;
3. improve personal appearance;
4. develop adequate social skills;
5. create the mastering of basic academic skills;
6. make the transition to a liberal arts college.

The requirements for admission and the costs were not specified in the university catalog. Interested persons may secure additional information by writing to the School of Developmental Education, Institutes for the Achievement of Human Potential, 8801 Stenton Avenue, Philadelphia, Pennsylvania 19118.

Westminster College

Westminster College, an accredited liberal arts school located in Fulton, Missouri, offers a program for young men with learning disabilities. The Program for Students with Learning Disabilities is available through Westminster's Experimental Division. The 4-year program described as "challenging, non-threatening, and individualized" culminates in a bachelor of arts degree, although the requirements for the degree for the handicapped student are not necessarily the same as those for the general school population. To earn the degree, the student must: (1) develop an in-depth understanding of the subject matter of a particular subject area, defined as a major; (2) develop an understanding of subject matter in at least two areas outside the major, and (3) complete 124 credit hours or the equivalent thereof.

The student's course of study, personalized to meet his needs and desires, will likely involve a combination of regular courses and tutorials. Many provisions are made to accommodate the special student: the evaluation of student performance is based on what he has learned, not on what he has not learned. Written examinations may be replaced by other demonstrations of student mastery. Traditional grades are not assigned, instead summary statements of the student's work are given. These summarys form the student's transcript. Various substitutes for textbook assignments may be used, such as films, talking books, and tapes; programmed learning machines are used and tutors are available.

REQUIREMENTS FOR ADMISSION

1. There must be an established diagnosis of learning disability.
2. The results of an untimed SAT test* must be submitted.
3. A personal interview is required.
4. A battery of tests must be administered by the university to establish achievement levels and to be used in research.

COSTS

Tuition, activity fees, room and board costs are $3,520 for one year. There is an additional $500 yearly fee for special students in the college's Experimental Division.

CONTACT PERSON

For additional information contact Dr. Gale Fuller, Director, Experimental Division, Westminster College, Fulton, Missouri 65251, Telephone: 1-314-642-3361.

*Parents should be aware that learning disabled student is eligible for untimed college board exams. A special registration form can be secured by requesting a College Entrance Examination for Handicapped Students from the College Entrance Examination Board, Box 592, Princeton, N.J. 18540 (fee $6.50). The Preliminary Scholastic Aptitude Test and National Merit Scholarship Qualifying Tests are also available in special editions for handicapped students.

Curry College

Curry College is a coeducational liberal arts institution located in Milton, Massachusetts. The Curry College Program of Assistance in Learning (CCPAL) has a short, but very successful, history of assistance to dyslexic young adults who desire a liberal arts college education. (An extensive description of the CCPAL program is available in Weber's book, *Handbook on Learning Disabilities,* 1974.) The CCPAL program was designed as a 1-year supportive program; its goal is "to develop within the enrollees the language-oriented, thinking-based skills which will allow them to function successfully on their own in the college setting" (Weber, p. 254). The sponsors of the program believe that deficiencies of language are the core problem area for the learning disabled student, and they, accordingly, have focused remedial and compensatory efforts in this area. An individualized, prescriptive PAL program is developed for each student.

The CCPAL program is short term and is provided in addition to the regular college program. All special program students carry a full academic load, participating in the regular courses with nonhandicapped peers; all special students are fully integrated into the life of the college community. The faculty, however, are notified of the attendance of the special CCPAL program students in their classes, and thus far, the understanding, supportive, and cooperative attitudes of the faculty have been a key factor contributing to the success of CCPAL students.

REQUIREMENTS FOR ADMISSION

1. The student must have normal intellectual ability, with his or her learning disability being the primary disabling problem.
2. The student must submit a psychological and an educational history.
3. A personal interview is required.

COSTS

The fee for the program is $1000 a semester in addition to the normal tuition and dormitory fees of about $4000 a year.

CONTACT PERSON

For further information contact Ms. Gertrude Webb, Curry Learning Center, Curry College, Milton, Massachusetts 02186, Telephone: 1-617-333-0500.

Wright State University

During the 1974–1975 school term, Wright State University initiated a pilot program for learning disabled students. From its inception in 1964, the university had made a concerted effort to extend its services to the physically handicapped student whenever possible. The new program represents an extension of its services to include the nonphysically handicapped but learning disabled individual. During the 1974–1975 academic year, 3 students were enrolled in the pilot program (one student dropped out but had the option to return at a later date). In 1975, 8 new students were accepted into the program, bringing the total enrollment to 10. The students range in age from 17 to 22 years. There are 7 men and 3 women.

The program provides support services in three areas: academic, tutorial, and counseling. Each student is assigned a professional academic advisor who works individually with the student through a process of evaluation and program development. For the first semester, the student's schedule typically includes no more than four courses: one is difficult, two are moderately difficult, and one is of minimal difficulty. Tutorial services available to the learning disabled student include personal tutoring, the use of proctors for examinations, and taped recordings of textbooks. The tutors are upper level or graduate students who are paid for their services, but the individual student is responsible for seeking the services of the tutors. Counselors are also available for the student. Initially, counseling sessions may be held as often as once a week. In a few instances when more counseling is necessary, it will be provided. The counselors, members of the staff of the Special Education Department, work closely with the students to help them weather the rough spots in their college program.

The program places the primary responsibility for success on the individual student, as the major objective is to help the handicapped student function as much as possible as "normal" students do. The responsibilities of both the student and the institution may be specified in a contract which is drawn up between the student and the coordinator of the program. Although the coordinator accepts the responsibility for providing services to the student, the student in turn agrees to use the services to his best advantage.

REQUIREMENTS FOR ADMISSION

1. The student must demonstrate a full scale IQ of 115 or better on the Wechsler Adult Intelligence Scale or a score of 120 or better on either the Verbal or Performance portions of this test.

2. A teacher evaluation form must be submitted by one English teacher, one math teacher, and one additional content teacher from the student's high school.
3. Additional information, such as school, medical, or family history, which describes specific strengths and weaknesses must be included with the application form.

COSTS

Current tuition is $560 a quarter for out-of-state applicants; the costs for a state resident are $260.00 a quarter.

CONTACT PERSON

For further information contact Dr. Marlene Bireley, W475B Millett Hall, Wright State University, Dayton, Ohio 45431, Telephone: 1-513-873-2677.

DeAnza College

DeAnza College is a state community college in Cupertino, California, which admits educationally handicapped students, including the learning disabled, to its program. The school offers five specialized services: (1) an Education Diagnostic Clinic, (2) a corrective physical education program, (3) a counselor enabler program, (4) a convalescent home, and (5) a program for the developmentally disabled.

Of these, the Educational Diagnostic Clinic and the corrective physical education program are most relevant to the learning disabled. The Educational Diagnostic Clinic offers diagnosis, remediation, counseling, and tutoring to students with learning problems. A comprehensive evaluation of the student, who may be self-referred to the clinic or may be recommended by a clinician, an agency, or an instructor, will be done to determine the student's potential and to determine whether he can benefit from participation in the program.

The course of study conforms to the standard curriculum (but the learning disabled student will receive counseling and on-going tutorial assistance). With counselor's guidance, the student will be channeled into those classes in which his disability will be a minimal handicap or he will receive intensive preparation for essential or required courses that are likely to be difficult. The program's objective is to provide continuing educational and/or vocational training to help the learning handicapped achieve their maximum potential.

The DeAnza College program has been in operation for 3 years; conceived as an experimental program, it is now well established and is the prototype for at least 15 other similar state community college programs.

REQUIREMENTS FOR ADMISSION

1. The student must live in the district in which the community college is located or be a legal resident of a neighboring district without a comparable program.
2. The student must have average or above average ability.
3. The student must undergo a complete assessment and evaluation at the College Educational Diagnostic Clinic.

COST

A student activity fee is $7 a year. Tuition is free; all students commute.

CONTACT PERSON

For further information contact Ms. Judith Triana, Learning Disabilities Specialist, 21250 Stevens Creek Blvd., Cupertino, California 95014, Telephone: 1-408-157-5550.

REFERENCES

Ansara A: Language therapy to salvage the college potential of dyslexic adolescents. Bull Orton Soc 22:123–139, 1972

Weber RE (ed): *Handbook on Learning Disabilities.* Englewood Cliffs, New Jersey, Prentice-Hall, 1974

CHAPTER 9
Curriculum for the Secondary Learning Disabilities Program

The most problematic area of concern for the secondary-level learning disability specialist lies in the area of instruction. The definition, diagnosis, identification, and measurement of secondary level learning disabilities have been thorny problems for us. Those of instruction confront us in the face of almost nonexistent research (specifically concerned with the secondary-level learning disabled youth) and in the absence of any specific technologies.

It will simply not do to apply the techniques of elementary school-level learning disabilities to the problems of the secondary-level learning disabled pupils. Some useful approaches apply to all learning disabled individuals. But the reader will surely agree that, for the most part, approaches useful at the elementary level are not directly transferable to the secondary school.

Programs, curricula and supplementary materials, diagnostic prescriptive techniques, and the like, specifically intended for secondary learning disability pupils remain to be developed. We thus recommend that the reader accept our current philosophy concerning the programming for such pupils: *adapt existing programs and materials from regular education so that they can be used effectively for instructing the learning disabled youth at the secondary level.*

The values of these materials for secondary learning disability pupils will be greatly enhanced by their deployment along the lines that we have discussed in our earlier chapters. In this chapter we will

133

provide, in the absence of other clearly supporting evidence, our own guidelines and approaches to curriculum and supplementary material selection. Hopefully, the near future will see greater sophistication in the selection and usage of such materials and the development of specific technologies for secondary-level learning disabilities.

We suggest that core and supplemental curricula materials be identified for each of our priority instructional areas: reading, mathematics, spelling, and written communications skills. The general criteria to be used to assess the potential utility of various curricular systems are:

1.   The curriculum will include a comprehensive, structured, developmental sequence of the subject matter content.
2.   The appearance and format of the program should be appealing to the older student.
3.   The scope and sequence of the program should be clearly delineated and preferably presented in a behaviorally objective format.
4.   The program should have an accompanying curricular management-evaluation system.
5.   The program should focus on mastery of basic skills.

For us, core and supplemental materials serve different instructional purposes, although the difference between the two types of materials often lies in the way we use them rather than in the author's or publisher's original intent. Core curricular programs are the focus of daily instruction for the very low functioning student. Supplemental materials will be used intermittently with him as the need arises, and as an extension of or in addition to the core program in order to increase and vary the opportunities for the student to apply the skills he is learning and to help maintain interest and motivation. On the other hand, the student in need of remedial rather than basic developmental instruction, may use both types of programs but is very likely to spend more time with various supplemental programs selected for remediation of specific skill deficits.

The core and supplemental curricular programs should be the mainstay for all secondary learning disabilities classes; we suggest each classroom be stocked with these materials at the very least. To be sure, many other available incidental materials may also be used peripherally—including some teacher-made material that may be excellent. In addition, the teacher may need to use some of the curricula from the regular classes, particularly if she is preparing a student to reintegrate in a regular course of study, and these will vary considerably from school to school.

Our current inventory of secondary core and supplemental curricula is presented in Table 9-1. We stress that these are the curricular materials we are using currently. We are not completely satisfied or totally comfortable with this selection: there are gaps and weaknesses, but hopefully new and better programs and materials will appear in the future. These curricula were the best that we found for secondary learning disabilities programming.

Table 9-1
Inventory of Secondary Curricular Programs

Subject Area	Core Curricula, Publisher	Management System	Supplemental Curricula
Reading	Phoenix Reading Series, Prentice Hall	Developed by Montgomery County (Pa.) Intermediate Unit Learning Disabilities Staff	Specific Skill Series, Barnell Loft The Thinking Box, Benefic Press New Practice Readers Reading for Concepts, Webster/ McGraw-Hall Reading Attainment System, Grolier Educational Corp.
Math	Heath Mathematics Program, D. C. Heath	Developed by Montgomery County (Pa.) Intermediate Unit Learning Disabilities Staff	Arithmetic: Step by Step, Kit A, Kit B, Continental Press Spectrum Mathematics
Spelling	Continuous Progress in Spelling, The Economy Co.		
Language arts	Keys to Good Language, The Economy Co.	Developed by Montgomery County (Pa.) Intermediate Unit Learning Disabilities Staff	Newslab Science Research Associates

Some cautions: we have found that the Heath mathematic program is generally applicable for grades seven through nine, but is inappropriate for the senior high student. Therefore, at the senior high level we approach mathematics instruction very pragmatically through consumer and career education using a variety of materials. On the other hand, the Phoenix Reading Program, Continuous Progress Spelling, and Keys to Good Language can be used, for the most part, from grades seven through twelve.

Also, no handwriting program is included in Table 9-1. Although handwriting assessment was included as part of the placement evaluation, we do not consider handwriting an instructional priority. We seriously question the appropriateness and effectiveness of handwriting instruction for the adolescent or young adult unless the student is exceptionally motivated for this purpose. For students with penmanship so poor that it interferes with their ability to communicate through writing, we urge typing instruction; for students whose handwriting is so slow that they can't keep up with class discussion and lectures, we suggest the use of a recording device in place of note taking by hand. Corrective approaches to handwriting problems are discussed extensively by Hammill and Bartel (1975) and by Otto, McMenemy, and Smith (1973), but the reader will find, as we did, that most existing evaluative and corrective techniques are definitely geared toward the elementary student.

We have already said that our current curricular inventory is subject to changes. Different core programs may be selected, and our teachers are free to try supplemental materials at will. In the following pages we have compiled a listing of reading, math, English, and spelling materials for possible use in secondary learning disability classes (Table 9-2)–the results of our own materials search. Although we do not endorse these materials, many of the items are being reviewed at the present time. We offer the information as a resource for other secondary learning disability teachers.

REFERENCES

Hammill DD, Bartel NR: *Teaching Children with Learning and Behavior Problems: A Resource Book for Preschool, Elementary and Special Education Teachers.* Boston, Allyn & Bacon, 1975
Otto W, McMenemy RA, Smith RJ: *Corrective and Remedial Teaching.* Boston, Houghton-Mifflin, 1973

Table 9-2
Materials Survey For Secondary Learning Disabilities Classes

Title	Publisher, Date	Grade Level	Reading—Core Content	Comments
Point 31	Readers Digest, 1975	Adolescents; reading level 0–4.9	Decode book, audio lessons, reader magazines, activity book, evaluation program, teacher's manual	A structured program that develops decoding skills through the fourth-grade level. The material and format are specially designed for the adolescent reader.
Phoenix Reading Series	Prentice Hall 1974	Reading Level Level A 2–3 Level B 3–4 Level C 4–5	Photo reader, action reader, teacher's guide, spirit duplicator, masters, tests.	Provides a structured developmental approach to reteach phonics and other basic reading skills by presenting real-life stories and experiences in a photographic newspaper format.
Developmental Reading Diagnostic/Prescriptive	Paul S. Amidon & Associates, Inc., 1975	1–12	Placement tests, pre & post tests, learning materials, teaching ideas, teacher's guide	A total reading program including all elements that lend themselves to the effective teaching/learning of reading for those who have not mastered fundamental reading skills
Hip Reader	Book-Lab, Inc., 1969	Secondary reading level 1–4	Books, teacher training materials	A high-interest, low-vocabulary basic remedial reading program presenting materials and situations pertinent to adolescents

Table 9-2 (continued)

Title	Publisher, Date	Grade Level	Reading—Core Content	Comments
+4 Reading Booster	Webster McGraw-Hill, 1972	4–9	Tape cassettes, pupil code book, teacher's manual	A tightly-structured, corrective reading program for students who have not mastered fundamental word perception and comprehension skills necessary for effective textbook learning and academic success
Reading Attainment Systems 1 and 2	Grolier Educational Corp., 1975	Reading level 3–6	120 color-keyed reading selections in each kit, skill cards, reader record books, instructor's manual, wall chart	High-interest reading selections and built-in motivational materials for self-study; allows students to progress at their own pace
The New Streamlined English Series	New Readers Press, 1972	Reading level K–5	Skill books, correlated readers, student checkups, teacher's manuals, teaching aids, supplemental reading material	Designed to teach adults who have no reading skills; each lesson includes phonics, reading sight words, comprehension checks, structural analysis, and vocabulary development; Writing lessons reinforce reading concepts and develop spelling skills

Reading—Supplementary

"And Hereby Hangs the Tale . . ."	Mid-America Publishing Co.	Reading level 3–8	Books	High-interest, low-vocabulary materials
Auto Phonics	Educational Activities, Inc.	Grade level 7–9	Cassettes, markers, call cards, master cards	Bingo-like games based on words associated with driving to improve spelling, vocabulary, speech, and listening skills
The World of Adventure Series	Benefic Press, 1964–1965	Reading level 2–6; grade level 4–9	8 reading texts, activity books	High-interest content, easy-to-read vocabulary action adventure stories
Your Own Thing	Leswing Press, 1973	Grade level 7–12	13 paperback books	High-interest content, low-vocabulary stories that portray ethnic groups through believable characters and language
Scholastic Action	Scholastic Book Services, 1970	Reading level 2–4 grade level 7–12	Records, posters, skill books, teacher's guide	Develop word attack and comprehension skills; multimedia approach; students must have some reading skill
Double Action	Scholastic Book Services, 1973	Reading level 3–5; grade level 7–12	Reading books	A follow-up program to Scholastic Action; reading improvement for those who can read at the 3.0 level
Adult Readers	Readers Digest Services, 1965	Reading level 1–4; grade level 7–12	Paperback books, 3 levels	Low-vocabulary, high-interest level stories with short exercises at back of each book to promote vocabulary building, comprehension, and word attack skills

Table 9-2 (continued)

Title	Publisher, Date	Reading—Supplementary		Comments
		Grade Level	Content	
Spectrum of Skills	Macmillan Company, 1973	Grade level 1–8	Workbooks	3 sets of workbooks: word analysis (5–6), vocabulary development (3–7), reading comprehension (4–8)
Success in Language	Follett Publishing Co., 1964	Grade level 7–12	8 booklets, comprehension checks	Designed for slow learners in secondary school; high-interest materials to develop listening, speaking, writing, reading, language, and social skills
Teen-Age Tales	D. C. Heath Co., 1964	Reading level 3–6; grade level 9–12	9 reading texts, teacher's manual	Developmental skills program
The Turner-Livingston Reading Series	Follett Publishing Co., 1974	Reading level 4–6	6 workbooks	Deals with understanding basic social behavior, language, and arithmetic in life situations
Venture	Follett Publishing Co. and Advanced Learning Concepts, Inc., 1975	Reading level 4–6.5	Reading texts, sound film strips	Sports themes in high-interest, low reading level books
Reach: The Reading Extravaganza of American Cycling Hydroplaning Show	The Economy Co., 1971	Grade level 4–9	Cassettes, workbooks, readers	Reteaches basic reading skills; focus is on word attack skills, vocabulary expansion, and positive attitude toward reading

Reading in High Gear	Science Research Associates, 1964	Grade level 7–9	Worktexts	Adult interests are stressed
City Limits I, City Limits II	McGraw-Hill, 1968	Reading level 5–7	Short stories, paperback books	Story content—young adults living in the inner city and the problems they face
Clues to Reading Progress	Education Progress Corp., 1972	Grade level 5–8	Magazine-type booklets, audio cassettes (12), taped tests	For those who have not yet mastered primary-level reading skills
Sports Mystery Series	Benefic Press, 1974	Reading level 2–4; grade level 4–12	8 books	High-interest reading
Target Today	Benefic Press, 1975	Reading level 2–6; grade level 4–12	4 books, pretests, placement tests	Each book contains 100 short stories relating to real-life situations.
Laurie Newman Adventures	Creative Education, 1975	Grade level 3–8	Books, cassettes	Adventure stories
Learning Your Language	Follett Publishing Co., 1964	Reading level 3.5–7.1; grade level 9–12	Books	Reading, writing, listening, and discussion skills—novels, poems, stories, etc.
Morgan Bay Mysteries	Field Educational Publications, 1965	Reading level 2–4.1; grade level 3–10	Hard-bound mystery books	Designed to motivate readers, develop vocabulary; evaluation exercises
EDL Skill Development Controlled Reading	McGraw-Hill, 1973	Grade level 3–13	20 skill sets (300 lessons), filmstrips, ditto masters, cassettes, study guide	Adapted from books and magazine; many deliberately controversial lessons for critical and interpretative reading

Table 9-2 (continued)

Title	Publisher, Date	Reading—Supplementary Grade Level	Content	Comments
Newspaper Reading	Gary Lawson, 1967	Grade level 9–12	Workbook	Can be used with any newspaper
Plays for Reading	Educational Development Corp., 1974	Reading level 1–8	2 plays	Oral language program to strengthen word analysis, word identification, vocabulary, comprehension, and use of figurative language; different reading levels structured in each play
Racing Wheels Readers	Benefic Press, 1974	Reading level 2–4; grade level 2–12	6 books	High action books for low-level readers
The Tempo Series	Macmillan Co., 1974	Reading level 3–8; grade level 7–12	4 texts with accompanying activity guide	Magazine format; oral and written activities which accompany each text
Cracking the Code	Science Research Associates, 1968	Grade level 4–9	Reader workbook	Teaches decoding to students who have not developed independent word attack; high interest, low vocabulary materials
Crossroads	Noble & Noble, Publishers, 1969	Grade level 7–10, reading level 4–9	Softbound texts, records, activity books	A multimedia reading motivation program; supplementary reading library available

Title	Publisher/Date	Level	Materials	Description
Go: Reading in the Content Areas	Scholastic Book Services, 1975	Reading level 2–7.5	Skills text, teaching guides, ditto masters	Basic reading skills applied to concepts in elementary and high school texts
Face-off Red Line/Blue Line Supplementary Reading Program for Intermediate Grades	EMC Corp., 1973	Reading level 5–6; grade level 6–12	Books, tapes, skillsheets, activity sheets, answer sheets	High-interest, action-packed material with topics related to hockey
Getting it Together—A Reading Series About People	Science Research Associates, Inc., 1973	Reading level 2–6; grade level 9–12	Books and workbooks	High-interest, low reading level material; each book has same subject, sequence, etc., but is written at different level
Guide Book to Better Reading	The Economy Co., 1968	Reading level 2–6; grade level 1–12	Workbooks	Stress on phonic analysis, structural analysis, context clues; low-vocabulary, high-interest level reading
Language Experiences in Reading	Encyclopedia Britanica Educational Corp., 1974–1975	Grade level 1–6	Books, cards, sound filmstrip, teacher's manual	A multimedia program that stresses a language-experience approach to reading; bilingual instruction
Guidebook to Remedial Reading	The Economy Co., 1968–1969	Reading level 2–6	Workbooks, progress tests, placement exam, readers, teacher's manual	Low-level vocabulary with high-interest subject matter; stresses phonetic analysis, structural analysis, and context clues
Heath Urban Reading Program	Educreative Systems, Inc., 1970	Reading level 5–7; grade level 7–9	Paperback books, records, filmstrips, activity sheets, teacher's guide	Designed to motivate students by presenting stories about the problems of young adults

Table 9-2 (continued)

| | | Reading—Supplementary | | |
Title	Publisher, Date	Grade Level	Content	Comments
Happenings	Field Educational Publications	Secondary reading level 4.2–4.6	Books	Series of high-interest, low-vocabulary books with exercises to help reinforce comprehension and recall
New Dimensions	Educational Developmental Laboratories, a division of McGraw-Hill, 1973	2–13	Cassettes, filmstrips, study guide, ditto masters	Individualized skill-based multimedia reading program designed to motivate students by using high-interest materials
Action Libraries	Scholastic Book Services, 1971	Secondary reading level 2–4	Eight kits, five books per kit, spirit masters	To be used alone or with Action and Double Action programs, reading material for low-functioning students
Individualized Directions in Reading	Steck-Vaughn Co., 1975	1–6	Modules, learning stations, teacher's set, pre & post tests	Pupil-centered system of criterion-referenced inventories of self-instructional learning materials covering phonics analysis, structural analysis, and comprehension
Kaleidoscope Readers	Field Education Publications	Secondary reading level 2–9	Books, lesson plans, progress tests	High-interest, low-vocabulary readings on topics such as careers, dating authority, drugs, hot rods, social relations

Interesting Reading Series	Follett Publishing Co., 1961	Secondary reading level 2–3	Books, screening tests	Series of high-interest, easy-to-read books
A Time for Action	Scholastic Book Services, 1970	Grades 7–12; reading level 2–4	Records, books, plays, short stories, teaching guide	High-interest, low-vocabulary materials to develop basic word attack, reading, and comprehension skills through reading, role playing, discussion, and writing
Breakthrough	Allyn & Bacon, Inc., 1971	Reading level 1–6	Series of paperback books, teacher's guides, reading skills, activities masters	Varied selection of stories, biographies, articles, and poetry interesting and relevant to the older student
Webster Classroom Reading Clinic	McGraw-Hill, 1962–1972	Grade level 6–12, reading level 4	Complete program: skill cards, word wheels, vocabulary games, vocabulary cards, workbooks, teacher's manual	Famous novels geared to 4th-grade level: Poe, Stevenson, Buck, London, etc.
The Young America Basic	Lyons & Carnahan, 1974	Grade level 1–4	Printed material, skillbooks, ditto masters, charts, tests, teacher's manual	11 levels from pre-primer to grade 4 language arts skill development

English—Supplementary

Living Your English	D. C. Heath and Co., 1964	Grade level 7–12, reading level 4–6	Workbooks, teacher's manual	Designed for slow learners; grammar is taught through simple relationships of everyday life rather than in the traditional sense

Table 9-2 (continued)

English—Supplementary

Title	Publisher, Date	Grade Level	Content	Comments
Learning Your Language	Follett Publishing Co., 1956	Reading level 4–6; grade level 6–9	Books	6 books with 120 lessons each based on a single theme to develop reading skills and language disciplines; a novel, stories, essays, biographies, poems, and drama
Language Exercises	Steck-Vaughn Co.	Grade level 1–8	Workbooks, texts	Remedial work for slow achievers at upper levels; grammar series with simple instructions and practice problems on each phase of language instruction
English That We Need	Frank E. Richards Publishing Co., 1974	Grade level 6–9	Workbook	Consumable worktext offering instruction in simplified grammar for the educable student; Contents include: the alphabet, capital letters, the dictionary, sentences, contractions, abbreviations, homonyms, paragraphs, letters, and oral English
More English That We Need	Frank E. Richards Publishing Co.	Grade level 6–9	Workbook	Consumable worktext for the educable student in four units, punctuation marks, correct usage, written English, and oral English

Title	Publisher	Level	Format	Description
English the Easy Way	South-Western Publishing Co., 1974	Grade level 9–12	Worktext	Remedial instruction or review in vocational education programs or adult education classes; includes grammar, punctuation, spelling, and word study
English Grammar	Behavioral Research Laboratories	Grade level 8–9	Books, test booklets, teacher's manual	A programmed, 2-volume, grammar course to introduce students to descriptions of ways in which words are used in context and to demonstrate syntactic functions in language; Begins by introducing the product and parts of a relationship of nonverbal symbols; Gradually, words replace nonverbal symbols and include all elements from noun and adjective through sentence analysis
English for Today	McGraw-Hill, 1962–1966	Grade level 6–12	Books	Developed for bilingual students, but these 6 books may be used for remedial programs in written and spoken language arts skills
Success In Language and Literature—A	Follett Publishing Co.	Reading level 5–8; grade level 9–12	Booklets, workbooks	High-interest, low-vocabulary series that focuses on ideas and experiences common to disadvantaged students; stresses class activities

Table 9-2 (continued)

Title	Publisher, Date	Grade Level	English—Supplementary Content	Comments
Success in Language and Literature—B	Follett Publishing Co.	Reading level 5–8; grade level 9–12	Booklets, workbooks	Series of 6 booklets that build on the concepts and language skills introduced in Part A; designed to help students develop practical, written, and oral language skills; contents emphasize environmental factors and the influence of peers, community, communications, media, and economic conditions
R.S.V.P.—Reading, Spelling, Vocabulary, Pronunciation	Amsco School Publication	Grade level 4–9	Workbooks	English workbooks designed to develop understanding of words and an interest in their discriminating use; in short reading sections the lesson words appear in boldface type and are underscored; reading selections deal with animals, natural science, people, safety, and hobbies and vocations
Modern Short Biographies	Globe Book Co., 1970	Grade level 7–12; reading level 5	Softcover texts	Includes a collection of 31 true stories of American personalities that emphasize the multiracial origins of America and the contributions of all groups

Title	Publisher	Level	Materials	Description
Basic Foundation Series in English	Continental Press	Grade level 7–12; reading level 7–9	Workbooks	4 workbooks containing 64 lessons providing practice in basic English skills; Recommended for selective use in programs for the disadvantaged and slow learner
Practical English Grammar	Creative Visuals, 1974	Interest level adolescent and adult	Filmstrips, cassettes, worksheets, templates	Traditional rules and usage, drill sentences grouped with a common theme; concentrates on common problematic words; may be used for review and adult retraining
Adult Basic Education Books	Steck-Vaughn Co.	Grade level 7–12 and adult	Worktexts	3 worktexts on English fundamentals—alphabet, grammar, verbs, capitalization, punctuation, sentences, reading, and writing
Gateway English	McGraw-Hill, 1967–1969	Grade level 7–12	Books, transparencies, records	A 3-year program of developmental literature and language arts for "less able readers;" 4 anthologies per grade level contain poems, plays, stories with transparencies, recordings of songs and poems
Guidebooks to Better English	Economy Co.	Reading level 4–9; grade level 5–12	Workbooks	Remedial English program that allows student to work at own pace; includes simplified usage, grammar, and mechanics
Organizing and Reporting Skills Kit	Science Research Associates, 1974	Grade level 4–8	Study cards, skill cards	Teaches students how to write reports—research, planning, and basic skills

Table 9-2 (continued)

English—Supplementary

Title	Publisher, Date	Grade Level	Content	Comments
Graph and Picture Study Skills Kit	Science Research Associates, 1974	Grade level 4–8	Skill cards, key cards	Teaches students to use visual aids in books, magazines, etc., to interpret data in tables, graphs, charts, and diagrams
How To Series	International Teaching Tapes, Educational Progress Corp.	Grade level 4–7	Audio tapes	Series of lessons on how to use the dictionary and other resources, use the library, study, and make a speech
Troubleshooter I	Houghton-Mifflin Co., 1975	Grade level 9–12	Paperbound books, pre & post tests	Nongraded basic skills program for remedial work; consists of 8 student-directed texts: sound out, sound off, spelling, word attack, word mastery, sentence strength, punctuation, and English achievement
Troubleshooter II	Houghton-Mifflin Co.	Grade level 9–12	Paperbound books	Provides further practice materials in areas of Troubleshooter I and develops more advanced language skills
The Write Thing	Houghton-Mifflin Co., 1974	Grade level 7–12	Posters, tapes, booklets, photoprints	Multimedia approach to get students to write; uses topics of interest to stimulate responses

Title	Publisher	Grade level	Materials	Description
Report Writing Skills	Coronet Instructional Media, 1972	Grade level 5–9	Audio cassettes, response books	Designed to improve research, organizational, and composition skills used in writing formal reports and to present bases for making critical judgments; each cassette is a self-contained lesson on choosing a topic, research, note taking, planning and organizing, outlining, etc.
Write Away	McDougal, Littell and Co., 1973	Grade level 6–8	Kit with teacher's manual, photographs, and writing assignments	On the back of each picture is a brief, unstructured, and open-ended writing assignment designed to get students to write
Lessons In Syntax	Educational Activities, Inc.	Grade level 5–12	Student workbooks, teacher's manual	For developmental or remedial use in teaching written constructions based on transformational grammar
The Writing Bug	Random House, 1974	Grade level 4–7	Cards, cassettes, filmstrips	A multimedia approach to stimulate students to write units on describing, explaining, and storytelling
Play It Cool in English	Follett Publishing Co.	Grade level 7–12	Workbooks, kits	3 English programs designed for slow learners and culturally disadvantaged students
Individualized English/ Programmed Instruction	Follett Publishing Co., 1974	Set J: reading level 5–8, grade level 7–9; Set H: reading level 6–9, grade level 10–12	Exercise cards, diagnostic and mastery tests, teacher's manual	Programmed materials provide instruction on how to overcome weaknesses in the use of language; exercise cards cover principles of English with emphasis on grammar and usage, sentence structure, punctuation, and mechanics

Table 9-2 (continued)

| | | English—Supplementary | |
Title	Publisher, Date	Grade Level	Content	Comments
Unigraph Laps	Unigraph Products	Grade level 3–8	Ditto masters	Self-contained packets of instructional materials on language, grammar, and punctuation
English in Action	Regents Publishing Co., Inc.	Grade level 5–8	Workbook	Basic course with emphasis on spoken English; contains many pictures to help ensure quick vocabulary development and comprehension; simple explanations, easy reading selections, many exercises, 8 review sections
Keys to Good Language	The Economy Co., 1975	Grade level 2–6	Exercise books	Nongraded English program to develop necessary skills for written and oral communication. The lessons: follow a progression of thinking skills that range from simple memory to complex evaluations; organized to follow a diagnostic-prescriptive pattern and incorporate the process of inquiry; organized according to clearly defined performance objectives.

Title	Publisher	Grade level	Format	Description
Lessons for Self-Instruction in Basic Skills: English Language	California Test Bureau, McGraw-Hill, 1966	Grade level 5–8	Reusable booklets	Programmed booklets for review work on the basic elements of grammar
Lessons for Self-Instruction: Mechanics of English	California Test Bureau, McGraw-Hill, 1966	Grade level 1–12	Reusable booklets	Programmed booklets to develop mechanics of English, sentence patterns, and spelling
Laidlaw Language Experiences Program	Laidlaw Brothers, Division of Doubleday & Co., Inc., 1973	Grade level K–8	Books, activity	Multigraded language arts series based on student involvement
Writing Our Language	Scott, Foresman and Co., 1976	Grade level 4–8	Paperback	Develops the concept of and skills and motivation for legible handwriting; can be used in class or individually

Spelling

Title	Publisher	Grade level	Format	Description
Spelling Word Power Lab	Science Research Associates, Inc., 1966	Grade level 4–7, reading level 4–7	Learning wheel, response book, check tests, achievement surveys, key cards	Emphasizes specific spelling problems such as suffixes, consonant blends, special plural endings; divided into 4 laboratories—roughly grades 4, 5, 6, and 7; material presented on a learning wheel, student response book

Table 9-2 (continued)

Spelling

Title	Publisher, Date	Grade Level	Content	Comments
A Spelling Workbook Series	Educator's Publishing Service	Grade level 2–12	Workbooks	Corrective program for spelling and reading
Word Book Spelling Series	Lyons & Carnahan, 1974	Grade level 2–8	Workbooks, spirit masters	Linguistically oriented; 4 levels emphasizing sound, structures, and meaning of language; phonics-oriented approach to spelling
Spelling Growth	The Economy Co.	Grade level 2–8	Books	Phonetic approach stressing auditory, visual, meaning, and kinesthetic techniques
Spelling Our Language	Scott, Foresman and Co., 1973	Grade level 1–8, reading level 1–8	Books, acetate overlay; proofcheckers available	Books 3–8 can be used in independent study designed to develop: spelling, vocabulary; ability to identify and use English spelling patterns; relationship of handwriting to spelling; use of dictionary, glossary, thesauri, etc.
Spell/Write	Nobel & Noble, Publishers, 1971–1973	Grade level 1–8	Hard- or soft-cover books, diagnostic and mastery tests, duplicating masters	Inductive approach to spelling generalizations; spelling list teaches reliable phoneme-grapheme patterns first; also incorporates handwriting

Reading Road to Spelling	Harper & Row, 1970	Grade level 1–8	Hardbound or paperback books	For slow or average students; emphasis on spelling and language skills; objectives specified in each lesson, but not in behavioral terms
Spelling	Behavioral Research Laboratories	Grade level 1–8	Texts, test booklets, teacher's manual	A programmed series in which one sound maintains the same letter representation until child masters it; illustrations with clues aid student in answering
Gateway to Correct Spelling, revised	Steck-Vaughn, 1975	Grade level 7–12	Worktext, teacher's manual	High school speller; exercise format
Ginn Individualized Spelling Program	Ginn and Co., 1974	Grade level 2–8	Individualized spelling kits with cards	6 kits containing 28 levels; each kit has roughly a 3-grade range and contains approximately 425 cards for preassessment and instruction; teaches word and language concepts, nongraded, individualized
Harbrace Spelling Program	Harcourt Brace Jovanovich, 1974	Grade level 1–8	Workbooks	Program built on a spelling-pattern base; starts with consistent and moves to less predictable relationships; also covers handwriting, tracing, writing stories and sentences, and analyzing word structure, etc.
Botel Spelling Program	Penn Valley Publishing Co., 1965	Grade level 1–12	Dictionary speller, student record book	For slow or beginning speller

Table 9-2 (continued)

Title	Publisher, Date	Grade Level	Spelling Content	Comments
Demon Spelling Words, Phondise	Educational Activities, Inc., 1968	Grade level 2–8	Record or cassette	Words are grouped by grade level; they are not representative of rules so they must be memorized; average is 15 words per grade level; systematic, intensive review of these words
Dr. Spello (2nd Ed.)	McGraw-Hill, Webster Division, 1968	Grade level 4–9	Worktext	Corrective reading and spelling skills worktext; content includes vowel and consonant sounds, 2-letter consonants, silent letters, endings, prefixes and suffixes, homonyms, contractions, etc.
Basic Goals in Spelling	McGraw-Hill, Webster Division, 1972	Grade level 1–8	Text, workbook, filmstrips, Webstermasters, sound symbol charts, teacher's edition	No grade level designations, flexibility within texts with multilevel teaching devices to help teachers individualize instruction, practice in spelling by analogy
Basic Spelling Series	J. B. Lippincott Co., 1973	Grade level 1–8	Workbook	Ungraded series of workbooks uses a phonetic/linguistic approach to spelling, listening, speaking, reading, writing, punctuation, handwriting, proofing, and dictionary activities included

Math—Core

Title	Publisher	Grade level	Materials	Description
The Learning Skills Series—Arithmetic	McGraw-Hill, Webster Division, 1975	Grade level 5–12	Text, workbooks, Teacher's Edition	Part of series for "Children With Learning Difficulties"; 4 books, each for a different unit, designed for individualized instruction
Mathematics for Individual Achievement	Houghton Mifflin Co., 1974	Grade level K–8	Text, ditto masters, workbooks, pre and post tests	Available in regular or metric; recommended as a core program for students to work at own pace; designed for mastery of basic skills; separate book for each level, levels loosely correspond to grades

Math—Supplementary

Title	Publisher	Grade level	Materials	Description
Target Series	Mafex Associates, 1971	Grade level 7–12	Workbooks	Variety of exercises for applying arithmetical concepts to family, social, and employment situations
Understanding Decimals	Enrich, 1973	Grade level 6–12	Teaching machine	Teaches students the decimal system, how to figure and check, and estimating size of answer to facilitate computation; linear programming format; close teacher supervision necessary
Individualizing Mathematics	Addison-Wesley Publishing Co., 1970	Grade level 7–12	Text, consumable booklets, activity cards, testing program	3 sequences, roughly coinciding with grades 7, 8, and 9, have motivational phase, mainstream phase, in-depth phase, and complete testing program; designed for remedial use

157

Table 9-2 (continued)

Title	Publisher, Date	Grade Level	Math—Supplementary Content	Comments
SRA Mathematics Learning System	Science Research Associates, 1974	Grade level K-8	Text	Informal approach relates math to real world with photos; teaches basic computational skills, metric system, and geometry; kit includes material for diagnosis, instruction, practice, testing, recycling, extension, and maintenance
Useful Arithmetic Volumes 1 and 2	Frank E. Richards Publishing Co., 1975	Grade level 9-12 and adult	Text	Applied arithmetic; unit includes grocery bill, cost of transportation, eating in restaurants, and other everyday situations
Success With Mathematics 1, 2, and 3	Addison-Wesley Publishing Co., 1974	Grade level 7-9	3 texts, masters, skill cards	For low achievers; each lesson begins with activity requiring little or no written work, followed by discussion and drill
Non-graded Mathematics Topic—Texts	Charles Merrill Publishing Co., 1974	Grade level 3-9	Ditto masters	To be used with Merrill Skill tapes; set has 8 titles, e.g., base ten system, addition of whole numbers, operations with fractions, etc.
Refresher Mathematics	Allyn & Bacon, Inc., 1974	Grade level 7-12	Text	Refresher or remedial text in general mathematics with emphasis on the fundamental operations of arithmetic; includes keyed inventory tests, diagnostic tests, reviews, and maintenance tests

Title	Publisher	Grade Level	Materials	Description
Special Ed Programmed Arithmetic Lab	Mafex Associates, 1975	Grade level 7–12	Tests, exercise cards, practice cards	Identifies areas of weakness and gives remedial work; individualized instruction
Mental Computation	Science Research Associates, 1971	Grade level 2–7	Booklets	Develops skill of computing without use of pencil and paper; each skill introduced by a word problem followed by steps for solving problem mentally; independent exercises included
Metric Measurement Program	Science Research Associates, 1975	Grade level 1–12	Activity cards, audio tapes, measuring kit, masters	Provides experiences in measuring length, area, volume, mass, and temperature; minimal reading skills needed
Math from Rock Bottom	Charles Merrill Publishing Co., 1974	Grade level 5–8	Booklets, study guides, cassettes, narrative books, teacher's guide	Cartoon-illustrated narrative; main character "invents" counting and 4 arithmetic operations; tape permits poor readers to follow along; study guide reinforces concepts
Mathematics for Schools—An Integrated Series	Addison-Wesley Publishing Co., 1970–1974	Grade level K–7	17 consumable and nonconsumable paperback books, teacher's resource books, child marking answer books	Reflects British "open-ended approach"; children begin with a real situation and progress through doing and discussion activities into practice activities
Mastering Mathematics Series	Sadlier, Inc., 1971	Grade level K–8	Booklets	"A non-graded program for reluctant learners and students with reading problems"; 5-book series—each with teacher edition, readiness and beginning books

Table 9-2 (continued)

Math—Supplementary

Title	Publisher, Date	Grade Level	Content	Comments
Mathematics Drill Tapes	International Teaching Tapes, 1972	Grade level 1–8	Tapes, student activity sheets	160 taped lessons for drills in basic computational skills; program divided into 8 subject unit sets, e.g., addition, subtraction, multiplication, division, etc.
Holt's Elementary Math	Holt, Rinehart and Winston, Inc., 1970	Grade level 1–8	Transparencies	8 levels, each with 6 units; unit 1 is basic (concept of sets, fractions, etc.), unit 8 covers geometry, decimals, statistics, etc.
Numble	Educational Aids and Supplies of Tomorrow, Inc., 1974–1975	Grade level 2–9	Game	A crossword-puzzle numbers game using addition, subtraction, multiplication, and division
Twin Choice and Come Out Even	Holt, Rinehart and Winston, Inc., 1974	Grade level 1–8	Cards	10 decks of cards to help pupils sharpen computational and problem solving skills
Think Metric	Educational Activities, 1974	Grade level 4–8	Filmstrips, records, cassettes	Teaches metric system in relation to standard measure; involves conversion using length, weight, capacity; can be used one-to-one, or for small or large group instruction

Title	Publisher	Grade level	Format	Description
The Metric System	Addison-Wesley Publishing Co., 1974	Grade level 4–8	Softbound book	Supplement to math or science program; introduces the metric system through activities and investigations
TUF	Avalon-Hill Co., 1969	Grade level 3–12 and adult	Game	Based on number sentences or equations that can be played in a group or individually
Think Metric	South-Western Publishing Co., 1975	Grade level 6–8	Workbook	Self-teaching text workbook designed to give the student practice using metric denominators; provides a review of decimals then concentrates on various base units of measurement characteristic of the metric system; student can proceed at own pace
Using Money Series	Frank E. Richards Publishing Co., 1973	Reading level 1–4; interest level 7–12	Workbook	Work dealing with practical finance
Dominoes, Decimal-Fraction	Responsive Environment, 1971	Grade level 5–8	Game	Sturdy plywood dominoes that show common fractions, percentages, decimal fractions, and pictorial fractions for matching
Dominoes, Fraction	Responsive Environment, 1971	Grade level 5–7	Game	Introduction to fractions; written and pictorial fractions for matching
Going Metric	Addison-Wesley Publishing Co., 1975	Grade level: Set C, 5–7	Ditto masters	Introduces the metric system through activities

Table 9-2 (continued)

Math—Supplementary

Title	Publisher, Date	Grade Level	Content	Comments
Cross Number Puzzles	Ideal School Supply Co., 1971	Grade level 1–12	Puzzle cards	6 boxes with puzzles involving finding end number; similar to magic square
Decimal Numbers	Grolier Educational Corp., 1972	Reading level 4	Books	Teaches conversion of numerical fractions to decimals and vice versa, placement of decimal point, rounding off decimal numbers, calculating percentages, etc.; basically a drill unit for 4-th grade reading level; recommended for remedial use
Basic Mathematics	Educational Activities, 1972, 1973, 1974	Grade level: Set 2, 6–9	Records or cassettes, worksheets	Each recording teaches 4–8 complete single concept, self-directing, and self-correcting lessons; answers are given after each lesson; can be used for class drill or independent study
Continuous Progress Laboratories	Educational Progress Corp., 1972	Grade level 1–8	Cards, cassettes	Each grade level has a program, each program has a set of tapes at grade level, lesson cards, teacher resource materials, and student progress books

Arithmetic Series	Milliken Publishing Co., 1975	Grade level 4–6	Duplicating masters	Independent activities that require minimal supervision
Basic Mathematics	Charles E. Merrill Publishing Co., 1974	Grade level 7–9	Duplicating masters, pre and post tests, "roundups," supplemental pages	Cartoon format and daily learning success to motivate low achiever; each lesson is to be completed in 1 class period without homework assignments; each kit covers 1 year
Arithmetic Step by Step—Kit B	Continental Press Co., 1971	Grade level 3–6	Duplicating masters	For remedial use and for students with learning problems; 10 units—counting, place value, addition, subtraction, multiplication, division, fractions, money, measures, graphs, decimals, percentages; each unit has 3 levels and a short diagnostic pretest
Animated Arithmetic	Mafex Associates	Grade level 1–8	Paperback workbook	Computation and word problems presented via cartoon characters; suitable for independent study
Arithmetic (Intermediate Series) Holt Adult Basic Education Series	Holt, Rinehart and Winston, Inc.	Grade level 4–7	Paperback books	Basic elementary curriculum in arithmetic from initial concepts through the 4 arithmetical operations; not enough information available to determine whether it can be used for core program
Metric System Skills	Educational Activities, 1974	Grade level 4–8	Tapes, records	Developmental series of skills and drills on fundamentals of the metric system

Table 9-2 (continued)

Math—Supplementary

Title	Publisher, Date	Grade Level	Content	Comments
Mathematics Skill Builders, 3rd ed.	South-Western Publishing Co., 1975	Grade level 7–9	Workbook	Thorough review of fundamentals of math; practical exercises and 80 tests written in script
Mathematics in Living	Pruett Press, Inc., 1975	Grade level 7–9	Books	Relates to everyday situations in: Buying, wages and budgets, banking and loans, credit, and taxes
Supermarket	Fern Tripp	Grade level 5–7	Worktext	Simple everyday math problems in grocery buying including making change, check writing, can size, weight, etc.
Sum Up	Educational Aids and Supplies of Tomorrow, Inc., 1974	Grade level 3–12	Game	2–8 players compete against each other and time to create high-scoring mathematical equations; each round calls for a different type of equation involving addition, subtraction, multiplication and division
Practical Applications in Mathematics	Allyn & Bacon, Inc., 1975	Grade level 7–12	Text	Comprehensive practice book in general math; good for supplement to basal text in arithmetic or general math; includes relevant consumer application exercises

Title	Publisher	Grade level	Materials	Description
Mathematics for the Consumer	South-Western Publishing Co., 1975	Grade level 10–12	Textbooks, problems and drills, tests	Everyday consumer problems for students of varying abilities; 5-step learning plan and a planned program of review ensure mastery of new skills and retention of previously learned skills
Mastery Arithmetic Drills and Tests	Addison-Wesley Publishing Co., 1974–1975	Grade level 1–9	Duplicating masters	Drills, exercises, reviews, and practices for use without extensive teacher direction
Know the Essentials of Math	Addison-Wesley Publishing Co., 1974–1975	Grade level 1–6	Duplicating masters	Used for review, practice, drill
Dyna Math	Macmillan Company, 1975	Grade level 6–9	Texts, manipulatives, cassettes, ditto masters	For underachievers; offers alternative to basal instruction through "hands on" activities, self-directed and self-pacing materials, and special nonreading materials to review and upgrade computational skills
Elementary Math	Charles E. Merrill Publishing Co., 1974	Grade level 1–8	Duplicating sheets	For classroom use; each page is to be completed after the concept has been presented from the classroom textbook
Essentials of Mathematics, Skills and Concepts	Ginn, 1975	Grade level 7–12	Texts	Teaches below grade-level readers and slow learners basic math skills through games, activities, experiments, pictures, and diagrams; minimal, simple reading and highly visual

Table 9-2 (continued)

Title	Publisher, Date	Grade Level	Content	Comments
		Math—Supplementary		
Explora Tapes—Mathematics	International Teaching Tapes, 1975	Grade level 4–12	Tapes	Provides enrichment materials and allows students to study on their own and in-depth those math concepts not included in the usual math class; activity sheet encourages students to participate as they listen to the cassette by answering questions, drawing pictures, examining illustrations, or making models
Foundation Mathematics	McGraw-Hill, Webster Division, 1975	Grade level 9	Text, workbook	Gives the slower math student practical content he can understand and the non-college-bound student math he needs in his daily life and work; reviews decimals, percentages, and fractions as well as "business" mathematics
Fractions	McGraw-Hill, Webster Division, 1966	Grade level 6–8	Text	A complete unit on fractions for introductory drill, makeup, review, remediation
Educational Development Lab	McGraw-Hill, 1974	Grade level 7–8	Cassettes, answer books, ditto masters, manipulatives, filmstrips, games, diagnostic tests	Diagnosis, review of prerequisite skills, and concept introduction through modeling, key concept development, concept enrichment, practice and reinforcement, and skill drill

CHAPTER 10
Secondary Learning Disabilities: An Epilogue

We have attempted to provide the field of learning disabilities with an overview of some of the critical issues, current practices, and potential avenues of approach to the pressing problems of the secondary-level learning disabled youth. We have done so from the standpoint of the practitioner more than from that of the theorist, and from the vantage point of those who are directly responsible for day-to-day teaching activities with the learning disabled. Thus, our book has dealt with practical rather than theoretical problems for the most part; although, inevitably, one must confront theory particularly when dealing with certain aspects of learning disabilities.

The reader, we are sure, will come away with a feeling of dissatisfaction from many of the positions we have taken concerning the diagnosis and education of the learning disabled. We believe that this is all for the good, for opinions rather than facts are being discussed in the field of learning disabilities currently, and these opinions should be challenged. Teachers and support personnel in the field of learning disabilities will have to live with dissonance and dissatisfaction until we have the facts. Dissonance and dissatisfaction should help to generate the facts. Meanwhile, two facts confront us now: there are secondary learning disabled youth, and many of them are not being adequately helped. Let us amplify some of our earlier comments concerning what should be done to help them.

We believe that the goals for the secondary-level learning disabled pupils should be mastery of basic skills in written language and in mathematics. We have established full sixth-grade competency in these areas as the criteria for these goals. We believe that the field of learning disabilities has or is developing the technical capabilities that make their achievement possible for many, if not all, secondary-level learning disabled pupils. We believe that the secondary-level learning disabled pupil should be the educational charge of the learning disability specialist until the pupil's basic skill competencies are established. We do not, however, believe that the learning disability specialist has much to offer in the content areas of instruction at the secondary level. We recommend that these be managed by the instructional staffs of regular education. The learning disability specialist may serve as a consultant to the secondary school faculties concerning the possible techniques and prostheses that will help the secondary learning disabled pupil better adjust to the mainstream. But he has little to offer at the current time toward the advanced instruction of pupils. Assistance in such instruction is more likely to come from curriculum specialists and the educational psychologist. Knowing this, let us not cheapen our skills by offering them when they do not apply.

As to our positions, we believe that they have much to recommend them, despite the disagreements they will engender. These positions clearly establish the field of learning disabilities as a legitimate area of special education instruction and inquiry. They clearly delimit the youth to be served to a manageable number and yet do not commit us to some contrived figure based on expediencies or guesses. Our positions show that we accept the tenets that have been fundamental to the conceptualization of the field of learning disabilities, but eschew many of the unwarranted premises that have accompanied them.

Our positions establish as the appropriate field of operation for the learning disability specialist at the secondary level those areas with which the specialist is most familiar: the training and development of basic skill competencies. The areas of subject matter are left to those best able to deal with instruction therein—traditional faculties at the secondary level. We recognize the need for mainstreaming and integration and yet also the too-often-scorned fact that intensive problems need intensive care and remediation, which only specialized situations and instruction can provide. Finally, we offer programming based on what we regard as the most appropriate technologies and instructional strategies of the day—instructional objectives, criterion-referenced measurement, and mastery learning—which we have field tested with considerable success.

We hope and anticipate that this book will have some useful applications—even if it does not solve the complex ills of a most complex problem. It is not enough, we know. But it is a beginning.

PART III

Selected Bibliography of References

Ansara A: Language therapy to salvage the college potential of dyslexic adolescents. Bull Orton Soc *22:* 123–139, 1972

The adolescent with a specific language disability often has a high degree of potential ability but has been misunderstood and neglected for years. The author believes that if "his primary problem is recognized and dealt with appropriately, the dyslexic adolescent becomes free to establish and pursue goals that can include college. Although much precious time has been lost and much needless 'school trauma' endured, it is still not too late to salvage the college potential of the dyslexic adolescent through language therapy."

Throughout the school years, the dyslexic has been learning and storing vast amounts of information. This knowledge, however disordered, can be tapped and reorganized. Therapy must not only deal with language, but with academic skills as well.

The author gives concrete examples of techniques successful in language therapy. One method, adapted from Orton's work with stutterers, involves using a pencil to coordinate eye and brain during reading. After some proficiency is developed with this procedure, syllabication, still using the pencil, is introduced. The concept of phrase, first orally and then in reading, is taught next. Spelling, sentence construction, and handwriting are then introduced.

With the improvement of language arts skills, the dyslexic gains new confidence, freedom, and perspective. The author stresses "overlearning" of skills so that the student will have an edge and "be more sure of academic success when he is on his own."

Ansara A: The language therapist as a basic mathematics tutor for adolescents. Bull Orton Soc 23: 119–139, 1973

The language therapist who teaches the dyslexic (defined here as "an otherwise healthy and normal individual who has specific problems of a primary nature with learning to read, write, spell, or manipulate symbols") may find that the youngster has problems with math as well as with English. Ansara believes that the same insights used in teaching language skills may prove helpful in teaching basic mathematics. Traditional teaching devices are of no value to the child who, due to his perceptual difficulties, is transposing numbers, omitting steps in a sequence of operations, or misaligning columns of numbers. The author cites various studies in which arithmetic deficits and dyslexia are associated.

The student must be given a sequence and a structure that will permit him to recognize the patterns of the material to be organized. The experiences that develop the sequences and structures must be designed to "(1) circumvent or overcome sensory modality deficits; (2) circumvent the problems with spatial or temporal relationships or sequencing; (3) develop organization and integration; and (4) provide the associations that will ensure memory." Each experience must allow the learner to construct logical rules which he can apply to more difficult material as he progresses. It is most important to avoid a repetition of the kind of teaching that has proven unproductive in the past.

A sample of a basic arithmetic curriculum for dyslexics is presented in this paper, along with two case studies of boys who have derived great benefit from the method. In the author's view," all dyslexic children should be considered as high risk in arithmetic and later mathematics until their performance in school has demonstrated otherwise."

Behan EF: A resource-room program at the junior high school level. In *Successful Programming: Many Points of View.* Proceedings of the Fifth Annual Conference, ACLD, Boston, 1968

This paper details a junior high school special education program in which a resource center served as a spanning program between the self-contained special class and an average homeroom section. The project was planned for children with average or better potential who still needed to receive some part-time help following work at lower grade levels with itinerant teachers. The program was put into effect at Edgewood Junior High School, Highland Park, Illinois, and served 10 students per year. Most of them already had been in some type of special education program.

At the start of the program, the instructor met with every child and his parents, as well as with the regular teachers who were also seeing these children. Time for these special classes had to be taken from study halls, art, music, or gym. However, if a student was extremely low in an academic subject, he was removed from all those periods and given a total curriculum at a lower level. Each child was seen for 5 hours a week, with a maximum of 4 or 5 children in the center at the same time. Whenever possible, 2 students who were compatible worked together on a task of mutual interest.

The materials used were judged on the basis of whether they were suited to accomplishing their intended purpose, were appropriate to the age and ability level of the child, and were new and appealing to the student. More important than the materials alone was the teacher's ingenuity and ability to adapt them to each student's needs.

The suggestion was presented that it might be possible to plan for a fifth year of high school. The child could take a normal but lighter than average load each semester, which might even enable him to work on a competitive basis in a normal classroom.

Berlin WH Jr: The police badge and the NH child. In Anderson L (ed): *Helping the Adolescent with the Hidden Handicap.* Los Angeles, Association for Neurologically Handicapped Children, 1970

Berlin, police chief of a small California city, discusses acting out behavior and how it often brings children in conflict with the law. Youngsters act out because they don't believe that they're equal to other children. They are seeking compensatory gratification and protesting their inequality when they display antisocial behavior. He suggests that it is universally agreed within law enforcement agencies that children should not be incarcerated or institutionalized if there is another way to solve the problem.

Four cases are presented that involve neurologically handicapped juveniles in various infractions of the law. In one case, a police officer was alert to the fact that a 10-year-old boy was in the company of several 7-year olds when he got in trouble. The officer requested that the youth write a simple sentence and copy some designs. When he was unable to do so, the officer recommended that he be tested, and it was revealed that the child was neurologically handicapped. Therapy and training were initiated.

In another case, a brother and sister, 7- and 8-years old were truancy problems. A visit to their apartment by the investigating officer revealed aimless scrawling all over the walls—no pictures or words. He recognized that these children were performing below their age-achievement level. Testing confirmed that they both had neurological problems as well as emotional difficulties.

In the third case, a reverse reaction to a drug was the clue that a 14-year-old girl might have a neurological impairment. With this handicap, small doses of a drug sometimes have this effect, but large doses produce a normal reaction. The author believes that for every girl with neurological handicaps, there will be 9 boys, and that both boys and girls in their acting out often seek narcotics.

The fourth case involved a boy with neurological handicaps who had been diagnosed early and received special training, but who nevertheless became a police problem. The department understood his difficulty but could really do nothing but witness his self-destruction.

The solution to these types of problems is felt to be in continued medical research so that some day these defects can be corrected. It is suggested to parents that their child carry identification indicating any neurological handicap and use of certain medications, if such is the case. This should help law enforcement agencies to handle the child in the best possible way if there is ever a conflict with the law.

Berman A, Siegal A: Delinquents are disabled: an innovative approach to the prevention and treatment of juvenile delinquency. Final report of the Neuropsychology Diagnostic Laboratory at the Rhode Island Training Schools, 1974

The authors have reviewed research on the relationship between behavioral disorders and neurological or perceptual abnormalities. They point out the importance of learning more about the neuropsychological characteristics of delinquents in order to institute effective and realistic rehabilitation. Delinquent behavior cannot be changed only by psychological or sociological techniques when the problem is a neurological or perceptual distortion or deficiency. "A crucial rehabilitation element, then, becomes the ability to distinguish among delinquents, often with similar behavioral symptoms, who will require alternative kinds of rehabilitation programs."

The subjects of the study discussed in this paper were 45 adolescent boys incarcerated at the Rhode Island Training School and an equal number of nondelinquent controls matched by age, race, and socioeconomic background. All subjects were examined using the Halstead Neuropsychological Battery for Adults, Halstead–Wepman Aphasia Examination, Reitan's Sensory-Imperception Examination, and WAIS and WISC batteries. Significant differences were found between the two groups on almost all of the Wechsler scales and on the majority of Halstead's, showing that the delinquent group had marked impairment in most critical adaptive abilities. The most severe deficits occurred in the areas of concept formation and utilization, verbal symbolic manipulations, and perceptual organization. The use of discriminant functions based on five neuropsychological predictors (Impairment Index, Verbal IQ, Performance IQ, and Trails A and B) allowed correct classification of 87 percent of the delinquents as youngsters.

The authors stress two statistics which highlight the severity and persistence of the problem of delinquency among adolescents and teenagers: the average, and decreasing, age for first-time incarceration has fallen to below 13 years of age and the recidivism rate among juvenile offenders now approaches 85%.

Current treatment programs have apparently had little success, it is time to change our approaches.

The authors suggest a series of recommendations on early identification, mandatory screening and evaluation, analysis of skill deficits and appropriate remediation, reordering of goals and expectations in vocational training, rehabilitation and follow-up, and training of teachers and rehabilitation counselors.

Boeser R et al.: *A Program for Students with Learning Difficulties: Social Studies—Ten, Eleven, and Twelve.* Bloomington, Minnesota, Bloomington Public Schools, 1969 (ED 075-442)

A social studies program for grades 10, 11, and 12 designed for students with learning difficulties is described in this paper. Students chosen for the course were generally below average in scholastic ability and achievement; in need of individual help and attention; deficient in reading, writing, speaking, and other skills; unable to keep up with the regular class; and suffering from feelings of inferiority due to repeated failures.

It was felt that these children would respond best to a "problems" approach to American history. The basic method was to identify problems in contemporary society, study them, trace their development through history, and then recapitulate in terms of the present situation. A multimedia approach was used.

The course objectives were evaluated by student self-evaluation, teacher-student conferences, teacher observation and evaluation, teacher-made tests, and standardized tests. Attitudinal tests were also felt to be important.

The guide is divided into three sections, each corresponding to a grade level. Each unit of study covers problems, activities, and materials; the materials are specially developed for students with learning disabilities. Objectives are listed for each section and activities are briefly suggested for each unit.

Bowe A et al.: *Special Education Curriculum for Junior and Senior High School.* Syracuse, New York, Syracuse City School District, 1970 (ED 068-466)

The curriculum presented here was developed so that a combination of materials, information, and skills could be introduced to special education students as preparation for the working world. The first half of the guide presents a curriculum for junior high special education. Topics covered are math, communication skills, social adjustment, personal grooming, the world of work, occupational information, occupational skills, and homemaking. The second half covers senior high. Topics are the same, except for homemaking. Each topic is divided into general objectives, content, activities, and resources (books, records, films, and filmstrips). The Appendix includes job application forms. No provision is made for evaluation.

The guide is not to be thought of as representing the entire curriculum, but only as one integrated segment of the total curriculum.

Bright GM: The adolescent with scholastic failure. Bull Orton Soc 59–65, 1969

The author, a doctor involved in adolescent medicine, expresses the belief that, in many cases, problems such as stealing, running away, headaches, and other physical symptoms are the result of scholastic failure. The concerned physician should evaluate the somatic complaint of a teenager from the standpoint of the total individual. The medical history should include questions about attitudes and feelings toward teachers and school. It is sometimes advisable for the doctor to call the school to find out about the child's academic performance and social adjustment. A careful neurological evaluation should be considered as essential as routine laboratory tests. It is equally important for the physician to spend time alone with the youngster to give him a chance to talk about his feelings and fears.

When a school problem does exist, steps should be taken to alleviate the problem as quickly as possible. Some children may benefit from a tutor or from adjustments in the educational program. If the problem involves a learning disability, the greatest benefit that can be provided to the child is early detection. Teachers and physicians must be on the alert for the bright child who is having trouble with reading and spelling or with workbooks or copying from the blackboard. They must be aware of the kinds of errors he makes—rotations, reversals, confusion over look alikes, and bizarre spelling. Any clue that points to the possible existence of a learning problem should never be ignored. Early evaluation and remediation can be the difference between a life of academic success and one of failure.

If the professionals who deal with children are sensitive to their needs and are willing to help, many of the so-called problem children can be redirected toward happier and more productive lives.

Brunner J, Starkey J: Interpersonal relationships and the self-concept. A paper written at Northern Illinois University, DeKalb, Illinois, 1974 (ED 089-515)

The authors attempted to prove the hypothesis that high school students in special education programs for learning disabilities or emotional disturbances have a lower self-concept than those enrolled in remedial or average classes.

They tested 65 high school students using the Scale of Fundamental Interpersonal Relations Orientation—Behavior. Six areas were examined:

expressed behavior of inclusion, control, and affection, and wanted behavior of inclusion, control, and affection.·

The results revealed that the hypothesis was incorrect. The remedial group scored lower than the learning disabled adolescents in the area of expressed control. The remedial group also scored significantly lower than the emotionally disturbed students in wanted behavior, lower than the average students in expressed control, and lower than all groups in wanted control and wanted affection.

The authors concluded that students enrolled in remedial classes have lower self-concepts than average or special education students.

Brutten M: Vocational education for the brain injured adolescent and young adult at the Vanguard School, in *International Approach to Learning Disabilities of Children and Youth.* Proceedings of the Third Annual Conference, ACLD, Tulsa, 1966

The Vanguard Upper School is designed to prepare teenagers with learning diabilities for entry into the job market with confidence and with valuable skills. The students, unable to keep up with their peers in a normal classroom setting, are referred either from primary special education classes or from normal classes where they received remedial help. The philosophy of the school is that the learning disabled youngster in his teens is capable in some line of endeavor, and that the special educator must locate, identify, and nurture this unhindered capability and help the youngster bring it to fruition. The encouragement of a teenager's ego development is felt to be every bit as important as developing skills in deficient areas. His areas of aptitude, interest, and high-level motivation are exploited in an attempt to resolve underlying deficiencies and engender success.

An integral part of the program is the vocational rehabilitation and guidance service. It is felt that in our changing society many opportunities in technical and preprofessional fields will be opening up, and that people with learning problems can be trained to fill these positions. Occupations such as data processing, library science, public health, and space exploration, lower-level jobs which are methodical and repetitive in nature rather than creative and abstract, will not call for college-level personnel and may be handled by these LD students with the proper training.

The job of the vocational counselor is to match job requirements with a student's aptitudes and abilities. The Vanguard Career Guidance Center has created certain prototype testing models which simulate realistic work demands and conditions, and these models are being consolidated into a formalized job evaluation battery. The student is given a programmed experience, which is carefully controlled, that allows him to "advance through carefully graduated life experiences without the possibility of suffering failures that trigger frustration reactions."

Use is also made of a simulation laboratory: a synthetic environment is substituted for a real one so that it is possible to work under control laboratory conditions. This provides an objective picture of the patterns of difficulty and suggests areas for remedial action. "Gaming" is another technique often employed to gain information about the student's capacity to handle interpersonal relationships, especially with authority figures.

The overall objective of the Vanguard Career Guidance Center is to demonstrate that the workshop setting can serve as a major strategic step towards advancing the rehabilitation program of the disabled youngster. The emphasis is on building personal and social qualities and helping students reconcile their attitudes toward their choice of occupation and their future adjustment to the working world. Training is in fields that show considerable growth potential and hold promise for entry level jobs. Flexibility and adaptiveness, two qualities so necessary for job success, are encouraged for every student in the program.

Bursuk LZ: *Sensory Mode of Lesson Presentation as a Factor in the Reading Comprehension Improvement of Adolescent Retarded Readers.* New York, City University of New York, York College, 1971 (ED 047-435)

The author compared the effectiveness of two remedial reading approaches with adolescents from ages 14 to 16, with IQs ranging from 92 to 114 and reading approximately two years below grade level. Ss were classified according to learning style preference and then were exposed to a predominantly visual reading approach (V) or an experimental aural-visual (A-V) approach.

The hypotheses tested were that: (1) adolescent retarded readers taught by a combined aural-visual approach will achieve a greater gain in reading comprehension than those taught by a predominantly visual approach; and (2) there will be a (significant) relationship between sensory modality preference and emphasis of instruction with reference to comprehension. (The A-V approach will be more effective in improving comprehension for "auditory learners" and those without a sensory preference than for "visual learners"; the mainly visual approach will be more effective in improving the comprehension of "visual learners" than that of "auditory learners" and those with no preferences).

Bursuk makes several assumptions in her rationale. One is that verbal comprehension skills (especially in retarded readers) may be expected to transfer from listening to reading. Another is that listening instruction is an "efficacious approach to utilize for development of thinking skills."

Tenth-grade students were tested on the California Test of Mental Maturity, Form A (nonlanguage section) and the California Reading Test. Students who met initial LD initial screen criteria were selected for the study. STEP Reading and Listening Tests were administered to the entire subject population of 132, and this information was used to subclassify the subjects as to modality preference. After classification, groups of 30 were established and further separated into experimental and control groups differing as to remedial technique used; there was a total of 90 Ss. Tests yielded no significant intergroup differences as to test performance.

After a semester of instruction differing as to emphasis on visual or aural comprehension, all subjects took Form X of the California Reading Test. Both hypotheses were confirmed. Bursuk concluded that the mode of instruction should be consistent with students' preferred learning style. If this is not possible, an integrative, multimodal approach is preferred.

Butts P, Sanders J: *Motivated Reading: A Supervisor's Manual for a Tutorial Reading Program. Part 1: Information on Operating the Program.* Madison, University of Wisconsin, Research and Development Center for Cognitive Learning, 1972 (ED 073-445)

This manual contains information on how to conduct a tutorial reading program for upper elementary and junior high school students who are reading on a second- or third-grade level. Included is a plan for motivating these students using the Stoats "Motivated Learning" reading procedure. Non-professionals can learn the methods involved with only brief training, making it ideal for inner city schools where more individualized tutoring is needed.

Part 1 of the manual presents information on operating the program, including how to arrange instructional schedules, prepare materials, select students, select and train tutors, and supervise the program. Part 2 provides the supervisor's materials and a tutor's guide, sample lesson materials, record sheets, tutor materials, and training materials. These may be duplicated for tutor training and student instruction.

Cole N: School habilitation program for secondary students. Rehabilitation Lit 28: 170–176, 1967

A school habilitation program that attempts to offer a meaningful and purposeful curriculum for students who have neither the incentive nor the ability to participate in the regular secondary school program is described in this paper. The program is coordinated by the special education department and the District Office of Vocational Rehabilitation; the staff consists of master teachers within the secondary schools, school rehabilitation specialists, and vocational adjustment coordinators. Three phases are involved: classroom, laboratory, and placement.

In the classroom phase, students learn the basic skills through a practical and individualized approach. All subjects are presented in relationships that relate to the students' lives and future occupational options. In addition to basic skills, subjects such as leisure time, humanities, and job preview are covered.

The laboratory phase provides a formalized program of work evaluation and adjustment training in laboratories equipped for that purpose. In the domestic laboratory, students are prepared for occupations such as kitchen helper and janitor's assistant. The industrial laboratory concentrates on jobs such as gardener or welding assistant. Instructional materials such as audiovisual equipment, written contracts, and overhead transparencies are furnished by the materials laboratory. In addition, an individualized program of work adjustment is designed for each student in an effort to remediate any deficiencies in employability.

In the placement phase, students are assigned to actual jobs in the community. Each student receives training on the job during his senior high school years on a half-day basis. Even after graduation, further counseling is available to the student as needed.

Throughout the program, parents and students are counseled and extensive work is done with community agencies. Services such as medical and psychiatric evaluations and skilled trade schooling are also available.

Colella HV: Career development center: A modified high school for the handicapped. Teaching Exceptional Children 5: 110–118, 1973

In Nassau County, New York, the Board of Cooperative Educational Services operates one of the nation's few modified high schools for handicapped adolescents. Called the Career Development Center (CDC), the school enrolls 265 students, ages 15–21, who have been labeled brain injured, learning disabled, or emotionally disturbed. All have a history of academic failure, poor school adjustment, and behavioral disorder. The underlying purpose of the CDC is to prepare adolescents to adapt to the environmental stress of daily living. The premise is that deviant behavior is capable of being modified and that through concrete and success-oriented activities students can be motivated toward change. The school offers instruction in performing arts, outdoor education, practical sciences, driver education, horticulture, and technical trades. In contrast to many ongoing special education programs, the center attempts to prepare students to return to the community.

The basic assumption is that these students want success and approval. Therefore, the attitudes and behavior of the staff, not those of the students, are the first to be modified. The environmental circumstances also are altered so that the student will want to change. The student's week is made up of 40 periods of instruction—18 in occupational education, 12 in core subject academics, and 10 in enrichment, which involves a variety of electives; the school day is 6 hours long.

The work experience counselor is the central liaison between industry and the school. He often creates job opportunities where none existed previously and counsels both the student and the employer.

One of the electives available is outdoor education, a 2-day camp experience which has proved to be of great value to the student's growth in making friends, breaking dependencies, developing attitudes of cooperation, and creating feelings of good will that are carried over into the classroom.

The philosophy on testing is that it is important that youngsters prove their value to themselves, not to educators. "Testing should only occur where one needs information that cannot be gained in any other fashion, and where one has an applicable need for such information."

Parent participation is encouraged in group learning experiences which are supervised and guided by a professional staff. The goal of these group sessions is the fostering of meaningful group interaction.

The success of the program may in part be measured by the fact that average daily student attendance has risen considerably. Another benefit of the Career Development Center is that it has fostered an attitude of mutual responsibility for the student between the program and referring school districts.

Crossover assistance to children with handicaps (COACH). Personal communication from Central Dauphin School District, Harrisburg, Pa.

The COACH program is designed to provide academic aid to seventh- and eighth-grade students unable to cope with the scholastic demands of junior high schools. The students included in the program were those identified as low achievers and/or learning disabled. A low achiever was defined as a student achieving one or more grade levels below actual placement. Academic levels were determined by SRA achievement test results. Students who had specific learning disabilities were identified by teachers who were provided a 2-week indepth in-service course in this topic; the actual definition of learning disabled and the screening criteria employed were not stated in the paper.

The experimental program focused on math and social studies. Elementary teachers were selected and trained in theory and methods for working with learning disabled students in these two curriculum areas. Two hallmarks of the program were a philosophy of continuous progress development from the student's own baseline of academic achievement (the unrealistic, and often harmful, standard of performance on grade level was disregarded for these students), and a multimedia instructional approach.

The program's major objectives were that the students: (1) demonstrate less frustration with the secondary environment; (2) demonstrate increased motivation in working with the usual curriculum content; (3) achieve measurably higher scores in basic skills than students in control schools, based on pre- and posttesting using SRA achievement batteries (confined to the math and social studies areas); and (4) function with less disruptive behavior in the junior high classroom.

The program brought about many changes in classroom procedures, including a shift from traditional lecture and/or textbook approaches to small group instruction utilizing a variety of instructional approaches, e.g., audiovisuals, manipulatives, simulations. Learning disabled students were referred to the learning therapist normally assigned to the junior high school, who assisted teachers in coping with the learning problems.

The results of the Central Dauphin School District project were very encouraging. Discipline problems were lessened markedly. Student attitudes toward school improved as perceived by both teachers and parents. Academic gains were registered by a large percentage of the students. The criterion for success was simply a reversal in the trend toward academic deterioration. Therefore, just "holding the line" in math and/or social studies was indicative of positive results; any "gains" were doubly rewarding to the students and project staff. During the project's second year (1973–1974) the number of seventh graders who gained academically in math and social studies was 73 percent and 83 percent, respectively. For eighth graders, 86 percent and 65 percent of the students improved in math and social studies, respectively. In math, 27 percent of the seventh graders and 14 percent of the eighth graders made no gains or lost ground; in social studies, the percentage of students who regressed was 17 at the seventh-grade level and 35 at the eighth-grade level.

de Hirsch K: Two categories of learning difficulties in adolescents. Am J Orthopsychiatry 33: 87–91, 1963

de Hirsch differentiates between two categories of learning difficulties in adolescents. As a group, the adolescents were all underachievers in terms of their intellectual endowment, little interested in school work, and anxious; some were quite hostile.

Despite the overt homogeneity of the group, de Hirsch maintains that they fall into two categories. Group A contains adolescents who have severe psychological disturbances that impede academic success. These students generally have good intellectual potential but are strikingly infantile and passive. Although they may experience little difficulty in the early school grades, their performance begins to deteriorate as they move toward the higher grades. Many in this group are highly articulate and many are avid readers. Nevertheless, they do poorly in all school subjects. "Essentially boys in Group A are passive and infantile individuals with little or no psychic energy to invest." Their lack of ego strength and their physiological immaturity are particularly noteworthy.

Remedial work for this type of student emphasizes achievement of identification with the teacher and finding some area of interest. Much of these youth's learning is fragmented and diffuse. The discrepancy between potential and performance tends to persist; prognosis is not good.

Adolescents in Group B display evidence of a residual language disability; such as higher performance score than verbal score on the WISC, spelling difficulties, and poor quality of written work. "In the main, they are fairly inarticulate youngsters for whom language is not a convenient tool."

Psychologically, the youngsters in Group B have a very low frustration tolerance and can be quite explosive. They often are defiant and openly angry. Their feelings are not repressed or submerged as are those of the boys in Group A.

In summary, the adolescent boys dichotomized by de Hirsch are often viewed as one undifferentiated group by other professionals. However, she contends that a separation is necessary because for Group A individuals academic difficulties stem from ego impairment and severe character disorder, whereas for Group B individuals scholastic dysfunction (based on residual language dysfunction) precedes and precipitates the overt psychological problems. Different instructional treatment programs are indicated.

Deshler D: Learning disability in the high school student as demonstrated in monitoring of self-generated and externally generated errors. (Doctoral dissertation, University of Arizona) Ann Arbor, Michigan, University Microfilm, 1975, No. 75-4135

This study attempted to differentiate between the learning disability adolescent and the non–learning disability adolescent by investigating some characteristics which relate specifically at the high school level. A Bayesian approach to psychometric test data was used in the identification of learning disabilities, as well as a comparison of the performance by students on selected tasks.

Five school-related tasks requiring the monitoring of self-generated and externally generated errors were designed to discover whether a monitoring deficit would be a good indicator of learning disabilities.

Two groups of students (36 in each group) were selected; one group was known to exhibit learning disabilities, the other was "normal." The same tasks were administered to both groups and were scored to determine if the groups could be differentiated on a variety of error measures. The results indicated that: (1) on the creative writing task, significant differences were found between the variances and means on the measures of errors, errors detected, percent errors detected, and nonerrors detected for the learning disability and non–learning disability groups; (2) on the editing task, significant differences were found between the means and variances on the measures of errors detected, percent errors detected, nonerrors detected, and percent errors corrected (for both groups, no significant difference was found on errors corrected); (3) on the yes-no spelling task, a significant difference was found between the two groups in detectability of errors; and (4) on the vocabulary task, a significant difference was found between the two groups on their detecting of errors in vocabulary usage (however, the LD group did better on this task than they did on the spelling tasks).

Analysis of results suggests that these tasks were effective discriminators and that the component disability of monitoring is diagnostic at the high school level. However, these results should be treated as preliminary in nature and suggestive for future research efforts and refinements.

Dillner MH: The effectiveness of a cross-age tutoring design in teaching remedial reading in the secondary schools. (Doctoral dissertation, University of Florida) Ann Arbor, Michigan, University Microfilms, 1971, No. 72-15, 671

A group of senior high school remedial readers was selected to serve as tutors in reading for junior high school students with reading problems. It was hoped that the experience would cause the senior high students to "question preconceived notions about their academic abilities, improve their self-concept, expand their social relationships, develop a more positive attitude toward school, and improve their reading skills." The study was carried out during most of a 1-year school term. The control group consisted of 13 senior high students of comparable ability who had no tutoring responsibilities.

Standardized reading and self-concept tests were given to the experimental and control groups in pre- and posttesting in order to assess growth. The tutoring took place once a week, with the tutors having a training session the day before in order to plan the lesson. A short seminar followed each session in an effort to evaluate and improve the tutoring techniques.

Although the tutors gained in many areas, the only significant differences between the two groups were in reading skills (in poetry comprehension) and in self-concept (autonomy). No significant difference existed in the relationship between reading and self-concept, or between the two groups in the relationship between reading and attitude toward school. But when each group was looked at separately for this factor, the experimental group exhibited a relationship between growth in reading and growth in attitude toward school.

Implications suggested in this dissertation were that the classroom teacher has the main responsibility for the success of the program, but that cross-age tutoring has much applicability for the average classroom.

Dorney W: The effectiveness of reading instruction in the modification of attitudes of adolescent delinquent boys. J Educational Res 60: 438–443, 1967

The study's purpose was to examine to what extent reading instruction mitigates the maladjustment of adolescents who are retarded in reading, and also to evaluate changes in the behavior and attitudes toward authority figures of adolescent delinquent boys after they received reading instruction.

The 37 subjects were males between the ages of 16 and 20 years, born and educated in New York City, with no history of drug addiction, psychosis, alcoholism, or any acute auditory or visual defect or foreign language problem. The subjects' IQ range was 85 through 110 on the Hillside Short Form of the Wechsler-Bellevue Test, and the subjects were all at least 2 years retarded in reading as measured by the California Reading Test.

The 37 boys were divided into 3 groups equated for age, IQ, ethnic background, and reading ability. Group 1 was given 50 sessions of reading instruction, group 2 was given 50 sessions of swimming instruction, and group 3 was given no instruction at all. The results of the experiment were organized according to the effects of the swimming and reading treatments on attitudes toward authority figures, behavior, and reading ability. In changes in attitude, the largest improvement took place in the reading group.

A follow-up study was done on each boy 18 months after the end of the experiment to determine court involvement. Only 2 subjects in the reading group had been involved with the courts. This was the lowest rate of recidivism of the 3 groups.

The author feels that these results emphasize the importance of reading instruction, not only for the agencies that service delinquent youth, but also for school systems in the country that have to program for juvenile offenders.

Drake C, Cavanaugh J: Teaching the high school dyslexic, in Anderson L (ed): *Helping the Adolescent with the Hidden Handicap.* Los Angeles, California Association for Neurologically Handicapped Children, 1970

Drake and Cavanaugh express the belief that effective remedial work begins with a proper and honest diagnosis of the basic problem or problems involved in underachievement. The lumping of all scholastically handicapped students into one group is not an effective way of treating the problem. The subject of this paper is the adolescent dyslexic—the student of normal or high intelligence and sound emotional health who is underachieving in the language arts areas because of late or irregular development of perceptual motor functions. He is often spoken of as having specific language disability or minimal brain dysfunction. Most adolescents in this category are boys, usually from families with patterns of late or poor language development.

Impairments in language acquisition may occur in biologic language, speech, decoding skills, coding, or second languages. This last area seems to encompass between 6 and 10 percent of the total school population and probably represents the largest single group with one identifiable pathology. Within the broad spectrum of language disability children, there are many different behavioral manifestations which should shape the remedial method used for the particular symptoms being expressed (e.g., the "verbals" and the "nonverbals").

Characteristics of dyslexic students who want to succeed in school are discussed. Included are low ego status, paralysis of efforts, supersensitivity to external clues, time panic, ambivalence over intelligence, and dependence. The basic remedial tool for all these areas is success. The student must be able to succeed at some level, no matter how low it might be at the start; he has to reverse all the negative feelings he has about his capabilities and self-worth. Quiet firmness is the most effective mode of teaching since strong negative outbursts are especially difficult for the dyslexic to tolerate. A balanced remedial program should also preclude dependency relationships in order for the student to learn to rely on himself. He must be made aware of the fact that he has intelligence and is not "dumb" as he believes himself to be.

In conclusion, any remedial program for language disability youngsters must consider the following: adequate diagnosis; remediation beginning at the appropriate level; discovery of the real as opposed to the superficial breakthrough point; encompassing of a large number of activities related to total growth; teaching of total language skills, not just reading; a highly structured approach to reading, spelling, and writing; assurance that success occurs at every step along the way; a diversity of "set" involved in all teaching; learned language skills that are practiced until automatization is perfected; correction of auditory and visual problems; and planning in advance for the continuous growth of the student.

Educators, administrators, school boards, and taxpayers must be educated to the job that must be done and the tools that must be used to help these students learn.

Early M: Taking stock: Secondary school reading in the 70's. J Reading 16: 364-373, 1973

This article provides an overview of the "state of the art" of the teaching of reading at the secondary level. Unfortunately, from the author's vantage point, reading instruction has changed very little over the years despite the repeated exhortations of many reading specialists. Reading instruction per se (instruction in reading and study skills) generally still does not extend beyond the eighth grade. High school instruction is highly departmentalized, with teachers who are skilled in teaching reading generally to be found only in the English departments. Reading instruction in the content areas is quite rare, as teachers do not yet acknowledge their responsibility for teaching reading along with their content material.

Early's statement of reading goals for illiterate adolescents is particularly germane to the topic of secondary learning disabilities. The goal, she says, is "to raise them to levels of functional literacy that will help them to cope with the paperwork of our bureaucracy." She also believes that once such students have reached functional literacy levels they should no longer be assigned to reading skills courses or study centers. The best approach to continued reading instruction, particularly for the older adolescent, may be through work study programs where the utility and importance of reading become obvious.

Edgington R: A hard row to hoe. Academic Ther 9: 231–233, 1973–1974

The author is concerned with the difficulties that face the learning disabled teenager who is expected to cope in a regular grade placement. Being a teenager is difficult enough without being crippled by a lack of skills needed to deal with peers, adults, society, and the environment.

College would result in failure for many of these students, and so the educational system should help prepare them for gainful employment. Certain basic skills must be learned by these teenagers, and the schools could help by providing such a curriculum at their own interest level.

Language, mathematics, and social skills are the three areas Edgington feels deserve particular attention. Language skills provide a foundation for other skills and activities. Some objectives in the area of language are cited in the paper, for example: "write consistently and legibly his name, address, phone number, date of birth (and/or age), parent or guardian's name, address, and phone number, as well as those of previous employers."

Arithmetic skills are basic to functioning in society. The learning disabled student should be taught to perform such functions as, "write numerals and common signs, such as decimal point, cent, and dollar signs clearly."

The learning disabled student has a great need to be accepted socially, yet this is often impossible as he has trouble relating to peers and supervisors. Communication is basic to his survival, and the handicapped student must recognize this and do something about it. Lists of verbal and nonverbal goals are given by the author.

Edgington hopes that teachers find her lists of objectives useful in their attempts to help the learning disabled student cope with the world around him.

Evans HM: Remedial reading in secondary schools—still a matter of faith. J Reading 16: 111–114, 1972

One of the most common approaches to the problem of disabled readers in the secondary schools is some form of corrective or remedial reading course. However, the evidence to support the effectiveness of such courses is scanty and often questionable. Two assumptions behind these programs are that a majority of students enrolled will show a significant gain in reading ability, and that such gain will be sustained after the course is over. It is also felt that academic performance will improve as a result of increased reading ability.

Some criticisms of study methods and interpretation of data are discussed. One involves the use of the pretest/posttest study technique, especially when there is no control group. Another concerns the use of mean gains to determine and report the results of special reading instruction.

On the basis of current research, Evans concludes that the majority of student participants are not greatly benefitted by remedial reading programs. Longitudinal studies are rare and their results are discouraging; too often the advantage of the treatment group quickly disappears. Evans concurs with Balow's sentiments that severe reading disability demands long-term treatments, not the short-term and/or intensive efforts to which we are accustomed.

The research suggests two conclusions: (1) there is only questionable support for the beliefs that existing programs are a solution to the problem of the disabled reader, and (2) unless supportive instruction follows remediation, any benefits gained from the program will be lost and will not reflect favorably on the student's past classroom performance.

Faigel HC: The medical needs of neurologically handicapped adolescents. *In* Anderson L (ed): *Helping the Adolescent with the Hidden Handicap.* Los Angeles, California Association for Neurologically Handicapped Children, 1970

Adolescence is an extremely emotional, often difficult time in any youngster's life. School and peer pressures are felt very strongly, and the need to be "like everyone else" makes it painful for the child who is in some way different. The author, a pediatrician, believes that it is most important for a teenager to have a good relationship with his doctor, especially in the area of confidentiality. The physician should view his patient as an adult and should be a good listener if he is to gain the youngster's trust.

Faigel feels that children with neurological handicaps, as represented by a lack of physical and muscular coordination, respond quickly and well to physical therapy. Success in learning fine motor skills may give the youngster the emotional strength to attack other learning as well. The assistance of a specialist in rehabilitative medicine—testing, prescribing therapy, and evaluating progress—is important.

Various drugs are used in the treatment of neurologically handicapped children, including stimulants, tranquilizers, antidepressants, and anticonvulsants. A high-protein diet and a nourishing breakfast are extremely beneficial for optimal functioning. When the individual's emotional problems are severe, therapy should be sought for him and for other family members. Group therapy sessions are often helpful because the youngster is made aware of the fact that many other teenagers also have difficulty in adjusting.

The team approach to the total needs of the neurologically handicapped adolescent and a willingness to experiment and improvise are viewed by the author as important aspects of medical care for these youths.

Feshbach S, Adelman H, Burke E: Empirical evaluation of a program for the remediation of learning disabilities in culturally disadvantaged youth, some issues and data. Los Angeles, University of California at Los Angeles, Department of Psychology, 1967 (ED 034-805)

The Fernald School at UCLA has undertaken a research demonstration and training program concerned with the remediation of learning problems in culturally disadvantaged children. The study described here was designed to evaluate the impact of an intensive, individualized remedial program on the learning skills, aspiration levels, and self-attitudes of culturally disadvantaged children. It also compared their learning problems with those presented by a middle-class population.

The subjects were advantaged and disadvantaged elementary and junior high school students who participated in a 6-week summer remedial program and a full academic year program.

Preliminary data pointed to a number of significant propositions and conclusions: the lower class family places a high value on education; the child and his family value school achievement; disadvantaged youth, especially older boys, manifest considerable anxiety and fear of failure; and what has been regarded as a conflict between the morals of middle-class teachers and lower-class children is really a conflict in manners. The data showed that disadvantaged children with learning problems were responsive to individualized instruction programs; the full-year program group at the junior high school level showed the most improvement.

Frank DF: Are we really meeting their needs? Academic Ther 8:271–275, 1973

In 1972, the Department of Health, Education and Welfare estimated that the limited productivity of educationally handicapped adults is causing this country to lose three billion dollars a year in gross national income. The problem is magnified by many unknowns; in the author's opinion, educational leaders do not know the number of students with specific learning disabilities nor do they know the severity of these disabilities. He feels that what is needed most is a standardized method that will enable us to determine, with a reasonable degree of accuracy, who these youngsters are and what specific disabilities or problems they have.

Since this is a national problem, Frank suggests that the basic diagnostic parameters should be established at the federal level along with the criteria which would ensure that all youngsters are correlated to the same population baseline. The method, materials, and guidelines should be developed and provided by a federal agency to ensure conformity throughout the educational system and should be applied on a mandatory basis.

The establishment of this effort at a federal level will clearly assign one specific organization with the responsibility to identify the total problem, to establish a fact-gathering agency to calculate the magnitude of the problem, and to develop a group of experts and administrators who could guide our legislators in matters pertaining to the problems of learning disabled children. This last point is significant not only at the federal but at the state, county, and municipal levels. Very few elected officials have knowledge about learning disabled children. Financial assistance is being received for less than 2 percent of the children with learning disabilities in contrast to the 35–40 percent afflicted.

Friedman SB: Medical considerations in adolescent underachievement. J S
    Psychol 9:235–240, 1971

Friedman's paper is concerned with the physician as a consultant in cases of academic underachievement in adolescents. His first point is that the pediatrician differs from the neurologist in many important ways. Such factors as diversity in training, background, and professional philosophies, can cause them to arrive at unlike conclusions when evaluating the same case; educators must keep this in mind.

Physicians play an important role in the academic multidisciplinary team, but, according to this paper, they often need guidance from the nonmedical personnel. They are too accustomed to being "team captains" rather than members. The author also believes that pediatricians should have clinical experience in the schools included in their training.

Any physical illness, whether or not it is disabling, will lead the student to problems in school; absence in itself is harmful. The author reports on a study which proved that mothers who are physically disabled or have a high incidence of medical problems tend to keep their children home from school for even minor complaints. Therefore, when a child is often absent his mother's health should also be considered.

The author warns against the careless use of the minimal brain damage diagnosis. He feels that the term itself is not exact enough; it can allude to many disorders. Parents and their children tend not to understand the term and quite often confuse it with something like insanity. The diagnosis will change the child's life; he will probably be overprotected by parents and his self-image will become damaged. "The benefits of remedial and special educational programs must be carefully weighed against some of these undesired side effects."

The author feels that the use of the specialized neurological examination when diagnosing minimal brain damage is questionable. He also feels that the use of the EEG has been overrated: "the main function of the EEG is to rule out the existence of a major unsuspected neurological problem, and not to establish the diagnosis of minimal brain damage." He strongly believes that the use of these devices, as well as the services of the physician, should be studied much more thoroughly.

Getman GN: Visual training as a useful resource. Part I: Is adolescence too late? *In* Anderson L (ed): *Helping the Adolescent with the Hidden Handicap.* Los Angeles, California Association for Neurologically Handicapped Children, 1970

The question presented by Getman is whether or not adolescence is too late to begin visual training. The author feels that it definitely is not, provided that the youngster is amenable to the idea and is willing to cooperate. The author defines vision training as learning how to see what one is looking at, steering and guiding oneself to get to the object or place viewed, and performing the motor action needed to complete the process. He believes that "vision is much more than sight; it is a learned procedure of interpreting what is seen and therefore can benefit from proper training." Vision training without confirmatory motor action, or motor activity without visual judgments of one's location in relation to one's surroundings, will not bring about the desired learning processes.

With a trainee who is willing to work at developing visual and motor skills, there is no age limit to learning. "All they need is the desire, and the proper clinical guidance by those who understand the total dynamics and the developmental role of vision and movement."

Giffin, M: How does he feel? *In* Schloss E (ed): *The Educator's Enigma: The Adolescent with Learning Disabilities.* San Rafael, California, Academic Therapy Publications, 1971

From a psychiatric point of view, a child with a learning disability is structurally damaged—he has an ego deficit. Unlike autonomous ego function in a normal child, the ego deficit manifests itself in the learning disabled child as a deficiency in speech, language, perception, or memory.

Parents and preschool teachers deal with these misperceptions from the beginning. These children do not respond to the nursing experience; they do not respond to the usual kinds of home environment; they are hypersensitive or distractible; and they are often hyperkinetic. These children are damaged intrapsychically by the interactions that necessarily occur out of their frustration, both with themselves and with their parents. They are also damaged by the parental need and society's need to deny the presence of difficulty.

The child is faced with the disabling factors of his handicap, and added to all of this is the impact of adolescence. Giffin views adolescence as a special form of reality. Adolescents are mercurial and variable; these variants of personality are in all adolescents, not just handicapped youngsters.

The author feels that the problem we have with these children is to listen to the confusion of their emotions. Their problems with thought, learning, and behavior are recognized most of the time. Their feelings, however, are often forgotten. This is the area in which we need to move. The sensations, desires, and emotions of children are too often ignored. There is no education, no learning without emotion. There is no child without emotion. The problem is communication. It is necessary to refine our focus to the feelings of the adolescent, whatever his academic skills. It is the author's opinion that every adolescent with a learning disability has a psychiatric problem as well.

Gnospelius AP: Selecting media for learning disabled students. Audio-visual instruction 20:4, 24–25, 1975

This paper describes project OPEN (Optimal Procedures for Evaluational Needs), one of the few Title VI-G secondary programs in the country, is located in East Junior High School, Brockton, Massachusetts. A major goal of the project is to maintain the learning disabled child into the regular classroom. Remediation provided by the resource room as needed.

According to the U.S. Office of Education, a learning disability is, "a disorder in one or more of the basic psychological processes involved in understanding or in using spoken or written language. . . . They include conditions which have been referred to as perceptual handicaps, brain injury, minimal brain dysfunction, dyslexia, developmental aphasia, etc."

In surveying the instructional materials available for learning disabilities, the author found very little for the older LD student; much of the material is diagnostic rather than remedial; there is no single source of secondary materials; and print materials are abundant.

To compensate for these gaps, OPEN employed a media specialist to select and modify existing materials for use with secondary LD students. Also involved in the selection process were classroom teachers (for content analysis) and the learning disabilities specialist (for the remediation analysis). The media specialist was involved with the modality and technical analysis. All materials were selected by group decision, and the materials had to be available in several forms in order to accommodate different learning styles.

A supplemental selection checklist is presented for selecting print, nonprint, and multisensory materials. The criteria are classified under two headings, "essential" and "desirable." If the material fits the objective, meets the criteria, and the price is right, it can be requested for preview. If the teacher is then satisfied, the purchase can be made.

It is felt that when students with learning disabilities are given materials which fit their learning styles, they will be better able to succeed in the classroom.

Gordon S: Reversing a negative self-image. *In* Anderson L (ed): *Helping the Adolescent with the Hidden Handicap*. Los Angeles, California Association for Neurologically Handicapped Children, 1970

In Gordon's view, the existence of a negative self-image is the major stumbling block to the ultimate adjustment and employability of the neurologically handicapped youngster. Major areas of importance in reversing this negative feeling considered in this article include: a reasonably good relationship with one's parents; friends; self-awareness of assets and limitations; a wide range of things to do and interests; savoir faire; and a minimum of functional academic skills.

Gordon feels that most neurologically handicapped children need protection, and that parents should not hesitate to offer it when needed. Parents need to be understanding of their child's difficulties in making friends, learning in a competitive setting, and accepting his own handicap. The emphasis in the home situation should be on guided independence, with an effort made to avoid chronic struggles of will. Overprotection can be very destructive, but so can treating the child as though he were like everyone else. His problems must be faced openly, and efforts made to work around them. Inappropriate or obnoxious behavior should not be reinforced if the youngster is to learn to live in society.

Friends play an important role in improving one's self-image. The author feels that whenever possible, the handicapped child should try to make friends with peers in regular classes or in the neighborhood, rather than limiting his social contacts to other handicapped people. This is best accomplished in well-structured, noncompetitive activities which are not threatening to the child.

Neurologically handicapped youth often seem to lack self-awareness, especially with respect to their impact on others. This is probably due, in part, to their impaired capacity for abstraction. "Thus, direct instruction, guidance, learning by doing, etc., seem to be indicated, rather than expecting the youth to be able to anticipate behavior or profit from previous related experience." Having a thorough knowledge of his handicap and what kinds of situations are best avoided can help prevent unpleasant occurrences with resulting aggressive or embarrassing behavior.

Leisure time activities can be a source of great pleasure and can help in developing positive feeling about one's self. A child who is compulsive or who perseveres can become quite an authority in areas that involve collecting—either tangible things or facts. Any interests should be encouraged and skills developed in those areas. Success in any endeavor can help offset feelings of failure in the classroom.

In the area of knowing the "right thing to do," the author believes these children should be exposed to magazines and books reflecting social mores and styles of dress, as well as being taught manners at home. He feels very strongly that they must be given a comprehensive education in sex and the language associated with it, so that they won't be subjected to ridicule by their peers.

A minimum of academic skills is viewed to be a sixth-grade level in reading and math. Most important in the teaching of neurologically handicapped children is individualizing instruction to suit the needs of each child.

In conclusion, success in life will depend on the individual's attitude about himself to a much greater degree than on the natue of his disability.

Gordon S: Sex education for youth with learning disabilities. *In Progress in Parent Information, Professional Growth and Public Policy:* Proceedings of the Sixth Annual Conference, ACLD, Fort Worth, 1969

Gordon feels that the field of special education is, in general, based on a series of false assumptions, all carefully documented by research. We say that the special child cannot cope with anything abstract, cannot generalize, and has a short attention span. Perhaps this inability to focus on abstractions or generalizations is due to the fact that the child hasn't been taught at the point that he is most receptive.

A handicapped child has areas of adequacy.coexisting with areas of inadequacy. That he has difficulties abstracting doesn't mean that he lacks the ability to abstract. As an adolescent, his most devastating problem may be that he is an isolate—he has no friends.

The handicapped child has to know more about sex than the ordinary child. He has to know it sooner. He has to be able to anticipate what other children will say to him; he must not appear naive. He has enough trouble being handicapped and making friends. He cannot appear naive in this sexual revolution in which we live because almost everything is sex oriented. We tend to protect the handicapped child because of the fear that if we tell the child something about sex too soon, he will act out. There is no evidence that this is true. You cannot harm a child by giving him information. Even pornography is not harmful, according to the author. Children who read pornography and are interested in it are those who have not had a sound sex education at home. The children who are involved in sexual acting out have no way of gratifying their curiosities and have usually grown up in a rigid "moral" home.

The handicapped adolescent who wants to know the meaning of a four-letter word cannot find this information through group interaction. You must tell him what obscenities mean, or let him read what they mean and he will not use them as a weapon.

The author's three rules concerning communication of sexual information are (1) answer all questions frankly, including explanation of obscenities; (2)

communicate that sexual activity is a private matter; and (3) explain that there is no such thing as an abnormal thought, feeling, or impulse. All thoughts are normal. Guilt is the energy for the compulsive repetition of thoughts that are unacceptable to the individual. It is all right to have any possible thought about sex, but it is not necessarily all right to put these thoughts into practice.

Gordon S: The brain injured adolescent. East Orange, New Jersey, New Jersey Association for Brain Injured Children, 1966

Gordon's booklet provides a guide for the parents of learning disabled adolescents. The opening section discusses the characteristics and special needs of the brain injured child. The bulk of the paper is a list of practical suggestions for parents to aid them in understanding and helping their children.

The author has drawn on the questions asked by parents over the years and has come up with 18 topics of discussion, each with specific suggestions. The importance of social experiences and how to arrange appropriate situations, as well as why and how to structure and guide the "world" of the learning disabled are the first two topics.

Other points include: teaching social skills, providing the adolescent with success, leisure time activities, choice of friends, how much television, what about driving a car, is psychotherapy helpful, and the question of sex. Fantasies, coping with repetition, resentment of other children, success in school, reverse psychology, the future, and what to tell the child about his condition are also delineated.

Gow DW: Dyslexic adolescent boys: classroom remediation is not enough. Bull Orton Soc 24:154–163, 1974

The author has worked with dyslexic adolescent boys of above average intelligence, defining above average as over 105 WISC. His functional definition of dyslexia is a condition wherein a student is unable to write, spell, and read as well as he can think.

The language disabilities, along with classroom failure and pressure from parents and teachers, are just more problems added to those inherent in adolescence. The academic morale and self-concept of these dyslexic adolescents are low; their attitude is seldom friendly—previous experience has made them suspicious and hostile.

In addition to their reading disability, these youths are hampered by their inability to translate spoken words into thoughts they can understand. They also suffer from maturational lag, both physical and emotional.

The author warns that unless these children's self-confidence and self-esteem are raised, they will probably wind up in trouble-prone situations. He suggests a highly structured academic environment coupled with an athletic program. He has found a great deal of success in approaching the problems of social confidence with a weekly session called interpersonal relations. The boys meet in large groups of 35 to 40, in which they gain confidence from speaking before the group and from the praise they receive. They devote time to cooperative problem-solving sessions and in the process begin to view themselves as an integral part of the group.

Hagin RA: How do we find him? *In* Schloss E (ed): *The Educator's Enigma: The Adolescent with Learning Disabilities.* San Rafael, California, Academic Therapy Publications, 1971

The syndrome of specific language disability is a discrepancy between expectancy and achievement in the use, comprehension, and written expression of ideas. Adolescents with specific language disability have difficulty with one or more of the language arts. These difficulties occur despite intact senses, adequate intelligence, conventional instruction, and normal motivation. When these children are examined with psychological, neurological, and perceptual tests, the following characteristics are found: lack of neurological organization corresponding to cerebral dominance; visual-motor difficulties; auditory problems; body image problems; tactile figure-background problems.

The author's experience leads her to conclude that careful, individual, clinical diagnosis is necessary to locate and differentiate the child with specific language disability. She suggests observations of the following characteristics: highs and lows in functioning; methods by which the child handles language; handwriting (with particular emphasis on how the child grips the pencil); approaches to reading; spelling methods; difficulties he has had with other kinds of symbols; and spatial abilities. Careful clinical evaluation requires supportive information concerning the child's developmental history, neurological functioning, psychiatric status, psychological and perceptual abilities, and his educational skills.

The author reports on the follow-up of 3 children with specific language disability. At adolescence these children are seen at their most difficult time, for there is an interplay of constitutional factors, developing psychological needs and defenses, and external pressures and supports. Teaching that is founded in careful, multidisciplinary diagnosis is important to the realization of the child's potential abilities.

Hartlage LC: Differential diagnosis of dyslexia, minimal brain damage, and emotional disturbances in children. Psychol School 7:403–406, 1970

The study reported here examines patterns of responses made by children on the WISC, Bender-Gestalt, and Wide Range Achievement Test (WRAT).

Eighty-one children were classified into nonoverlapping categories from the records of 200 cases referred for diagnosis of school difficulties over a 2-year period to a university medical center pediatric neurology clinic. The subjects were 61 boys and 20 girls who were classified into the diagnostic categories of dyslexia, minimal brain damage, or severe emotional problems. The children's ages ranged from 6 years, 9 months to 14 years, 4 months, with IQs ranging from 85 to 133. Almost all of the children were from middle-class homes, had no social or cultural deprivation, and had been exposed to good educational opportunities.

The use of formalized Bender-Gestalt prediction scores seemed to be of little value in the identification of dyslexic children in a mixed sample. Neurological evaluation was also of little value in distinguishing children with dyslexia from those in other diagnostic groups.

A potential instrument for superficial differentiation of the three diagnostic categories appeared to be the WRAT reading discrepancy score. The major diagnostic problem is to distinguish dyslexic children from minimally brain damaged children, the large mean discrepancy differences on WRAT reading scores between these two groups suggests that the test differentiates between these two types of handicapped pupils.

Herbert JR: Specific language disability in secondary schools. Bull Orton Soc, 24:135–140, 1974

The Specific Language Disability program carried on in Prince George County Schools, Maryland, extends from kindergarten through 12th grade. At the junior and senior high levels, the program approximates a resource room model with the specific language disability teachers working with small groups of students for portions of the school day. Students received daily instruction in basic language skills—preferably at the beginning of the school day—with additional basic skills instruction including reading, writing, and spelling. Additionally, the specific language disability teacher helped students with content area work on a tutorial basis.

Evaluation included psychological and neurological examinations with "information derived from a writing sample, a spelling test, an informal reading inventory, and careful study of cumulative records."

The Specific Language disability program at the secondary level was designed for the development of basic skills, the adaptation of curriculum with as little dilution as possible, and the improvement of self-concept.

The remedial approach to language disability began with the letters and sounds of the alphabet. Writing, frequently from dictation, was stressed as such lessons provided "for application of spelling rules, reinforcement of organization and attention to detail, and self-monitoring." Ansara's "reading with a pencil" is another technique that was used. Gillingham and Stillman procedures were applied for instruction of long vowels. Additional teaching strategies for math and content subjects are also presented. The author views these learning disabled students as "learners" and holds appropriate expectations for them.

Herrick MJ: Disabled or disadvantaged: What's the difference? J Special Ed
  7:381–386, 1973

At present, learning disabled and culturally disadvantaged youngsters are viewed as two distinct and separate groups. The culturally disadvantaged are excluded by definition from programs for LD children. The author feels that the two groups are, behaviorally speaking, more alike than different and "that the specifics differentiating these two students were simply degrees of the same behavior."

The difficulties of the LD student are attributed to physical causes, the learning problems of the disadvantaged child are attributed to cultural factors. However, many professionals hold that cultural deprivation (or socioeconomic deprivation) may cause retardation and/or impaired cognitive functioning. "If the cognitive function resides in the central nervous system, then a deprivation-caused deficiency must be considered by the school as a learning disorder, for the organism takes in less information or it takes it in less efficiently and cannot progress according to the norm set up by the school."

Etiological factors, even if they could be pinpointed, are of little value in planning instructional strategies which must reflect the child's current repertoire of skill and achievements. Behaviorally, we cannot distinguish between the two groups at this time, thus we have no basis for excluding the culturally deprived from the category of LD. Every culturally deprived child is not also learning disabled; but many are and the fact of their low socioeconomic status should not prevent them from receiving much needed remedial services. Special education should provide for the deprived child with new forms of compensatory education.

Hogenson DL: Reading failure and juvenile delinquency. Bull Orton Soc
  24:164–169, 1974

To demonstrate that when school failure in reading begins in primary school the result can often be delinquent behavior during adolescence, the author proposes the following hypotheses: (1) continued failure in the most significant educational task challenging the child—reading—is a deeply frustrating experience when permitted to continue for several years, and usually such failure begins before the child develops the ability to think rationally; (2) continued frustration over prolonged periods of time will result in aggressive behavior directed outward toward society (delinquency) or inward toward the self (neurosis); and (3) confined delinquent boys who have failed in reading will have behavioral histories showing more antisocial aggression than confined delinquent boys who were able to read.

Two experimental populations of 48 boys each were randomly selected from two training schools. The data available for each boy included a complete social and behavioral history, including court transcripts and reports of behavior before confinement and while at training school; an individual Wechsler Intelligence Test; a Form K Stanford Achievement Test; a Minnesota Student Attitude Inventory filled out by each boy; a measure of Rokeach's construct dogmatism (Dogmatism Scale); and background information on each boy concerning family, community, economic, and ethnic variables.

The correlations between reading and aggression were 0.33 for one group and 0.40 for the other. A t-test for significance showed that both correlations were significant beyond the 0.05 level. This demonstrates an important correlational between reading underachievement and aggression. The court report proved to be the most reliable measure of aggression across populations. Dogmatic attitudes among the boys were not related to either reading failure or aggression. IQ was found to correlate with reading success. The present study was unable to correlate aggression with age, family size, number of parents in home, rural versus urban environment, socioeconomic status, minority group membership, or religious preference. Only reading failure was found to correlate with aggression in these two groups. IQ was equally related to reading among more or less aggressive boys.

The author recommends adopting the following proposals: (1) increase the size and efficiency of remedial reading programs, especially in primary schools, (2) redesign existing remedial reading programs to meet individual learning needs, (3) when necessary, delay reading instruction until the child is developmentally and cognitively able to understand failure (to at least age 5), (4) continue remedial reading and language programs as long as necessary, even through high school and into adulthood, and (5) if a child is failing in reading, carefully explain to him why; explain that it is not his fault, nor is he dumb, and that reading skill is not the best measure of his worth as a human being.

Huizinga RJ, Smalligan DH: The area learning center—a regional program for school children with learning disabilities. J Learning Disabil 1:502–506, 1968

The Area Learning Center is a Title III project, funded by the U.S. Department of Education, that is implementing a multidisciplined approach in dealing with children who have classroom learning problems. The Center accepts referrals only from the local school system. The referral information includes a school questionnaire filled out by the teacher which describes the child's academic progress, observations by the teacher, and the results of any school testing. Also included is a parent questionnaire dealing with the child's early developmental history, home behavior, the parent–child relationship, and release forms for medical and other special agency information.

When the referral is received, the case is delegated to a Center consultant who than visits the child in school and conducts some preliminary testing. If the consultant feels that enough is known about the child and his environment, an effective program for learning in the classroom is developed with the help of teacher and principal. However, if further diagnostic testing is necessary, the child is scheduled into the Area Learning Center for further assessment. Assessment is possible in four areas: intellectual, perceptual, academic, and personality. The Center's staff is comprised of reading experts, psychologists, and a corps of psychiatric, pediatric, and academic professionals.

After testing and observation are concluded, a conference is held with center personnel and appropriate school personnel. The resulting plan for action (prescription) is a composite of the thinking of all persons involved and is implemented by the school personnel with the continuing assistance of the center consultant.

Some conclusions and observations after the first year of operation are that: (1) of the 620 referrals, 45 percent had been retained during their school experience; (2) 79 percent of referrals were boys; (3) numerous health problems were detected and aided; (4) the interdisciplinary team approach coordinates services of many organizations and avoids duplication of efforts; (5) the majority of children have shown progress after work with the center; (6) the center is well accepted by parents and school personnel; (7) the teacher and principal are becoming more aware of the learning problems of children.

Hurwitz I, Bibace RM, Wolff, PH, Rowbotham B: Neuropsychological function of normal boys, delinquent boys, and boys with learning problems. Percep Mot Skills 35:387–394, 1972

Three groups of boys, 15 in each group, ranging in age from 14 years, 6 months to 15 years, 6 months, were compared in their performance on the Lincoln-Oseretsky Test of Motor Development. The first group consisted of students with learning disabilities with a mean IQ of 112 and coming from the lower middle or middle class. The second group included delinquent boys with a mean IQ of 101 who came from the lower socioeconomic class. The third consisted of normal boys, mean IQ of 116, from the lower middle or middle class.

Results indicated that adolescent boys with learning disabilities and juvenile delinquents were significantly retarded in their motor development when compared to normal boys of the same age. Tasks demanding rhythmical repetition posed greater difficulties than nonrhythmical ones for both clinical groups.

In a second experiment, two groups of 11-year-old boys, 13 in each group, were compared in tests of sequencing skills. One group was composed of delinquent boys having a mean IQ of 96 and from lower socioeconomic levels. The other group was composed of normal boys with a mean IQ of 118 and from middle class backgrounds.

Results indicated that delinquent boys consistently scored lower than normals on tasks of sensorimotor and symbolic sequencing. However, tests of spatial ability did not discriminate between the groups.

The authors feel that the statistical association between learning problems or delinquency and deficits in sequencing skills is suggestive. Neuropsychological disturbances, affecting in particular the child's ability to sequence sensorimotor events and symbolic stimuli, may define one general adaptive function in which the two clinical groups are deficient. This is compatible with the observation that both these groups also demonstrated a significant delay in motor maturity. The possibility is also raised that children with delayed or disturbed neuromuscular development are likely to be identified as delinquents when they grow up in a lower class context, and yet be identified as children with learning disabilities if they come from a middle class environment.

Kline CL: The adolescents with learning problems: How long must they wait? J Learning Disabil 5:262–284, 1972

It is estimated that 8 million children in the United States have severe reading disabilities. The author presents this as a complex problem with social and economic implications. It is his opinion that the existing school system is "irrational, ineffectual, authoritarian, inept, smug, defensive and undereducated."

The findings and recommendations of the Department of Health, Education and Welfare National Advisory Committee on Dyslexia and Related Reading Disorders were published in a booklet entitled "Reading Disorders in the United States." The author presents many of the conclusions and pertinent facts from that study.

There is a wide variety of grouping and characteristics of learning disabilities adapted from the chapter "Therapy of Learning Problems" in the book *Adolescents,* by Sandor, Forand, and Schneers: (1) chronic dyslexics; (2) the mini-effort group; (3) the over-indulged; (4) the can't-lose group; (5) the smart big brother group; (6) the afraid-to-be-curious; (7) the emotionally traumatized; (8) the afraid-to-know; (9) the love-to-be-loved group; (10) the psychiatrically ill. Diagnosis should be made by: standardized oral reading tests (Kline suggests the WRAT), process tests, and evaluation of emotional status and personality development by a psychiatrist or clinical psychologist. Family dynamics should be investigated.

The treatment that Kline recommends is the Orton-Gillingham multisensory method, modified for adolescents, as well as part of the Bywaters program of "therapeutic tutoring" for adolescents.

The author presents eight recommendations from the Report of the Joint Commission on Mental Health of Children that he feels could aid in solving some of the problems in the education system.

Kline emphasizes the importance of prevention and early intervention before the sense of frustration and failure is so deeply embedded and the anger so great that the children can't be reached at all. Finally, he feels that many programs are not researched thoroughly enough before implementation on a large scale (i.e., open classrooms) and that too much money is being wasted.

Kranes JE: Training adolescents with learning disabilities to be teacher aides. In *Management of the Child with Learning Disabilities.* Proceedings of the Fourth Annual Conference, ACLD, New York, 1967

The Education, Training, and Research Program for Adolescent Underachievers sponsored by New York University. The program trains adolescents as teacher aides for nursery school children. As reported by Kranes, the program included 9 adolescents, ages 18 to 20, with IQs from 64 to 95, and with an average academic achievement of fifth grade. The theory behind this program was that "in the setting where the nursery school child must begin to be more highly social, where his intellect unfolds almost from its beginning stages as he learns to solve problems, and where reason and discipline are a way of life, the aids would expand their thinking as they learned to perform and at the same time learned to reconstruct their own lives."

The aids participated in two types of sessions: an individual tutorial session of 1 hour a week which offered them time to discuss the problems that develop in nursery school placements; and a 2-hour a week child study seminar which provided for orientation in the nursery schools as well as specific training. There were usually two weekly written assignments, one bearing directly on the aides' problems and questions about their placements, the other dealing with abstract educational principles.

The aides' teachers reports indicated surprise and pleasure at the level of functioning of these students and the large amount of progress and emotional growth noted, apparently the result of the training program.

Kratoville BL (ed): *Youth in Trouble.* San Rafael, California, Academic Therapy Publications, 1974

This book is the direct result of a symposium in Dallas in the spring of 1974, which brought together experts in the fields of education, medicine, psychology, and juvenile justice. All these professionals were concerned with the problems of juvenile delinquency and its relationship to learning disabilities. There was an overall consensus of opinion that most children who come into conflict with the law, regardless of the infraction, usually have some underlying physiological problem responsible for their antisocial behavior. The failures of teachers, parents, and courts to detect these physical problems, as well as the use of punishment in an attempt to correct the behavior, are greatly responsible for the high (85 percent) recidivism rate in juvenile offenders.

School problems are almost always evident with these youngsters, and unless they are detected, diagnosed, and remediated early, additional severe problems are almost certain to occur. Children who do not fit into the mold or who cannot be reached by the usual methods have a great deal to offer in their unique way. These students must be allowed to develop at their own pace and must not be turned off to life or to their own potential by a society that doesn't quite know what to do with them.

Some of the suggestions that evolved from the symposium are highlighted: informing educators at the secondary level about the link between learning disabilities and juvenile delinquency; establishing alternative schools and programs as soon as possible; instituting training programs for probation officers, social workers, juvenile judges, and related law enforcement agencies so that they are better equipped to identify learning problems in the youngsters they deal with; educating parents to the special needs of their learning disabled children so they can better understand their problems and, hopefully, seek help for them; capturing the interest of PTAs and other child-oriented organizations so that they might focus their attention on the "youth in trouble" syndrome; and forcing community action on the part of school boards and legislators to meet the physical, emotional, educational, and vocational needs of the delinquent population.

Positive action must be taken to begin reversing the many wrongs that have been done to these misunderstood children. We must not allow such valuable lives to be wasted in the future.

Kronick D: Guidelines for parents. *In* Anderson L (ed): *Helping the Adolescent with the Hidden Handicap.* Los Angeles, California Association for Neurologically Handicapped Children, 1970

The author urges parents of minimally brain damaged (MBD) children to adopt a realistic and practical attitude about the present status and future directions of their youngsters. Parents of MBD adolescents must come to terms with the residual deficits of their children and determine or plan how to help them become better, more fully functioning people. Some areas of concern are self-awareness, social ability, grooming, independence, work patterns, maturity, and philosophy of life. It is as essential to devote effort toward increased effectiveness in thse areas of functioning as it is to spend time on academic improvement.

Elementary-level programming for MBD children concentrates on remediation and habilitation of disabilities. At the secondary level, emphasis should shift to strengths and the student's program should be designed to capitalize on strengths or at least on those areas of lesser handicap. A choice will have to be made between vocational and academic training—what proportion of the school day will be devoted to each area. The child should not be committed to an unalterable long-range plan too early in his school career, as this placement may be mistakenly based on an over-or underestimate of the child's abilities. Instead, the author suggests that the child's program be geared to his present abilities and that future employment plans evolve gradually through mid-adolescence. The appropriate secondary school stream for the MBD student must be consistent with the child's intelligence, aptitudes, motivation, and the severity of his handicap—as well as with the adaptability of the secondary school personnel and their willingness to modify their programs to his needs.

This paper, in essence, exhorts parents to help their handicapped children develop into total persons in preparation for adulthood.

Kronick D: *What About Me? The LD Adolescent.* San Rafael, California, Academic Therapy Publications, 1975

The adolescent is an active member of society. He is not limited to the home and classroom as are younger children. Therefore, Kronick believes that a book designed to provide insight and help in understanding this youth must deal with the many types of experiences he might or should encounter. The book is divided into two parts: the first contains eight chapters dealing with the world of the learning disabled adolescent; the second offers several papers designed to provide direction for parents and professionals.

In part one, the author raises questions about the lack of a psychology of learning disabilities. She is concerned with the application of traditional theories to the learning disabled youth; "what happens to a child whose family has led him to understand that it will protect him. From the comfortable knowledge of this protection, he ventures forth, only to learn that his unstable perceptions, poor coordination, errors in judgment, lapses in memory, and inability to deal with some forms of complexity, create for him a hostile and dangerous world." The child enters adolescence and with it a whole new way of life. How will he handle going from class to class, boy-girl relationships, or having many different teachers?

At some point for many learning disabled adolescents, educational alternatives seem to run out; a natural reaction of many parents is to offer their child a permanent refuge in the home. If he accepts, "he and his family will have chosen a living death." What can the parent do to foster healthy emotional growth? Kronick offers some examples and suggestions.

Socialization is an important part of the development of every human being, but how does the learning disabled adolescent fit in; how does he handle it? Can he find a place in the regular social activities of his school? What about school teams, parties, or camps? How does this youth fit in at home or in the community? How should parents handle the daily discipline? What should he be expected to accomplish in school? How should he be handled by the school administration? The author feels that numerous questions exist and she attempts to provide the reader with as many answers as possible.

Part two opens with the concern that many parents have over what will happen to the handicapped child when they are no longer able to take care of him. The author is an attorney as well as a parent and provides practical suggestions for estate planning.

Employers make provisions for hiring the physically handicapped such as the blind or crippled, as well as the mentally retarded. But what about the learning disabled youth who seems all right but cannot deal with jobs requiring normal perceptions and abilities? How can parents and educators prepare this individual for gainful and meaningful employment? What about college? Kronick delineates problems facing this population and some alternative programs which are proving successful.

Other chapters in this volume include: "The Specific LD Adolescent—Who is Responsible for Him"; "Different Points of View," a collection of helpful suggestions given to the author for dealing with her own child's problems; and five-part chapter about recognition, remediation, and restoration.

Landis J, Jones RW, Kennedy LD: Curricular modification for secondary school reading. J Reading 16:374–378, 1973

The article deals with a secondary-level reading program for poor (learning disabled according to the authors) readers. The reading program (developed under Title III funding) was designed to meet both the "subject matter needs and remedial needs of the learning disabled student." The dual responsibility for remedial instruction and for instruction in basic subjects was, in the authors' point of view, an excessive and unrealistic burden for the secondary school reading specialist.

A multisensory learning approach was substituted for the textbook-oriented instructional mode in the content subjects (English I, Mathematics I, and Science I). The content area teachers subsequently had to structure course content in terms of behavioral objectives and prepare appropriate auditory, visual, and/or kinesthetic learning aids and materials to facilitate the student's learning of content and skills.

A basic remedial reading program paralleled the new instructional program in which students, removed from the demands and pressures of the content reading situation, were able to profit from reading instruction in basic skills. The scope of the reading program included instruction in word recognition, comprehension, and study skills.

The project required the services of a reading specialist who, in addition to her regular duties, performed the following tasks that related to and were necessary for the total multisensory instructional approach: (1) wrote behavioral objectives in basic reading skills; (2) developed multisensory teaching aids for teaching basic reading skills; (3) identified high-interest, low-vocabulary materials; (4) worked with regular teachers to coordinate remedial instruction with content area instruction; (5) developed parent counseling procedures; and (6) informally evaluated students' attitudes toward reading.

As a result of their participation, students enrolled in the program passed their academic courses. The authors note that the courses were not "watered down" and differed in method of presentation, not content. Student self-concepts improved; apparently, success in content subjects sparked a renewed interest in and motivation for reading. Interestingly, many of the students in the program were disabled with respect to the reading requirements of their content courses but were able to read, at a considerably higher level and with good comprehension, nonschool and noncontent materials. The authors observed that elementary school techniques turned these kids off and suggested that reading drills should be kept to a minimum while innovative approaches are tried.

In summary, success in content subjectives provided the impetus for remedial reading and for general reading as well.

Lane D, Pollack C, Sher N: Remotivation of disruptive adolescents. J Reading 15:351–354, 1972

At Maimonides Community Health Center in Brooklyn, a demonstration model of a cross-age helping program was instituted. Eight adolescent boys were chosen by their teachers from the eighth and ninth grades on the basis of extreme acting-out behavior on the Burk's Behavior Rating Scale. The boys were of multiethnic backgrounds, and they all met the requirement that they be nontruants. Although they were all reading below grade level, they were trained in the use of the Intersensory Reading Program and assigned to tutor a very poor reading third- or fourth-grade boy who had been referred to the center for learning and behavior problems. Supervised by a college student, they tutored the younger students twice a week on a one-to-one basis for 7 months.

"Rap sessions" were held every other week for the tutors. Behavior modification procedures and modeling techniques were used at these sessions in an effort to improve behavior and heighten the self-image of the adolescents. After adequate rapport was established, discussions and role playing were used to direct changing of maladaptive behavior. Motivational concepts applicable to school achievement were modeled by two psychologists serving as group leaders; they encouraged the students to attempt new styles of behavior.

This was a demonstration study and not subject to rigorous statistical analysis. Before and after mean reading scores on the Metropolitan Achievement Test showed a 14-month reading gain by the younger children, a 19-month reading gain by the tutors.

Evaluation of the adolescents' behavior at the end of the project by the guidance counselors and teachers who had initially rated them showed a significant decrease in disruptive behavior. The adolescents' own evaluations indicated that they had profited from the program; they felt more confident about their own abilities, less angry, and more responsible.

Lane PR: Educational therapy for adolescent nonreaders. Academic Ther 6:155–159, 1970

The article recounts a small-scale remedial reading program for adolescent nonreaders. The author, drawing from the work of Dr. Cecelia Pollack, Director of Learning Rehabilitation Services at Maimonides Medical Center, initiated a remedial reading program in 1969 at the Montauk Junior High School under the auspices of the Maimonides Community Center.

Eleven nonreading seventh- and eighth-grade youngsters participated. All were disadvantaged, and all had repeated a grade at least once. Eight of the eleven exhibited severe behavioral problems in the school.

The Intersensory Reading Method developed by Dr. Pollack and used in this program featured "a gradual progression of phonic skills with strong reinforcements of learning, major use of linguistic work patterns, and a minimizing of contradiction in sounds of letters."

After 4 months, 9 of the boys showed marked improvement in reading. Average reading improvement for the group was 12 months (after 4 months of instruction) with some gains as great as 2 years and 5 months. Only 2 boys did not improve significantly and for them testing revealed severe learning disabilities. Among the 9 who made good progress, 7 had visual-perceptual, visual-motor, or auditory-motor problems.

Behavioral improvement was particularly good: truancy was cut in half; disruptive behavior diminished; and general classroom deportment, attention, and reading ability improved greatly.

Lane P, Miller M: Listening: learning for underachieving adolescents. J Reading 15:488–491, 1972

The authors believe that reading can be improved through listening and that with learning disabled children, reading can actually be taught through listening. Critical reading can be enhanced through training in critical listening.

The authors illustrate this belief in a study of a 14-year-old student who was functioning on a fifth-to sixth-grade level. He spent 1 hour, 4 days a week, for several months with a tutor who read aloud. The child's retention and interest were extremely high and his critical thinking skills improved greatly.

In another situation, a group of learning disabled students were highly motivated by a classroom program in which the teacher read one part of a play aloud to them each day as they followed the reading in their books. They later produced and acted in a play of their choice; this activity became a positive learning experience.

According to the authors, learning disabled children respond well to being read stories and in many cases are able to generalize from these experiences. It is the author's opinion that if a listening program is incorporated into the general curriculum, it will be instrumental in both raising the interest level and increasing the thinking skills of underachieving adolescents.

Lee W: How the public school can help. *In* Anderson L (ed): *Helping the Adolescent with the hidden handicap.* Los Angeles, California Association for Neurologically Handicapped Children, 1970

In this article, Lee presents the idea that programs for learning disability students on the secondary level often don't take into account the fact that many of these students have exceptionally high ability and many have only limited neurological involvement. He points out that: (1) learning depends on the interaction of a number of variables; (2) the best present-day techniques for diagnosing neurological difficulties are still inadequate; and (3) for secondary students, the original block in learning development has been overlaid with a great number of complicating difficulties and adjustments in the school setting.

Too many school programs based on controlling students' behavior rather than on providing for individual needs inhibit motivation and do not allow for the fulfillment of students' basic social needs. For a school program to be of maximum benefit, Lee feels that it must be based on a positive philosophy of how students can best help themselves to achieve their own goals.

The objectives of a program for the educationally handicapped must be stated in specific terms in order to allow for evaluation and improvement based on data feedback. Objectives should also be related to those of the school system, be realistic, be applicable to all academic levels, and be within the professional scope of the staff involved. The special education staff should be able to reach, as well as have an impact on, the total enrollment of the program. A statement of objectives represents a value judgment, and this judgment should be based on a well-developed program philosophy.

Some pitfalls to be avoided in developing a program, Lee states, are focusing on the past instead of on the present and future, focusing on failure instead of on success, and focusing on the needs of the system instead of on those of the students.

Lee believes that the student should be an active partner with both his teacher and counselor in the development of goals for himself, and these goals should be based on present abilities and an analysis of individual needs. The program should be structured so that a student cannot fail. If a grading system is adopted, only A, B, or Incomplete should be used. Critical to such a program is an emphasis on positive reinforcement. Punishment has no place in a learning disabilities curriculum. The element of curiosity is a strong motivating factor and must be considered when developing a program; imagination and innovation will turn the student back on to education.

Parent involvement is another important factor to be included. Parent counseling programs can be effective in establishing early parent-school contact and liaison, providing parents with important information related to their child's learning and development, and helping parents to understand themselves.

Since much ambiguity is often involved in a special education program, teachers should learn to expect it; they also need a high degree of social sensitivity, behavioral flexibility, and well-developed communication skills. It would also be helpful if they are innovative and creative. A need exists for well-organized and well-developed training programs for teachers of secondary special education programs, and, hopefully these will be offered by more colleges in the near future.

Concluding, Lee feels that evaluation is an important part of developing a program. The planning of this evaluation should be initiated with the establishment of the program and should detail specific goals that can be measured and analyzed by appropriate criteria. Only in this way can the special education program in a school improve and grow. Only then will the needs of its students be met.

Lehtinen-Rogan LE: How do we teach him?. *In* Schloss E (ed): *The Educator's Enigma: The Adolescent with Learning Disabilities.* San Rafael, California, Academic Therapy Publications, 1971

Children with special learning disabilities—perceptually handicapped children—can't achieve well without special help and understanding. The basis for their poor development is not always clear. According to the author, it may be related to "immaturity," because poor maturation of the central nervous system produces a lag in the development of some abilities. It may be the result of minimal brain damage occurring early in the child's life, and which may not have reduced the child's intelligence significantly but interferes with its expression. It may be the result of a genetic factor.

By the time a child with learning disabilities related to minimal brain dysfunction reaches the junior high school or high school level, many of the more obvious distinguishing features he may have had as a younger child have become less noticeable, if not less troublesome. This is due to the combined effect of physiological maturation, helping his central nervous system "catch up" somewhat, and to the learning that has occurred about the kinds of behaviors that are acceptable as well as about various compensations he may need to make in order to get along.

The author describes the most common characteristics of perceptually handicapped children: distractibility, inability to sustain attention, breaks in continuity of thought, poor feedback, overlooking or not noticing, poor organization, difficulty in selecting, lack of resourcefulness, and deficient memory.

Lehtinen-Rogan presents a series of suggestions for teachers of children with learning disabilities which emphasizes the importance of a humanistic atmosphere in the schools.

Lincoln Community High School, Illinois: Individualized multisensory approach to learning. Report from a Title III ESEA Project, 1972 (ED 064-835)

The project described was designed to meet the needs of potential high school dropouts exhibiting learning disorders. A multisensory approach to learning was employed in an effort to help these students acquire necessary levels of competence in English, mathematics, and science. It was hoped that success in these academic areas would encourage these students to continue in school and complete a vocationally relevant curriculum.

A variety of audio, visual, and kinesthetic instructional modalities were used in an attempt to make learning more meaningful and less frustrating for the learning disabled youngsters. The multisensory approach was based on the General Model of Instruction, which is a procedural guide for designing and conducting instruction, and on an Instructional Management Strategy, which includes procedures for large group instruction, small group instruction, laboratory instruction, and independent study.

Program source guides, explained in the paper, replaced textbooks and contained the basic information required for each course. They included instructional objectives, proficiency pretests, learning activities, self-tests, formative evaluation, and questing activities.

The role and responsibilities of the project teacher are discussed in the report and some sample forms are included. The reading, English, science, and math programs are also described. The program is evaluated in great detail, and the procedure used is also given.

MacIlvaine M, Cooper D: Some stories of real people, in Anderson L (ed): *Helping the Adolescent with the Hidden Handicap*. Los Angeles, California Association for Neurologically Handicapped Children, 1970

This chapter presents 7 case studies of people with various learning disabilities who overcame them and reached some degree of success. Several have completed college, one is a well-known writer, another a well-known actress. Several have dedicated their lives to helping children with neurological handicaps, and all have been gainfully employed. The disabilities covered include language disorders, motor problems, problems in visual perception and eye-hand coordination, dyslexia, visual and auditory perception problems, accidental brain injury, and impaired social perception.

In each case the problem, its diagnosis, and the compensatory measures taken are briefly described. The thread that holds these stories together is the fact that failure was not accepted by the parents, the professionals, or the handicapped persons themselves.

Maietta DF: The role of cognitive regulators in learning disabled teenagers. Academic Ther 5:177–186, 1970

The purpose of Maietta's paper is to acquaint teachers of learning disabled teenagers with the cognitive regulators (sensing mechanisms) involved in the learning process. It stresses the role of cognitive regulators as the bridge between cognitive styles of learning and the strategies required of teachers when these regulators are not functioning adequately. Youngsters with learning disabilities exhibit a dysfunction in one or more of the basic psychological processes involved in understanding or using spoken or written language. These may be problems of listening, thinking, talking, reading, writing, spelling, or doing arithmetic.

The major cognitive regulators involve focal attention, breadth of scanning, extensiveness of equivalence range, and leveling-sharpening. The two major tools for assessing their efficiency at the present time are observation of pupil performance and the use of standardized tests, notably the Detroit Tests of Learning Aptitude. Dysfunctions may be seen in pupil behavior in visual, auditory, kinesthetic, or tactile sensory inputs or in any combination of these sensory-motor stimuli. Some behaviors that reflect dysfunction of cognitive regulators are described.

In conclusion, Maietta contends that teachers should become more knowledgeable in this area and more perceptive in their observations. This will improve their effectiveness in selecting the appropriate strategy or learning task for each learning disabled student they encounter.

Maine HG: An experimental junior high school program. In *Successful Programming: Many Points of View.* Proceedings of the Fifth Annual Conference, ACLD, Boston, 1968

This paper considers the question of whether or not a child with learning disabilities can be helped when he has reached junior high school. Such a child has been promoted through the elementary grades even though he has been recognized as an underachiever.

The junior high school program described was initiated in New York in 1967. It involved a group approach to learning, based on many techniques used in the Orton-Gillingham method: a multisensory approach. During every school day, five special classes (four English, one math) were conducted, usually replacing the regular classes in those subjects; 12 to 15 students were seen each hour. Teachers made regular use of the sound pack (phonograms) and the booklet "A Guide to Teaching Phonics." Kinesthetic trace boards were designed for every desk.

The project used control and experimental groups. All the students initially received selected portions of the Purdue Perceptual Motor Survey, but only the students in two of the English classes received perceptual-motor training; those in the mathematics class also received perceptual-motor training but had no parallel control group due to program limitations. All experimental groups received 1 hour per week of calisthenics and trampoline exercises designed especially for the program. Emphasis was on improvement of overall body coordination, rhythm, and balance.

Students chosen for the special classes were achieving well below suspected potential in either reading or math. Spelling test scores and written Stanford Word Meaning grade scores were at least 2 years below grade level. Many students had varying degrees of neurological deficits. Participation was voluntary and parental approval was required. The only candidates eliminated were those whose emotional adjustment was a factor.

At the time this paper is written, the program has not been in effect long enough to evaluate it, other than to point out that no student has dropped out, even though they are all free to do so. Expansion of the program is planned and a senior high project is being developed as well.

Mauser AJ: Learning disabilities and delinquent youth.   Academic Ther 9:389–402, 1974

Learning disabilities and juvenile delinquency are certainly not synonymous terms, but they do seem to overlap. The incidence of learning disabilities in juvenile delinquents (JD) is higher than that among the nondelinquent population, yet the nature of this relationship is neither clear nor conclusive.

Learning disabled and juvenile delinquent youths share many common characteristics, including negative self-concept and a low frustration tolerance. Both learning disabilities and juvenile delinquency are more prevalent among boys; directional orientation problems are common to both populations; both LD and JD youths evidence a greater than normal occurrence of minimal brain dysfunction; the mean intelligence level reported is similar for both groups; school problems begin in the early years of school for LD and JD youths. Learning disabilities and juvenile delinquency cannot be attributed to a single cause; the etiology is quite complex for both and neither condition will respond to a single mode of treatment. Both learning disabled youths and juvenile delinquents lack positive personality characteristics.

The author discusses treatment programs, the school situation, the teacher's role, and guidelines for treatment. He concludes that some delinquency might be prevented if schools could identify students with learning disabilities and serious malformations of character and personality at an early age and deal with them effectively. In any event, "the delinquent child with a learning disability presents . . . a formidable challenge" that must be met.

McClelland J: Adolescents: it's never too late to learn. Bull Orton Soc 24:141–153, 1974

McClelland objects to a widely held conviction among educators that reading and spelling problems that persist into the adolescent years are unalterable and hopeless. She points out that many of these handicapped students remain in school, despite poor performance and continuous frustration, until they "graduate," posing serious management and behavioral problems along the way. Deterioration of behavior is likely to accompany continuing school failure. "However, some of these students refuse to 'go quietly' and cause a good deal of trouble along the way. They change from eager-to-please, cooperative young children, to frustrated, don't-give-a-damn adolescents."

Specific language disabilities are evaluated and diagnosed by inspection of past records (learning problems start early and persist), writing samples (particularly important), and reading (oral and silent) and speaking ability. From an inspection of a student's writing, the teacher can gain insight into spelling and grammar, as well as conceptual difficulties.

Various teaching methods especially suitable for the type of student discussed here are detailed. McClelland's conclusion stresses that ". . . success with these students will depend upon our skill as teachers."

McCoy LE: Braille: a language for severe dyslexics. J Learning Disabil 8:288–292, 1975

In this article, braille is suggested as an alternative language for students who are severely learning disabled. The case of Roslyn, a 15-year-old girl who could neither read nor write, is presented. Although she had a superior IQ, her reading and writing ability could not be improved beyond the second-grade level.

Roslyn's problems are demonstrated by the following: "maximum auditory memory of four digits; poor visual digit memory; hazy time concept; continued reversals of letters and numbers beyond age eight; confusion of right-left, east-west; poor fine motor coordination; EEG-borderline brain damage of very questionable significance; poor hand-eye coordination; low WISC Verbal scores; quiet-condition-below 50th percentile on the Auditory Discrimination test; noise-condition-above 70th percentile; and mixed hand and eye dominance."

Within 4 months of starting the braille program, Roslyn had exceeded her highest previous reading achievement and was beginning fourth grade studies. Although there were still problems, for the first time in her frustration-filled experience with education, Roslyn was making progress. This suggests an alternative method of instruction in communication for severe dyslexics.

McDonnell K: Bridging the achievement gap in negative learning adolescents. *In* Arena J (ed): *The Child with Learning Disabilities: His Right to Learn.* Proceedings of the Eighth Annual Conference, ACLD, Chicago, 1971

This paper describes a program for learning disability students, many of whom had a history of behavioral problems, at Hopkins Junior High School, San Jose, California. The study involved 25 children (21 boys and 4 girls), ages 12 to 16, who attended the clinic at Hopkins for 1 to 3 hours a day. They were selected by school psychologists from local junior and senior high schools. The staff consisted of 2 full-time certified teachers.

Initially, the student and his parents were interviewed and the program explained to them. Then the child was evaluated, his learning problems explored, and an individualized program of remediation established for him. He was encouraged to evaluate his own performance and discouraged from feeling sorry for himself. Emphasis was placed on developing a sense of humor. Group discussion of problems was employed and free movement within the classroom was permitted.

A point system was used to reward students for both work performed and acceptable behavior patterns. Each point was equal to 1 minute of free time, redeemable at the end of the week. This time might be spent in playing a game or getting some individualized help on a class project or test. All children were encouraged to help each other.

At the end of the 7-month study, gains were seen in the academic levels of the students as well as in their motivation, willingness to try, study habits, behavior, and ability to get along with other children. This improvement carried over into their performance in regular school classes. Perhaps the greatest gain for the students was their enhanced self-image and the reversal of a negative learning cycle.

McDonnell MK: The comparative effects of teacher reinforcement of self-esteem and of academic achievement on affective variables and achievement in learning disabled children. (Doctoral dissertation, University of Southern California) Ann Arbor, Michigan: University Microfilms, 1975, No. 75-25, 541

McDonnell's study investigated whether improvement in self-concept, academic achievement, school-related behavior, and attitude toward school were associated with teacher's reinforcement for desirable, affective, person-oriented behavior or cognitive task-oriented performance.

Subjects were 39 students, 10 to 17 years old. They were divided into eight groups. In four of the groups reinforcement was given for affective improvement (treatment A), and in the other four groups it was given for cognitive achievement (treatment B). Lessons were designed to ensure that the only difference between groups was due to treatment rather than to assignments.

Measures used were the Coopersmith Self-esteem Inventory (SEI), Peabody Individual Achievement Test (PIAT), Coopersmith's Behavior Rating Form (BRF), and Burks' School Attitude Survey (SAS). Four groups were pooled as one replication and four groups as another in order to assess interaction within and among groups.

The findings indicated that: (1) "there was no difference in posttest or change scores on the SEI among the self-concept ratings of children who received treatment A and B; (2) the PIAT showed no difference between groups in total achievement; (3) treatment B children reported more positive and negative attitudes on the SAS, yielding inconclusive results; and (4) treatment B children, reinforced cognitively, rated higher in posttest on observed esteem behavior, while both groups had positive scores."

Findings did not support the basic hypothesis that general improvement of performance would result from reinforcement of self-esteem, rather than from impersonal reinforcement of only cognitive achievement. On the contrary, in this study reinforcement for academic achievement was somewhat more productive for learning disabled children than was reinforcement for self-concept.

Miller WH, Windhauser E: Reading disability: tendency toward delinquency? Clearinghouse 46:183-186, 1971

The authors report a study of the relationship between reading disability and delinquency in secondary students. They point out that in many studies on the subject, a positive correlation between the two often exists. Both groups also share certain personality traits including impulsivity, lack of emotional stability, hostility, suspicion, low frustration tolerance, and a negative self-concept. The authors postulate that when a delinquent-prone youngster is unable to learn to read successfully, he may become delinquent as a result of failure and frustration. He needs to succeed in an area where reading is not a factor, and this may cause him to commit illegal acts.

In their opinion, "probably school failure is more highly correlated with delinquency than is any other condition such as poverty or a broken home." Therefore, it is most important for the schools to be aware of how much they influence a student's life; emotional satisfaction should be provided by ensuring successful learning experiences. Good developmental reading instruction must be given in the elementary school, and adequate remedial reading instruction must be available if it is needed later on. This can be one solution to the problem of helping the delinquent student achieve a satisfactory adjustment and get back on the right track.

Minskoff JG: Learning disabled children at the secondary level: educational programming in perspective. *In* Arena J (ed): *The Child with Learning Disabilities: His Right to Learn.* Proceedings of the Eighth Annual Conference, ACLD, Chicago, 1971

Traditionally, special education has focused on the middle range of children with learning disabilities. When these children go on to junior or senior high school, special education services are often discontinued or the children are channeled into inappropriate classes. Minskoff believes that we must create specific programs for learning disabled children at the secondary level. He suggests three curricula that might benefit many children with learning disabilities.

The first curriculum is called the Sheltered Workshop Approach. This would benefit children who are severely learning disabled and emotionally disturbed and/or those who have a severe disability in social functioning. These two types of children need a highly structured, but more simplified and less stressful environment. Training in social learning that is related to a job and general functioning in the adult world would be given, as well as training for specific types of jobs.

The second curriculum is Vocational Education. Children receiving training in this group are of average intelligence and do not have potential for college. These students do not have social problems. However, they might have learning disabilities in perceptual or academic areas. The essence of this curriculum is to fit each child's learning characteristics to specific types of jobs and functions; the child would be trained for jobs that interest him and that would use his strengths and aptitudes.

The third curriculum is Precollege. These children would be intellectually superior, yet, having learning disabilities. The curriculum is the regular precollege course with areas of weakness considered and circumvented.

To determine which curriculum fits each child, one must determine a child's pattern of strengths and weaknesses in such areas as social integration, language, reading, problem solving, perception, motor skills, and arithmetic.

There may not be time to remediate a secondary school child's learning disability and build the necessary skills and knowledge he needs to function after he leaves school. The author, therefore, recommends that when faced with the choice of concentrating on remediation of learning disabilities or on direct input of knowledge through intact areas, the educator should choose the latter as the major point of emphasis in a secondary curriculum.

Mordock JB, Novik E, Terrill PA: The Bender-Gestalt test in differential diagnosis of adolescents with learning difficulties. J School Psychol 7:11-14, 1968-1969

The investigation was designed to study the effectiveness of the Haine and Koppitz scoring systems in differentiating adolescents with demonstrated central nervous system impairment from those without such impairment. In addition to an analysis of Bender-Gestalt (B-G) scores alone, the authors examined their use in combination with intelligence measures since patients with right cerebral hemispheric lesions often score lower on performance than on verbal measures of intelligence.

Eighty-four adolescent subjects were selected from a suburban residential treatment center. All were achieving well below age expectation. Twenty-five had been diagnosed by physicians as demonstrating CNS impairment (mean age 14.33, SD 2.22). For 59 subjects (mean age 14.94, SD 2.30), medical and psychiatric examinations failed to disclose evidence even suggestive of encephalopathy.

Results of the data show that the significant differences between the scores of the CNS-impaired and psychiatric groups indicate that both scoring systems discriminate between the two clinical groups. Plotting the distribution of scores, however, demonstrated that neither scoring system is of much value in individual prediction. The authors feel that these results suggest that the application of either the Haine or Koppitz scoring systems to Bender-Gestalt performance does not appear worthwhile when evaluating adolescents with learning problems. It is suggested that the B-G be deleted from the school psychologist's diagnostic tests when attempting to make differential diagnoses of adolescents who resemble those in the present sample.

Muehl S, Forell ER: A follow-up study of disabled readers: variables related to high school reading performance. Reading Res Q 9:110–123, 1973

The purpose of this follow-up study was to investigate the high school reading performance of a group of subjects originally diagnosed as disabled readers and to relate this performance to selected variables obtained at the time of diagnosis: EEG classification, IQ, chronological age (CA), and parental background. An additional purpose was to determine the effects, if any, of varying amounts of clinic instruction on reading performance after diagnosis.

At the time of diagnosis, the 43 subjects in the follow-up group were about three grades retarded. The average grade placement at diagnosis was fifth; the average grade placement at follow-up was tenth.

Results showed that: (1) poor readers in elementary and junior high school, as a group, continued to be poor readers in high school 5 years after diagnosis; (2) there was no relationship between EEG classifications at diagnosis and high school reading, although a consistent trend favoring the reading performance of the abnormal-other EEG group compared to the abnormal positive-spike and normal EEG group was observed at both testing periods; (3) WISC verbal performance score and chronological age at diagnosis were significantly and independently related to high school reading. In relation to the below average reading performance at follow-up, the variation in WISC verbal IQ obtained at diagnosis not only significantly correlated with later reading performance, but in addition, the verbal IQ score range better predicted the below-average range in which the reading scores fell than did the performance IQ.

Results also indicated that early diagnosis, regardless of amount of subsequent clinic instruction, was associated with better reading performance at follow-up.

Mulligan W: A study of dyslexia and delinquency. Academic Ther 4: 177–187, 1969

This author is a probation officer with the Special Supervision Unit of the Sonoma County Probation Department, which unit instituted the screening of youngsters referred for delinquency in order to explore the possibility of dyslexia. Screening was begun because of concern about the apparent high correlation between delinquency and dyslexia (described as a defect of language: talking, reading, writing, spelling, speech).

In the spring of 1968, sixty juveniles were screened for chronological age, grade placement, and reading level. Results indicated that 10 were reading at or above grade level, 11 had no record available, and the rest were reading below grade level. Subjects ranged from the seventh to the twelfth grades, and from 13 to 17 years of age. Of the 49 subjects for whom there were data, 10 to 20 percent were reading at grade level and 80 percent were reading below grade level (inadequate readers). Reading levels were reported grossly as yearly (sixth, seventh, eighth, etc.) levels.

The screening battery included the following assessment devices: PPVT for IQ, WRAT for reading levels, gross and fine motor coordination, cerebral dominance, visual and audio discrimination, directional confusion, draw-a-man (himself), number recall, and rhythm sequence and retention test.

Preliminary screening revealed a large (significant) number of students who may have had learning disabilities—especially among those referred for delinquent tendencies such as truancy, running away, or acting-out behavior in the classroom or at home.

Nolen PA, Kunzelmann HP, Haring NG: Behavioral modification in a junior high learning disabilities classroom. Except Child 34: 163–168, 1967

This study was conducted at the University of Washington Experimental Education Unit, which was organized to provide for the study, assessment, and remediation of the educationally retarded. Because the Experimental Education Unit has diverse research responsibilities and because it provides services for teacher training as well as services for exceptional children, the behavioral deviances of children involved span a wider range than is normally found within the special education classrooms.

The data reported here were taken from the junior high school classroom during its first year of operation. Subjects were 8 students, between 12 and 16 years of age, admitted to the unit on the basis of having serious learning and behavior disorders. Individual programs were arranged for each child in the Unit's experimental classroom.

Although the stimulus program (an attempt to define and arrange academic responses) played an important role in the organization of an operant classroom, reinforcement contingencies were the major concern. Two principles guided the exploration of reinforcement contingencies in the unit's classrooms: (1) that "high probability behavior," which occurs at a high rate before educational or clinical intervention, consists of those things the student most often chooses to do, providing a source for "natural" consequences for the manipulation and acceleration of low probability behavior; and (2) that both high probability behavior and any other consequences assumed to be "secondary reinforcers" were ultimately acceptable in a traditionally organized classroom.

In order to determine the preferred "natural" consequences of high-strength behavior among a sample of junior high school learning-disabled students, teachers kept records of the students' selections from amongst an array of reinforcement options. The junior high students' preference for "traditional" reinforcers, e.g., handicrafts, typing, woodworking, organized games, and science units, surprised their teachers. Application of functional behavioral analysis produced impressive acceleration in response rate for many of the LD adolescent subjects and improved behavior outside the classroom. These gains were maintained in regular classrooms.

Page W: The disabled learner learns. *In* Anderson L (ed): *Helping the Adolescent with the Hidden Handicap.* Los Angeles, California Association for Neurologically Handicapped Children, 1970

A junior high school program for learning disabled students conducted by the Central Midwestern Regional Education Laboratory is discussed in this paper. The planners of the program felt that: (1) the child should be removed from the regular classroom, (2) a basis for success in academic learning had to be provided, and (3) the child's perceptual and language deficits had to be remediated.

Students were selected from the recommendations of their sixth-grade teachers or because they scored a year or more below grade level on the reading and arithmetic sections of the Iowa Test of Basic Skills. An elaborate screening and testing program proved to be of no value to the teacher in the actual operation of the classroom.

The primary purpose of the project was to establish a comprehensive remedial and developmental program to enable seventh and eighth graders to profit more fully from their junior high school learning experiences. One of the first steps undertaken was the strengthening of the student's self-image through individualized prescriptive teaching, in which responsibility for learning was shifted to the child. A perceptual training laboratory was provided to investigate self-learning and practical experience.

Three types of materials were originated and adapted: remedial perceptual materials, high-interest materials for low-level activities, and materials for the regular classroom designed to increase the perceptual abilities of all pupils.

Another objective was to effect attitudinal changes toward disabled learners among teachers, administrators, pupils, parents, and the public. It was believed that children will always choose positive rather than negative goals for themselves, and the teachers concentrated on these goals. It was also felt that there are certain skills and knowledge essential to each child, and it must be the objective of the teacher to teach all of this material, to all of the students, with 100-percent proficiency.

The teacher was to establish a tutorial relationship with each child based on the child's understanding of his goals. The child must be helped to determine a goal that is worthwhile for him and conforms with the school's goals. It is important that the teacher be sensitive to the student's needs and tolerant of behavior, as well as flexible in approach to and use of materials.

Two hours of each school day were used for physical education, music, art, industrial arts, and homemaking. The remaining 4 hours were devoted to academic subjects; the length of time spent on each depended on each child's needs. The classroom was self-contained and partitioned into sections. Two copies of as many kinds of learning devices as possible were kept in the classroom.

Children made their own worksheets and tests. Once they accepted the philosophy that the purpose of the school is to learn—not to impress the teacher or get a good grade—they sought help from whatever source was most efficient and convenient. Children also became tutors for lower-grade students.

An analysis of the program, conducted by a research team, indicated that this type of learning experience proved to be beneficial to the students involved. The author feels strongly that the junior high school years are an important time for students with learning problems, and special education at this point in their lives is critical for future academic success.

Page WR: Individualizing instructions for adolescents with learning disabilities. *In* Arena J (ed): *Meeting the Total Needs of Learning Disabled Children: A Forward Look.* Proceedings of the Seventh Annual Conference, ACLD, Philadelphia, 1970

The Kennedy Child Study Center in Nashville, Tennessee, was involved in a research project known as Project ENABLE. The remedial procedure found to be most beneficial for adolescents with learning disabilities in this project was a tutoring program in which the disabled learner became the tutor rather than the tutored. The role reversal gave the tutor some genuine prestige and perspective. It helped show the child that learning takes place when one determines the appropriate steps that must be taken, then is willing to go through those steps and get help when needed.

The tutoring did not have to be in the student's area of weakness or at the specific level at which he was deficient. It could range from helping a first grader learn to tie his shoes to teaching actual concepts. The student was trained to prepare lesson plans and organize his materials. An especially practical remedial procedure was having the children make their own materials, often upgrading or adapting materials designed for lower grades to the junior high level. First- and second-grade activity books often were used for ideas. Some students made up plays and skits; others created over-size rulers, thermometers, and charts as classroom aids.

In the author's view, the most valuable aspects of the project were that the pupils became involved in active, creative, and cooperative roles, and that the teacher was required to explain the purpose of each activity so that the child was able to teach it to others.

Page WR, Prentice JJ, Thomas DN: Program development at the junior-high school level, in Arena J (ed): *Management of the Child with Learning Disabilities: An Interdisciplinary Challenge.* Proceedings of the Fourth Annual Conference, ACLD, New York, 1967

An experimental program was established at Brittany Junior High School, University City, Missouri, in 1966 in order to deal more effectively with underachieving students with severe perceptual deficiencies. It was hoped that the program would provide remediation for these perceptual problems and restructure the school experience in an effort to provide a pattern of success. At the time, no studies could be found which dealt with underachievers at the junior high level, so information on learning problems at the elementary level was evaluated, and the findings were extended upward.

Screening of students included administration of the California Achievement Test, the Henmon-Nelson Intelligence Test, the Peabody Picture Vocabulary Test, the Detroit Tests of Learning Aptitude, and the Wide Range Achievement Test. In addition, a draw-a-person test, an autobiography, and an incomplete sentence test were included to measure self-esteem and attitudes toward school, family, peer group, etc. Teacher evaluations were also considered in the selection process.

The experimental group finally chosen consisted of 30 students (18 boys and 12 girls) representing the lowest achievers having the highest incidence of perceptual deficits on the test battery. They were removed from their regular classes (and the competition and frustration which accompanied attendance in them). A tutoring program was instituted in which the learning disability students became tutors to younger children. The youngsters devised many of their own teaching materials and each received much needed individual attention.

Areas in which specific procedures were developed were: open communication between student and teacher in gripe sessions, improved techniques for devising individualized instruction, effective parent involvement, and increased student responsibility for each other's learning and success. It was found that students were greatly motivated to learn due to the tutorial experience and to the individualized instruction they received.

Pearl S: Description of a secondary SLD teacher-training program and its clientele. *In* Arena J (ed): *The Child with Learning Disabilities: His Right to Learn.* Proceedings of the Eighth Annual Conference, ACLD, Chicago, 1971

This report describes the Educational Professional Development Act, a federally funded 9-month program designed to train 20 people with bachelor's degrees to become secondary learning disabilities (SLD) teachers and to attempt successful intervention with secondary students who displayed serious learning difficulties. The project was sponsored jointly by the St. Paul public schools, the University of Minnesota, and the Minnesota Department of Public Instruction.

The training received during the first half of the program included lectures, sensitization experiences, demonstrations, field trips, simulated tutorial experiences, direct instruction with university professors in remedial academics, curriculum preparation, feedback sessions with supervisors, and graduate courses at the university.

During the second half of the project, the trainees were sent in teams of 2, 3, and 4 to eight secondary schools which serviced 285 secondary learning disabilities students. The schools were a mixture of inner city, fringe area, middle class, and upper middle class schools. The trainees participated in screening students in the lowest 10 percent of the class in reading comprehension or vocabulary, examining achievement test scores, and looking for discrepancies between verbal and quantitative measures. Each trainee taught a maximum of 15 SLD pupils weekly. Trainees were closely supervised.

The greatest emphasis of the training program was on remedial academics. The experiences of the trainees in the eight placement situations are discussed, including problems, emphasis of instruction, and communication between team members.

The supervisory staff felt that the trainees who either worked together in the same room or who had good communication within their school developed the most relevant and flexible programs to meet the needs of their students. Those trainees who were operating in isolation from one another seemed to be most restrictive in their teaching and tended to follow the training model too closely.

Poremba CD: The adolescent and young adult with learning disabilities: what are his needs: what are the needs of those who deal with him?. In *International Approach to Learning Disabilities of Children and Youth*. Proceedings of the Third Annual Conference, ACLD, Tulsa, 1966

The author, a psychologist at the Children's Hospital in Denver, in addressing the Third Annual Conference of the ACLD, discusses adolescents who have been diagnosed in the later school years as having a learning disability. The need for early detection of learning problems is stressed, and the practice of promoting children to higher grades when they obviously lack the necessary prerequisite skills is criticized.

Poremba believes we will find more of these children in the future due to improved evaluative techniques and also because medicine is saving the lives of infants with various disabilities who will be entering the schools in the coming years. We must have programs for these children. Many youths who are considered emotionally disturbed have needs that are not being met by existing school programs. The pressure to succeed in the academic subjects necessary for college creates many hardships for students who should be getting vocational training instead, even at the junior high school level. Both the students and their parents must be made to understand the nature of the disability in order to avoid labels like lazy, obstreperous, and stubborn.

The author also believes that compulsory education, which forces students to remain in school until they are 16 but does not meet the needs of children with special learning problems, provides little benefit in terms of preparing them for useful lives in the future. A greater emphasis on manual and technical training at the higher levels of education could prove beneficial.

Poremba feels that in as many as 50 percent of the court cases of juvenile delinquency he observed, the defendants exhibited specific learning disabilities—often involving reading or math. The need for greater study of this problem is necessary to change the definition of delinquency and study its relevance to education. Children should be taught how to overcome their deficits rather than act them out in the community.

What is needed for the future is greater research, resources for training and evaluation of these children, legislation that is sympathetic to their needs, parental cooperation, and, most important, a citizenry that understands their problems and is willing to help.

Prawat RS, Gaines P: Paired-associate performance in normal and learning disabled youngsters. Psychol Schools 149–152, 1974

Two groups of students, one considered successful learners, the other learning disabled, were given a paired-associates (PA) test to assess school learning proficiency. The successful learners were 10 college students, 6 men and 4 women, ranging in age from 18.6 to 20.1 years. The LD group had 10 high school students, 6 boys and 4 girls, whose ages ranged from 15.8 to 17.6 years.

Two paired-associate lists containing word pairs (nouns) that were high, low, and moderate in "image provoking value" (according to the Paivio, Yuille and Madigan norms), were used. The first list contained 24 PAs, 8 at each imagery level. The second included 12 items and contained 4 PAs at each level of imagery. After the 24-item list was administered orally, half the subjects in each group were given instructions in imagery and sentence generation. They were told to either think of a sentence that included both words or make a mental picture that combined both objects. The control group was given no additional instructions. After this manipulation, the 12-item mixed list was presented, also orally.

After the first list, students were asked to describe how they tried to learn the associate. Nonelaborative strategies included rote, mnemonic, and verbal association. Techniques involving mental elaboration were verbal elaboration and imaginal elaboration.

Results indicated that the proportion of subjects in the normal and LD groups who reported use of elaborative strategies compared to nonelaborative strategies did not differ significantly. This does not support the data which indicated that PA performance is related empirically to performance on tests of school achievement. It is suggested that the LD group in this study was not deficient in the type of covert mental activity required for successful performance on such a task.

Additional data showed that: (1) the imagery value of word pairs constitutes a significant source of variance for both normal and LD groups, (2) the type of strategy used does seem related to imagery value, and (3) instructions to elaborate mentally did not make more of a difference for LD students than for normals. This may indicate that LD students are just as adept as normals at spontaneously elaborating input.

Quadfasel FA, Goodglass H: Specific reading disability and other specific disabilities. J Learning Disabil 1:590–600, 1969

Conflicting points of view have been expressed by various investigators (teachers, remedial instructors, neurologists, psychiatrists, educational psychologists) concerning the nature, cause, and treatment of learning disabilities. In this paper the authors present some of the conflicting opinions on issues relating to reading disability as a medical entity, the place of language skills among specific endowments and disabilities, and the clustering of symptoms accompanying specific deficits. These issues are considered in light of arguments and observations presented by various writers.

The authors believe that most cases of reading retardation must be understood in the context of variations in talent for the acquisition of special skills. They propose the classification of retarded readers into three categories, excluding those due to an acquired aphasia. The first category is symptomatic reading disability. This occurs in children who suffered cerebral damage before they developed language. The etiology may be known or obscure. There are often other neurological signs, or even motor and psychological deficits. There is no family history of reading problems. Reading errors reflect distinctive perceptual and associative defects.

The second classification the authors use is that of specific reading disability, which is primarily a deficit of functional organization. No brain lesion is known or suspected; there are no localizing neurological signs. The IQ is normal. A family history is often elicited. This deficit may be isolated or accompanied by other specific disabilities. Reading errors reflect distinctive perceptual and associative defects.

The third category, secondary reading retardation, applies to children with normal reading potential. The cause is exogenous, not due to any faulty structural or functional organization of the brain, and is secondary to limited schooling opportunities, poor general health, or emotional reaction to environment. The reading errors are nondistinctive.

The authors strongly believe that "one can understand primary or specific reading disability only if one sees it as part of a very common variation of function of the brain which makes one man less apt in doing certain things and given another man a great ability or talent to do so."

Rice D: Learning disabilities: an investigation in two parts, Part 1. J Learning Disabil 3:149–155, 1970

Rice reviews the "clinical diagnostic findings of a multidisciplinary study" of LD students, which have implications for program planning for all LD students. He defines learning disability as a "selective inability to learn reading, spelling, and arithmetic at the expected rate." Data for the study were gathered over a 2-year period at the Dyslexia Clinic at the Indiana University Medical Center. The diagnostic procedure was divided into five parts: (1) school history, (2) ophthalmological examination, (3) psychoeducational evaluation, (4) neurological examination, and (5) staff conference.

Significant deficit was defined as a standard achievement score (WRAT) 15 or more points below the full scale IQ (WISC), since this represents approximately 1 sp on both tests. Six deficit categories are discussed: reading, spelling, and arithmetic; reading and spelling; reading only; spelling and arithmetic; spelling only; arithmetic only; and no significant disability.

In reviewing the data, Rice made a number of observations: the ratio of male to female referrals is about 5 to 1; there is little support for other findings of a performance versus verbal WISC discrepancy of LD; reading deficit alone is rare (8 of 190 cases); only 57 percent of referrals showed significant deficits in one or more academic areas; of the 43 percent (82 cases) without significant academic deficit, 22 showed evidence of brain damage, 11 appeared to have emotional or behavioral difficulties in the classroom, 37 were of borderline (79 to 89 IQ) mental ability, 5 appeared genuinely retarded (below 70, WISC); 10 of the 190 cases resulted in psychiatric referrals before educational planning; approximately 20 percent of the study population appeared dyslexic (see Rabinovitch, who says that less than 25 percent of reading problems are incidences of dyslexia); except in category IV, there was significant evidence of visuo-motor difficulties (25 percent to 57 percent incidence) in all categories; and low incidence of uncorrected vision problems.

Rice says that the experience of the study team indicates that a study setting apart from the normal school setting causes serious communication problems. If schools used the talents of qualified people already available to them, better studies would result.

The study population consisted of 190 Ss ranging in age from 6-2 to 16-9. There were 157 boys, 33 girls. Grade placements at the time of evaluation included kindergarten and grades 1 through 10; the vast majority of the student referrals came from first (25), second (39), third (43), fourth (34), and fifth (24) grades. Only 3 kindergarteners were referred, and total referrals for grades 6 through 10 were limited (17).

Rice D: Learning disabilities: an investigation in two parts. Part 2. J Learning Disabil 3:193–199, 1970

This article deals with implications for school curriculum and program planning. Three questions are raised by the author about school programs and how these programs relate to learning disabilities: What parts of the public schools are relevant to the problem of learning disabilities? Which students appear to have significant learning problems? What can be suggested as worthwhile approaches to these learning problems?

Rice believes that through the years the goal of educators has been "a standardized educational prescription to fit all students, with thoughts of flexibility coming only after something seems to have gone amiss." Even in special education programs, he feels greater flexibility is needed to deal more effectively with individual differences and needs. He thinks that too much emphasis is placed on proficiency in reading at the expense of the rest of the student's education. He is also opposed to the schools' great reliance on chronological age as the main criterion for starting a child in school.

The second question concerns identifying learning disabled students. They may be referred to as brain damaged, language-learning impaired, visual-motor perceptually deficient, dyslexic, or as having a specific learning disability. It is estimated that from 10 to 30 percent of the total school population falls in this category. Educators can either create special classes for them out of expediency, evaluating and refining them as they go along, or they can apply all the information that is available about learning disabilities to create a curriculum that is relevant to all students from the very beginning.

Ten suggestions for resolving learning problems are offered: develop a true psychoeducational evaluation process; clearly define the basic purpose of education; become more involved with preschool education; identify and prevent reading disability early; permitting students to learn at their own pace, possibly without grades; carefully evaluate the teaching techniques used with disabled learners; carefully evaluate a school's initial approach to reading instruction; examine the effectiveness of remedial reading programs currently in use; explore alternate ways of imparting information when reading ability is seriously impaired; and finally, consider the efficacy of keeping these learning disabled students in the mainstream of education rather than in special programs that emphasize their "differentness."

Rice RD: Educo-therapy: A new approach to delinquent behavior. J Learning
    Disabil 3:16–23, 1970

A treatment model called "educo-therapy" was designed to remedy the
learning deficits and maladaptive behaviors of 10 delinquent girls, ages 13 to
15, in a Tennessee state institution for correction. The treatment model, used
in an experimental pilot project for 3 months, involved facets of several
different theories and procedures. The underlying basic philosophy of educo-
therapy held that each girl was worthy of respect and love. The treatment
philosophy stated that each girl should experience success in school (particularly in reading), learn modes of behavior that are socially acceptable, have her
self-concept enhanced, and learn to assume responsibility for the consequences of her behavior.

The goals of the treatment program were phased in three progressive levels,
each designed to meet basic developmental needs. The objectives were behavior modification through educational improvements, improvement of self-
concept, and social integration.

Improvement was evidenced in the language and reading performance of 9
subjects on a posttest of the Gates Reading Survey Test. Gains ranged from 2
months to 13 months in grade level. Full scale scores on the posttest of the
WISC were raised from 1 to 17 points. Improvements in personal appearance
and acquisition of social etiquette made the subjects more socially acceptable.

It was predicted that if the child could experience success in learning and
find gratification and reinforcement in academic achievement, many of her
maladaptive behaviors, which were most evident in the classroom, would be
remedied. One of the deficiencies of this study, according to the author, was
the lack of comprehensive posttesting. However, "in a subjective evaluation by
the staff of the conservative institution used in the study, enthusiastic support
was given to the belief that "educo-therapy" shaped academic learning into the
behavioral repertoire and provided an effective means of coping with disruptive
emotional behavior. A modified version of the pilot project treatment program
has been incorporated in the regular program of this institution."

It is the author's opinion that "in terms of institutional economics, this in-
depth, concentrated approach to educational remediation and behavioral
therapy is more economically feasible than long-term incarceration without
the treatment program."

Rosenthal JH: Self-esteem in dyslexic children. Academic Ther 9:27–39,
    1973

Subjects in this study of self-esteem in dyslexic children were 60 Caucasian
boys between the ages of 8 and 14 years. They were divided into 3 groups of 20
boys each. Group 1 contained 20 boys who had been diagnosed as dyslexic.

This group was divided into 2 subgroups: (1) those from families having some understanding of the problems and implications of dyslexia (DNM), and (2) dyslexics from families who had not heard the term and had no experience with the consequences of reading disability (DM).

Group 2 contained 20 boys having no school or reading problems and was matched as closely as possible for age, ethnic group, and socioeconomic class with the members of the dyslexic group. This control group of boys was selected by the dyslexic boys and their families to try to achieve close similarity of cultural and social backgrounds. Group 3 contained 20 asthmatic boys as closely matched as possible to the dyslexic group.

The Coopersmith Self-esteem Inventory (SEI) was given to each child. The questions on the test were taped for the dyslexic group. In an effort to determine the correlates between subjective statements and behavioral expressions of self-esteem, the researchers sent the Coopersmith Behavior Rating Form (BRF) to the teachers of all subjects.

The 10 DNM boys showed significantly higher self-esteem than the 10 DM boys. Teachers' estimates of classroom behavior showed no significant differences among the 3 major groups of boys, probably reflecting the teachers' awareness of the diagnosis and perhaps reflecting allowances made for the handicapped children. Two other possibilities are that asthmatic children, who usually do have psychological problems, were rated lower than healthy children would have been rated; and that the controls chosen by the dyslexics may have had psychological difficulties or other types of problems that lowered their behavior rating.

"The behavior rating scores for the DM and DNM dyslexic subgroups did not differ significantly; but a significant difference in the variance ratio indicated that the teachers of the DM subgroup had wider ranges of judgments about the classroom behavior of these children than had the teachers of the DNM subgroup. No significant correlations between SEI and BRF were noted among any group, indicating that all of these subgroups showed divergence between self-assessment and behavioral assessment by others."

In conclusion, the author stresses the importance of education for the family of the dyslexic youngster about the etiology and management of this handicapping condition.

Rourke BP, Yanni DW, MacDonald GW, Young GC: Neuropsychological significance of lateralized deficits on the grooved pegboard test for older children with learning disabilities. J Consult Clin Psychol 41:128–134, 1973

The reported study compares the performances of 10- to 14-year-old children (IQs between 80 and 120) exhibiting learning disabilities with those of adults with known cerebral lesions. The authors felt that if the "patterns of performance" of both groups were similar, then it would support the theory that cerebral dysfunction is a factor in learning disabilities. The paper outlines several studies of adults with cerebral lesions.

Related patterns were found between lateralized lesions and performance on the Wechsler-Bellevue. Using this information, the authors grouped learning disabled children according to lateralized motor deficits and then gave them the psychological tests. If the results of these tests paralleled the results of the adults with brain lesions, it would prove that the etiology of learning disabilities includes some cerebral dysfunction, as hypothesized by the authors.

The hypothesis was supported by the data; test results for the LD children were comparable to those of the previously tested adults. Learning disabilities did indicate, in the older child, some cerebral dysfunction. The authors do caution, however, that these results cannot be generalized to include younger children.

Schreiber A: An empirical approach at the secondary level. Academic Ther 6, 5–12, 1970

Schreiber discusses some of the newer modes of teaching that are being used in an effort to reach more students. Such methods as flexible and modular scheduling, programmed instruction, electronic laboratory-type classrooms, work experience programs, and vocationally oriented courses for the non-college-bound students are coming into much greater use than ever before.

In learning disability programs, new approaches relying on a psychoeducational team effort, prescriptive teaching, and modifying subject content so that it is tailored to meet the specific needs of a student are seen as the techniques of the future. The teachers in these programs must attempt to build a strong and lasting relationship with their students and communicate a feeling of empathy and unconditional acceptance of them. The students' strengths must be found and then capitalized on and the goal of returning them to regular classes as soon as they are ready must always be kept in mind. Reasonable experiences of success in areas of interest will hopefully carry over to deficit areas. It is also most important for the special education teachers to stay in close contact with the regular classroom teachers in order to disseminate pertinent information, as well as to be available for consultation.

The special education program at Capuchino High School, San Bruno, California, is briefly described in this paper.

Schweich PD: The development of choices—an educational approach to employment. Academic Ther 10:277–283, 1975

A program of occupational academics has been designed and developed by the staff of Archway School, Brooklyn, New York, to improve job opportunities for non-college potential learning disability students. Working on the assumption that the purpose of education is to make one self-sufficient, professionals developed a highly specialized work-study program for students 17 and older. Its objective is employment in a productive position, making the most of each student's strengths and abilities.

The program lasts 4 semesters. The first is strictly academic and includes reading, math, language arts, and occupational studies. The next 3 semesters include these academics in the morning and begin job placement in the afternoon. The goal of the program is not reeducation, but reorganization into usable form of what has already been learned.

Since the abilities to coordinate knowledge and to be flexible in adapting to job changes are of greater value than knowledge of many uncoordinated skills, an "educational" rather than a "training" approach to employment is stressed. All learning concentrates on skills applicable to clerical and semi-professional occupations. Curriculum instruction includes videotape seminars, peer mediation, employer-student workshops, and one-to-one teacher-student training. Instruction begins at a sixth-grade reading level with the expectation of a year of progress by the end of the program. The academic areas are time (how quickly one can perform his job) and communication skills are stressed.

The program has been in existence for 2 years on an experimental basis and has met with considerable success in placing students in appropriate work situations.

Scranton TR, Downs MC: Elementary and secondary learning disabilities programs in the U.S.: a survey. J Learning Disabil 8: 394–399, 1975

The authors report the results of a nationwide survey conducted to determine the level of development of elementary and secondary learning disability programs. Reactions from state special education officials concerning the disparity between programming at these two levels is presented.

The data reported reflected programs in 10,358 school districts in 37 states; the remaining states used incompatible data classification systems. Forty percent offered programs at the secondary level; nine percent offered programs at the secondary level. The disparity between the number of elementary programs and the number of secondary programs is reflected in the philosophies of state education department officials.

The justifications for the lack of secondary programs vary from state to state; many point to a general lack of readiness for secondary programs in terms of available technology, trained personnel, materials, etc. The belief that primary programs, through early identification and intervention, eliminate the need for secondary programs is also widespread. It appears that parental activism and/or specific legislation will be needed, in some cases, to spur the development of learning disability programs for secondary students.

It is pointed out that the Bureau of Education has stated as one of its goals "that every handicapped child is receiving an appropriately designed education by 1980." Based on data collected for this survey, the authors project that programs must grow at an approximate rate of 12 percent per year at the elementary level and at approximately 22 percent per year at the secondary level to reach 85 percent of the governments' expectation by 1978.

Silberberg NE, Silberberg MC: School achievement and delinquency. Rev Education Res 41: 17–34, 1971

Numerous groups have investigated the relationship between delinquency and reading disability. Because of such variables as differences in samples and definitions of delinquency, the results of these studies have been somewhat inconclusive and often confusing. In general, the evidence does seem to support a correlation between reading disability and delinquency.

As is the case with delinquency, there are many theories to explain the many causes of reading disability. Research indicates a common etiology for both problems. Whether the relationship between the organic and behavioral conditions is causal or merely correlational has not as yet been adequately examined.

There have been indications in the literature that delinquent boys exhibit a lack of abstract linguistic ability. The authors question whether highly abstract teaching methods are suitable for all children entering school. Once a child does enter school and is repeatedly frustrated by his inability to learn by the regular class methods, it seems quite likely that some form of protest behavior would result.

An alternative approach would be the expansion of the number of educational options available. Attempting to guide youngsters into the mainstream by emphasizing remedial work in the skills in which they are deficient seems to the authors contradictory and probably doomed to failure.

The authors have developed a bookless approach to education which relegates reading to the status of an isolated skill which is taught separately, while all other avenues of learning are used for the actual education of the child. Vocational curricula may be made more relevant by enabling students to enter into meaningful occupations through schools or privately financed training programs. Personnel policies in business and industry can be changed so that a high degree of literacy is not a prerequisite for positions in which literacy is not functionally necessary. Tangible rewards are important to the delinquent, and some programs have demonstrated that meaningful employment can reduce recidivism. Research findings indicate that academic success is related to getting a job and to the amount of training required to achieve proficiency in the job, but that success on many jobs after training is not related to school success.

The authors suggest that the children's talents do not need to be changed, but the values and institutions of our society must be redesigned to accommodate the variety of talents the children possess.

Strother CR: Who is he? *In* Schloss E (ed): *The Educator's Enigma: The Adolescent with Learning Disabilities.* San Rafael, California, Academic Therapy Publications, 1971

There has been so much emphasis on the early diagnosis and treatment of children with learning disabilities that the problems of the adolescent have been neglected, in the opinion of this author.

Educators differ about the etiology of learning disorders. One faction maintains that these learning disabilities represent a dysfunction that is of genetic, traumatic, or developmental origin. Another group maintains that the evidence is not sufficiently clear-cut to warrant the assumption that there is an underlying central nervous system disability. A third group maintains that a presumed or established central nervous system defect is of no importance because it does not help in working with the child. The author agrees with the second and third groups because of his distrust of the reliability of neurological diagnosis.

It is important to define the term learning disability for educational purposes. When an attempt is made to set up special facilities and educational procedures for these children, specific criteria must be agreed on. This must be done for admissions eligibility, for determining the kinds of programs that will be provided, and for funding decisions.

The advisory committee on the Education of the Handicapped has proposed the following definition on which the Office of Education is now basing its allocation of funds: Children with special learning disabilities exhibit a disorder in one or more of the basic psychological processes involved in understanding or using spoken or written language. These may be manifested in disorders of listening, thinking, talking, reading, writing, spelling, or arithmetic. They include conditions which have been referred to as perceptual handicaps, brain injuries, minimal brain dysfunction, dyslexia, developmental aphasia. They do not include learning problems which are due primarily to visual, hearing or motor handicaps, to mental retardation, emotional disturbance, or to environmental disadvantage.

At the junior high or high school level, there is a tremendous overlay related to this primary learning disability and it confuses the picture. It makes it more difficult to discriminate between the child with a primary learning disability and the child who is emotionally disturbed or the child who is a behavior problem because he is acting out.

Four major categories of disturbance and behavior that the teacher may find useful in his observation of children with special learning disabilities are visual and auditory problems, hyperactivity, conceptualization problems, and speech and writing problems.

Sundberg N: Vocational rehabilitation cooperation in school. *In* Anderson L (ed): *Helping the Adolescent with the Hidden Handicap.* Los Angeles, California Association for Neurologically Handicapped Children, 1970

The author describes a program in which the California Department of Rehabilitation and the Novato Unified School District work together in a two-part system: part one is a special education unit run by the school. Part two is the vocational rehabilitation unit, staffed by the school district and the Department of Rehabilitation. Key personnel are the program coordinator, vocational rehabilitation counselor, and the work coordinator.

Participants in the program come from LD classes or upon recommendation from school counselors. Rehabilitation arranges for a general medical exam and, if indicated, neurological or psychiatric testing. Vocational testing is also administered. Once accepted, some students are placed in a work experience; others, who are carrying a full academic schedule and are doing fairly well, are not placed. For them, the value of the program lies in the vocational testing and the vocational guidance available upon graduation.

There are two categories of work experience at Novato High School. One is the learning lab in which students are put in a work situation within the school district (e.g., cafeteria, library, school warehouse). These jobs are purely evaluative, and the student earns 5 units of credit for every 2 hours worked. The other is called occupational education. It covers true on-the-job training in the field the student will pursue, or part-time attendance at school and part-time attendance at a vocational or trade school. Credit is given for work experience which takes the place of school classes.

Fees for vocational rehabilitation services are based on how much a family is able to pay, although the preliminary testing is done at no cost to the client. The most important aspect of the program is believed to be the continuing concern and help the student receives after graduation or after he leaves school. He is followed for a full year beyond high school and, if more help is needed after that, he is transferred to a regular rehabilitation counselor.

Swanson S: Helping the learning-disabled in a high school setting. In *Successful Programming: Many Points of View.* Proceedings of the Fifth Annual Conference, ACLD, Boston, 1968.

Swanson's paper deals with a learning disabilities program in an Illinois high school. The students chosen for participation were those who had been in a junior high school learning disabilities program, as well as some who came from private schools and who had undergone a previous neurological and psychological evaluation. The program was planned as a resource unit where the students could go for certain periods during the day. Students came during their study hall periods and did not miss regular classes.

All students were integrated as much as possible into regular classes based on their abilities, interests, and needs. Decisions about which courses to take were left in the hands of the students themselves, with guidance available from the counseling staff.

Classroom teachers were informed about the special program and told which of their students would be involved. Many of these teachers were only familiar with special education classes in reference to EMH children, and were not familiar with learning disabilities or how they affected day-to-day functioning. After being briefed, the regular teachers joined a team effort with the learning disabilities teacher and the counselor in an attempt to provide the maximum benefit to the students in the program.

Audiovisual aids were relied on as teaching tools. Typewriters were available and programmed instruction workbooks in math and spelling were found to be helpful. Materials incorporating the initial teaching alphabet approach to reading were used, as were tapes and auditory memory drills. Many materials had to be individualized for each student.

Meetings were arranged with the parents to familiarize them with the nature and the goals of the program; conferences were held as often as necessary, and parents' suggestions were encouraged. Discussion groups were held to provide information about adolescent dynamics as well as about learning disabilities.

It was felt that there was a definite need for vocational and occupational guidance and counseling in the high school program since many of the children might not be able to go to college. At the time this study was written, such programs were being introduced into the curriculum.

Tarnopol L: Delinquency and minimal brain dysfunction. J Learning Disabil 3: 200–207, 1970

The author believes that the delinquent school dropout population from minority group ghettos contains a greater percentage of children with minimal brain dysfunction than does the total delinquent population. The term *minimal brain dysfunction* is used to designate the medical entity related to the educational term *learning disabilities*.

In this study, 102 males, ages 16 to 23 years, primarily from minority group ghettos, were examined and tested. Almost all had dropped out of school and had engaged in varying degrees of delinquency. A substantial number of untreated medical and dental problems were found. On the Wechsler Adult Intelligence Scale, 39 percent had significantly different verbal and performance IQ scores. The mean grade at which they dropped out of school was 10.5. Fifty-eight percent of this group was reading below the sixth-grade level on the Gates Test of Reading for General Significance. On the Bender Visual-Motor Gestalt Test, only one-third were in the normal range. Comparison of the Bender tests with the Oseretsky Test of Motor Proficiency indicated that most of their visual-motor problems were related to visual-motor integration and motor coordination. Comparison of the Bender test with the Closure Flexibility Test showed that only a small number of the visual-motor problems were related to disturbances of visual perception.

The author feels that these test results show that a significant degree of minimal brain dysfunction exists in the minority group delinquent school dropout population. This evidence should be used to encourage the revision of existing special programs for the minority poor which do not seem to be accomplishing their purpose. Too few of the intervention programs, which are aimed at raising the reading and educational levels of disadvantaged children, recognize that a significant segment of this population needs individual medical, psychological, and educational diagnosis followed by prescriptive teaching in order to learn. The earlier this is begun, the more successful the program will be.

Thompson A: Moving toward adulthood. *In* Anderson L (ed): *Helping the Adolescent with the Hidden Handicap.* Los Angeles, California Association for Neurologically Handicapped Children, 1970

Adolescence is a stormy, difficult time for all teenagers and their parents. The child who is neurologically handicapped has an even harder time adjusting to changes in himself and his environment. Some of the characteristics common to these youngsters which make life so difficult are their impulsivity, suggestibility, short tempers, impaired self-direction, low self-esteem, short sightedness, and poor social skills. This paper explores possible means whereby social conditions can be altered to make life less frustrating for these children and their families.

One area that might be changed is the matter of norms. Thompson feels that although learning problems are real enough and frequent enough, the present system is creating more problems unnecessarily by putting children in special classes when all they really need is a little more time to mature. The author believes that there is no defensible reason for classifying a developmental lag of 1 to 3 years in reading as a learning problem. This strict adherence to norms creates an inflexible school program which is another major deterrent for these children. She also states that by enriching what is offered to these children and allowing them to develop at their own speed, we could eliminate the majority of what we are calling learning problems.

Feelings of failure are very harmful to one's belief in oneself. There should be a way to deal with the exceptional child and his inability to adhere to norms without creating these feelings at a very young age. The author believes that "for the most part, failure is a name for the fact that we have asked children to do something that under the circumstances they cannot do."

In the area of authority, the idea is expressed that with these youngsters, punishment is an inadequate deterrent to undesirable behavior. Since there is often little association between behavior and experience, pain inflicted by authority figures due to infractions of the rules can easily cause resentment and suspicion of adults. It is up to society to find alternative methods of behavior modification for these children.

Happiness and self-respect must not be denied these children because of their differences. Some ways in which school and society can work together to help accomplish these are outlined. The list includes teaching social skills and self-direction as assiduously as reading and math, providing strong structures for those who lack inner strength, giving immediate reinforcement of approved behavior, focusing on the positive instead of the negative, and encouraging interests outside of the academic sphere where success is likely.

Tolor A: An evaluation of a new approach in dealing with high school underachievement. J Learning Disabil 3: 520–529, 1970

Underachievers in this study were subsumed under the label learning disabled. Tolor investigated the effect of three intervention strategies on perceived locus of control of reinforcement and grades for a group of junior and senior high school underachievers.

The author feels that the students' expectancy of internal (contingent on his own behavior) or external (contingent on external factors and independent of his own behavior) control of reinforcement was an important dimension of underachievement. He hypothesizes that: (1) underachievers tend toward greater externality than normal achievers; and (2) underachievers' academic performance will improve as a result of greater internality. Reduction in perceived internal control and a concomitant increase in perceived internal control will result in improved academic performance.

The subjects were 50 students (underachievers) randomly assigned to one of three experimental groups: tutorial, study skills group, and a computer group. All subjects received two 45-minute sessions each week for 8 weeks. The author expected the most benefits to accrue to the subjects of the computer training group.

The results indicated that the relationship between externality and underachievement was not significant. In addition, significant increases in internality were found for the tutorial and study skills group, but not for the computer group. Academic gains were not reflected in improved grades for any of the three groups.

Tolor A: Incidence of underachievement at the high school level. J Education
   Res 63: 63–65, 1969

The study reported here was undertaken because of the lack of available
data on the incidence of underachievement at the high school level. It was felt
that an accurate estimation of the percentage of underachievers was necessary
as a first step in the development of successful programs for these students.

The school records of 1263 sophomore, junior, and senior high school
students from an affluent community were examined for this study. An underachiever was operationally defined as a child who has: "(a) at least
average current intellectual functioning and (b) a placement on a standard
achievement test of at least one standard error of estimate below expectancy,
based on his own I.Q." Intelligence was measured by the group-administered
Otis Quick Scoring Mental Abilities Test (Gamma Test, Form FM). The
achievement tests were the National Educational Development Tests
(NEDT), which have five subtest areas: English usage, mathematics usage,
social studies, reading, natural sciences reading, and word usage.

Correlation coefficients between the Otis and the NEDT were computed and
regression equations developed. The mean underachievement rate for the
entire sample of students was found to be 26 percent. Some sex differences
were evident in that 28 percent of the boys were classified as underachieving in
comparison to 23 percent of the girls. Mathematics usage, when employed as
an achievement criterion, yields the highest degree of underachievement (29
percent), and natural sciences results in the lowest (20 percent). Although
underachievement as measured by deficiency in all subtest areas of the NEDT
is fairly rare, one-third of all students underachieved in two or more areas and
3 out of 5 students underachieved in one or more areas.

The author finds this high incidence of underachievement in an affluent community to be most alarming, especially since the 26-percent figure does not include students with below average intelligence. He urges intervention based on
an identification of the many causes of underachievement and more systematic
analysis and research of the underachievement problem.

Ullmann CA: Measures of learning disability for different purposes. J Learning Disabil 4:186–192, 1971

Definitions and measurement in the field of learning disabilities must be applicable both to scientific systems and to practical decision making. There is a
popular preference for intensive, norm-referenced measures such as age
scores and grade scores, and popular usage has led to their interpretation as if
they were extensive or criterion-referenced measures. The need exists in the
field of learning disability to employ measures pragmatically and selectively

according to purpose, whether for gaining scientific knowledge or for providing programs of service.

As more research leads to clearer definition of the concept of learning disability by each profession, effort must be made to assure that findings are translatable to allied disciplines. Each profession must understand its own frame of reference, as well as that of other disciplines and of those who are responsible for administering benefits and services. It is also important to understand the subjective standards parents and teachers use to decide when a child warrants special concern.

For systematic study, particularly when factors relating to growth are involved, some type of equal interval measure is preferable to measures using intervals of variable size; but for many practical purposes, criterion-referenced behavioral standards are useful, regardless of whether the units are equal. As interest in learning disabilities moves to the problems of maturity, it will become necessary to define deficits not only as discrepancies between actual and expected (currently a norm-referenced approach), but also as differences between actual and required (a criterion-referenced approach). As the child with severe learning disabilities grows up, norm-referenced measures become less useful and criterion-referenced statements gain in significance.

The development of techniques of absolute measurement may provide the advantages of both equal-interval measures and criterion-based standards. Ullmann believes that if this kind of measure can be used in conjunction with a construct of learning as it relates to LD, we may have a basis for developing a comprehensive system of diagnosis and evaluation for multiple purposes.

Vockell EL, Bennett B: Birth order, sex of siblings, and incidence of learning disabilities. Except Child 39:162–166, 1972

Records of 567 children between the ages of 6 and 16 years who were classified as learning disabled were examined from the files of the Purdue Achievement Center for Children. Data obtained concerned age, sex, IQ, ordinal position of birth, size of family, and age and sex of siblings. The group consisted of 113 girls and 454 boys. All subjects who were twins, who were adopted, whose parents were divorced, or whose background reflected some other traumatic event were excluded from further analysis. This left 95 girls and 387 boys. IQs ranged from 85 to 140 with a mean of 102.9.

The children came from families ranging in size from 1 to 9 children. The mean number of children per family for girls was 3.50, and 3.33 for the boys. Chi square analysis of the various birth positions within each family size indicates that none of the birth positions are over-represented at the 0.05 level of significance.

To examine the influence of the sex of siblings, the authors examined children from 2- and 3-child families in relationship to the number of brothers and sisters in their families. Chi square analyses indicate that none of the sibling constellations are overrepresented within a specific birth position.

These results provide no support for the hypothesis that birth order or sex of siblings is related to the incidence of learning disabilities.

Vogel AL: Teaching teenagers: integration of nine severe learning disabled children in a junior high school core program. Academic Ther 9; 99–104, 1973

A group of 9 children who were identified as having severe learning disabilities was located in a self-contained sixth-grade classroom in Park Ridge, Illinois. A team of teachers with learning disability experiences (academic specialists, a learning consultant, a coordinator of special education, a principal, and the district superintendent) were selected to implement integration of these children into a junior high school core program.

The team investigated the academic and social background of the 9 learning disability children. They were assigned 81 additional children who were divided into four heterogeneously grouped homerooms; three homerooms each contained 2 of the learning disability children, while the fourth contained 3.

Fundamental to the implementation of the program was the scheduling for individual students. A period of time was reserved for each academic teacher to meet with only the learning disabled children. The 81 children were divided into three homogeneous groups, with the learning disabled children making up a fourth; they had staggered academic sessions in the morning. In the afternoon they were heterogeneously grouped into classes of 30 for the nonacademic subjects.

The functional atmosphere resulting from the integration and grouping of the students was explained to all parents at a special meeting. Progress reports in the form of personalized letters were sent to the parents at midterm. New report cards were designed for the "low-achieving" and learning disability groups incorporating anecdotal records and letter grades which reflected achievement relative to the child's ability. Teacher–child conferences were held.

This program was evaluated as having many educational, attitudinal, and social rewards. The author contends that the integration of learning disability children in the junior high school, when compared to the stigma of the self-contained classroom, can be a realistic adventure into innovative educational programs.

Weiner PS: A language-delayed child at adolescence. J Speech Hear Disord 39: 202–212, 1974

This paper is a case study of Art, a 16-year-old boy first seen 12 years earlier because of his severe language difficulties. Current measures of his speech and language intelligence, reading achievement, and personal-social adjustment provide evidence of continuing deficits in the major language-related areas—speech and language, verbal intelligence, and reading. These deficits seem to have had adverse effects on his communication, educational achievement, and social adjustment.

The author's purpose in describing Art's case was to demonstrate that problems worthy of study arise from a consideration of the later functioning of language-delayed children. Many questions are suggested by his continuing difficulties; the most obvious is that of the frequency with which language-delayed children retain speech and language problems as they approach adulthood. Similar questions present themselves in relation to the children's use of language in the numerous areas of life in which it is important. Are there always difficulties in solving verbal intellectual problems or in reading when structure is deficient? What is the relationship between structural adequacy and adequacy of use?

Art's academic difficulties, coupled with his high functioning in the vocational training aspects of his school program, raise the question of the nature of an appropriate education. Specialized clinical techniques need to be directed specifically to the problems of the language handicapped. However, the most useful program for such children must go beyond speech and language—educational, vocational, emotional, and social aspects of adjustment need to be considered.

Weiss HG, Weiss MS: *A Survival Manual: Case Studies and Suggestions for the Learning Disabled Teenager.* Great Barrington, Massachusetts, Treehouse Associates, 1974

This book offers parents and educators alternative methods of teaching and helping adolescents with learning disabilities. In order to combat self-perpetuating feelings of failure and inadequacy, the authors present a student-centered approach in which these students become involved in diagnosing and overcoming their disabilities. All involved in the process must realize the importance of proper motivation and options other than total success or total failure.

The authors have developed the following functional descriptions of adolescent learning disabled students: "they exhibit a marked discrepancy between their level of ability and their educational achievement—there is often wide variation in achievement from subject to subject; they are often characterized by an attitude of disinterest and low motivation for academic tasks; their overall record generally shows consistent failure despite average to superior ability; in essence their school experiences have totally failed to meet their needs; the older the youngster, the more difficult it is to ascertain his specific educational pattern and the more likely he is to have built up inner emotional defenses.

In Part 1 of this manual, the authors present a series of case studies of adolescent students with various learning disabilities in order to illustrate ways of diagnosing, remediating, motivating, and assisting these youngsters in their specific needs. Among the specific disorders illustrated in the case studies are writing problems, problems in verbal expression, auditory processing problems, spelling problems, directional confusion and spatial disorientation, overall educational lag, and disorganized skills. The authors make recommendations to encourage learning strengths and to increase awareness of many different styles of learning.

In Part 2, the authors describe many medical-related conditions that often correlate with specific learning difficulties and poor achievement in school. Reproduced here is a checklist that teachers can use to gain insight into students' problems. One of the authors' main points is the importance of awareness of the kind of behavior suggestive of specific learning disability as opposed to emotional difficulties.

Presented also are examples of alternative styles of learning in the classroom and ways that teachers can accommodate the student who is unable to learn in the traditional ways. Also included are techniques the authors feel are effective in developing reading-associated skills that can be worked into any subject class.

The authors present a table of characteristic learning disability patterns displayed by adolescents: how these symptoms are seen at home and at school, suggested remediation techniques, and suggested ways of relieving intense academic pressure on the student while remediation is undertaken.

There are four appendixes to this manual: "Definitions of a Learning Disabilitation"; "Annotated Index of Tests and Measurements for Teacher and Professional Use, Grades 6–12"; "Bibliography of Alternative Reading Materials, Short Story Collections"; and "Bibliography of Books for Parents and Teachers."

White MM: A junior high school program for the learning disabled. In *Successful Programming: Many Points of View*. Proceedings of the Fifth Annual Conference, ACLD, Boston, 1968

White's article describes a junior high school class for LD children which is essentially a self-contained class within the junior high school structure. White maintains that it is not the teacher's job to get the child up to any particular grade level at the end of the year, but rather to help him learn how to learn. In this program 9 children were involved—6 boys and 3 girls (1 sixth grader, 5 seventh graders, and 3 eighth graders who ranged in age from 13 to 16). Their abilities varied greatly. Some had been in special education classes since second grade, and for some this was their first special education experience.

Each child's past records and the results of tests given when he entered the class were evaluated carefully. Techniques and materials were matched to his needs and were constantly reevaluated throughout the year. The seventh graders were in this class all day, except for certain nonacademic subjects. Eighth graders were each in a homeroom, where they also stayed for their first-period class (in this class, they were expected to meet class requirements and do their own homework).

The main focus of the special education class was teaching the use of symbols, which these children had not yet learned. The author felt that the students were not able to learn in groups—each must have his own program. Teacher aids were employed to work with the students on an individual basis. The ultimate aim was the satisfaction that comes from a job well done. Work had to be kept at a level below the frustration point so that a rebellious response was not aroused. One period per day the class met as a whole, either as a formal class experience or in a group therapy session.

According to the author, the tape recorder was of infinite value to the teacher, as were an abacus, small counting sticks, and number-facts flash cards. The work was slow, painstaking, and often frustrating, but White felt that it could be tremendously rewarding for the dedicated, interested teacher.

Wiig E: The emerging LD crisis. J Rehabil 38:15–17, 1972

Some problems of the college or working-age LD student are considered in this paper. These individuals are often hampered by their ineptness in social situations, possibly caused by a problem in perceiving social cues. Other characteristics include a poor attitude toward work and the unwillingness to ask for help or directions. Verbal and visual memory may be impaired as often as the ability to interpret spatial cues. All of these factors negatively influence the ability to perform specific academic and vocational tasks.

Early remedial intervention into the various perceptual problems associated with minimal brain dysfunction has produced significant results. However, it is generally observed that the rate of performance in these people is reduced, especially in tasks requiring high-level perceptual or motor skills. Academic or vocational failure or frustration may result unless specific adaptations are made in time requirements. Similarly, substantial performance in writing and adequate reading ability are needed for success in most areas, and in the case of college admissions, a foreign language requirement is often expected. For the person with learning disabilities, these are generally barriers to college admission unless a special exemption is made.

The author presents the idea that a prevention program, rather than one based on exemptions, would be an effective way of dealing with the problems of LD college students. Suggestions include: (1) a questionnaire to identify early learning problems, (2) administration of a foreign language aptitude test, and (3) an aptitude test for mathematics, and possibly an intelligence and memory scale when indicated. In some cases, exemption from the subject may be indicated, and in others, adapation of educational methods may be called for. This might include the taping of lectures, use of a class secretary to take notes, use of programmed self-paced instructions, use of oral or taped exams requiring oral responses, tutoring programs, and use of recorded texts and books such as those used by the blind.

In vocational and prevocational training, the author believes the emphasis should be on identifying and developing areas of strength in the individual, not on remediation of deficits. Testing for interests, aptitude, achievement, intelligence, and personality is valid; however, interpretation should be done by a learning disabilities expert along with the counselor or psychologist. Areas of strength should be matched with professional requirements. A team approach to vocational counseling also seems warranted in completing a job analysis for vocational placement since the LD student does not fit any of the standard vocational handicap categories.

Areas for change involve assessment, counseling, college requirements, and vocational possibilities. Potential employers and college administrators must be educated to the needs of people with learning disabilities, as must be vocational counselors in the high schools and in industry. New vocational areas must be explored as well before we can deal effectively with the learning disabled adolescent and young adult.

Wiig EH, Semel EM: Logico-grammatical sentence comprehension by adolescents with learning disabilities. Percept Mot Skills 38:1331–1334, 1974

This study was designed to evaluate whether logico-grammatical sentence comprehension deficits could be identified in learning disabled adolescents by using a set of 50 experimental sentences, designed by the authors, and by comparing performances to existing normative data for age peers. The study was also designed to evaluate whether concurrent validity existed between the experimental test and a widely used test of psycholinguistic ability (ITPA).

Subjects were 4 girls and 26 boys with learning disabilities diagnosed by a psychoeducational team. The youths ranged in age from 12 years 4 months to 16 years 1 month and attended middle class suburban public schools in grades six to nine. IQs ranged from 88 to 119. All exhibited academic retardation in one or more areas, all had normal auditory acuity and articulation ability, and none received speech or language therapy.

Results showed that a significant proportion of children with learning disabilities exhibit quantitative reductions in comprehension of logico-grammatical sentences. Findings also suggest that concurrent validity does exist between this receptive language test and the ITPA. A variance interpretation of the single correlations indicates that the unexplained variance in the performance on the logico-grammatical sentence test ranged from 65 to 86 percent.

It is therefore suggested that the present test measure abilities only partially assessed by the ITPA. The authors believe that their test may be used to assist in a comprehensive differential diagnosis of adolescent learning disabilities.

Wilcox E: Identifying characteristics of the neurologically handicapped adolescent. *In* Anderson L (ed): *Helping the Adolescent with the Hidden Handicap.* Los Angeles, California Association for Neurologically Handicapped Children, 1970

The author believes that our secondary schools are not ready for students with neurological handicaps. The reasons for this may include the relatively short period of time that professional attention has been directed toward the problems of these adolescents as well as the lack of communication between the individuals responsible for planning and administering programs and those professionals who work with adolescents.

Identification of previously unidentified neurologically handicapped adolescents, or reidentification of those youngsters who are moving up from elementary programs, is crucial if appropriate and realistic programs and goals are to be established. The criteria for identification include: hyperactivity, perceptual-motor impairments, emotional lability, general coordination deficits, disorders of attention, impulsivity, disorders of speech and hearing, disorders of memory and thinking, specific learning disabilities, equivocal neurological signs, and electroencephalographic irregularities. The author notes that these characteristics are not restricted to any one age level but are applicable across all age levels. However, she points out that "the observer . . . will not see the same manifestations [of each characteristic] as would have been seen in the same individual at an earlier age." Although the individual characteristics may be found in older or younger children, they are likely to differ in degree and expression.

Responsibility for identifying secondary neurologically handicapped students rests primarily with the counselor who helps the student select and schedule his courses. "Identification should be a continuing process during the first year of junior and senior school." The neurologically handicapped adolescents tend to have a long history of learning difficulties, often with frequent references to learning problems found in the students' cumulative folders. The counselor must help the students balance their academic programs between areas of competence and areas of difficulty so that the students' chances for success—and eventually graduation—are enhanced.

Williamson AP: Career education: implications for secondary learning disabled students. Academic Ther 10:193–200, 1974–1975

The author feels that career education (relating academic subjects to career options, encouraging personal growth, and instilling the desire to join the work force) has not been properly geared toward the learning disabled student in the secondary school. For years this student has been directed toward vocational training and away from the academic curriculum. The author feels, however, that the learning disabled youth might have profited more from academic instruction with curricular modifications; and vocational training might have developed a stigma from being so closely associated with the handicapped students, causing more capable students to steer clear of that area even though it might have proven beneficial to them.

Career education programs for learning disabled students should be heavily supplemented with basic literacy skills, including remedial reading. They should offer many options and not exclude the possibility of college. Curriculum emphasis must capitalize on the areas of strength, which in turn should be matched with jobs or professional requirements. Many colleges are accepting students with good grades in strong areas and are willing to grant exemptions in the areas of impairment. Since the student with learning problems often has resulting emotional problems as well, the program should also be geared toward helping him adapt to the stresses of daily living and working. By emphasizing the development of decision making abilities, problem solving techniques, and personal growth rather than simply developing proficiency in a particular vocational area, educators can help students adapt to numerous career opportunities as they present themselves.

Further study in this area should include research to determine the effectiveness of career education with learning disabled students, what type of program is best, when it should be started, and how well these students adapt to college. The author believes that the U.S. Office of Education and other funding sources should be made to see the need for allocating money for research in this area. Investigators' estimates of the total school population that has some degree of learning disability range between 2 percent and 30 percent. A group of this potential size warrants materials designed and field tested especially for their needs. Employers will need to be educated about the nature and needs of the potential employee with disabilities. Finally, students should be allowed to investigate human service vocations as well as technological areas, since these require a minimum of proficiency in high-level perceptual and motor skills.

Wissink JF: A procedure for the identification of children with learning disabilities. (Doctoral dissertation, University of Arizona) Ann Arbor, Michigan, University Microfilms, 1972, No. 72-31,838

The purpose of the study was to test the feasibility of a "Bayesian revision of the subjective probabilities" technique in identifying children with learning disabilities. The Bayesian technique involves a "mathematical means for estimating the probability of the existence of learning disabilities in a child when component disabilities are expressed in conditional probabilities or likelihood estimates."

Procedurally, the investigation involved five major project activities and/or objectives. Objective 1 involved a review of the literature in order to establish a list of factors (component disabilities) which were characteristic of learning disabled children (K through grade 12). Objective 2 involved the organization of the factors into a systematic framework; a "process" classification was used to categorize the identified factors under five headings (sensory orientation, memory, reception, expression, and integration). Objective 3 involved constructing a questionnaire by which the author intended to solicit the subjective clinical judgments of a group of specialists in the area of learning disabilities in a learning disability and a non-learning disability population. Objective 4 involved applying Bayes' theorem as well as other statistical measures to the returned questionnaires. Objective 5 involved a supplementary pilot investigation concerning the interrelationship of the component disabilities.

Of the 100 learning disability specialists polled, 41 did not respond, 19 disqualified themselves or gave reasons for nonparticipation, 40 responded to the first part of the questionnaire, and 26 responded to both parts of the questionnaire. In general, the 40 learning disability respondents agreed about the relative weightings assigned to the component disabilities as demonstrated by coefficients of concordance. Of the 40 factors, the three most discriminating component disabilities were attention deficit, auditory-visual coordination deficit, and visualization deficit, indicating that these factors may be particularly important for identifying learning disabled individuals.

Regarding processes: sensory orientation and integration processes contain the most effective identifier variables; reception and expression processes have the least effective identifiers; and the memory process, which contains the fewest component disabilities, yielded little useful information.

Index